AF573383

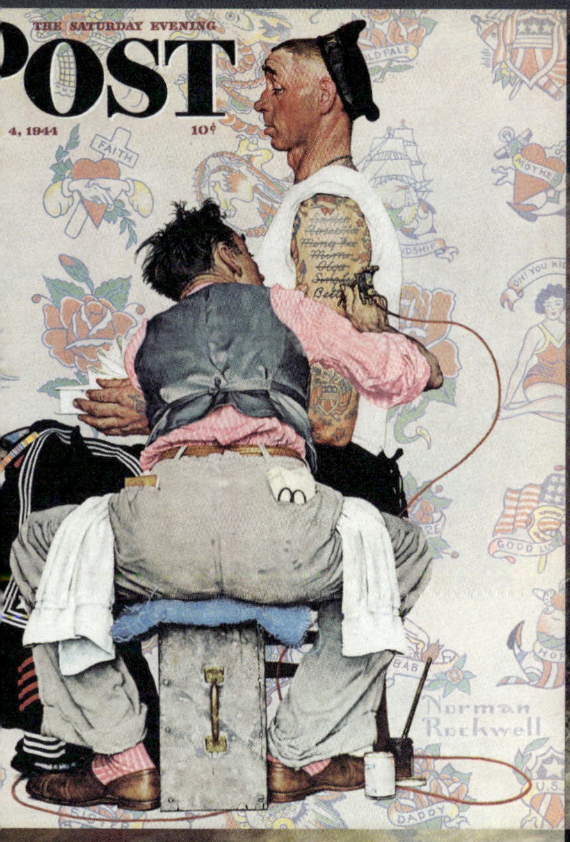
THE SATURDAY EVENING
POST
4, 1944
10¢
Norman Rockwell

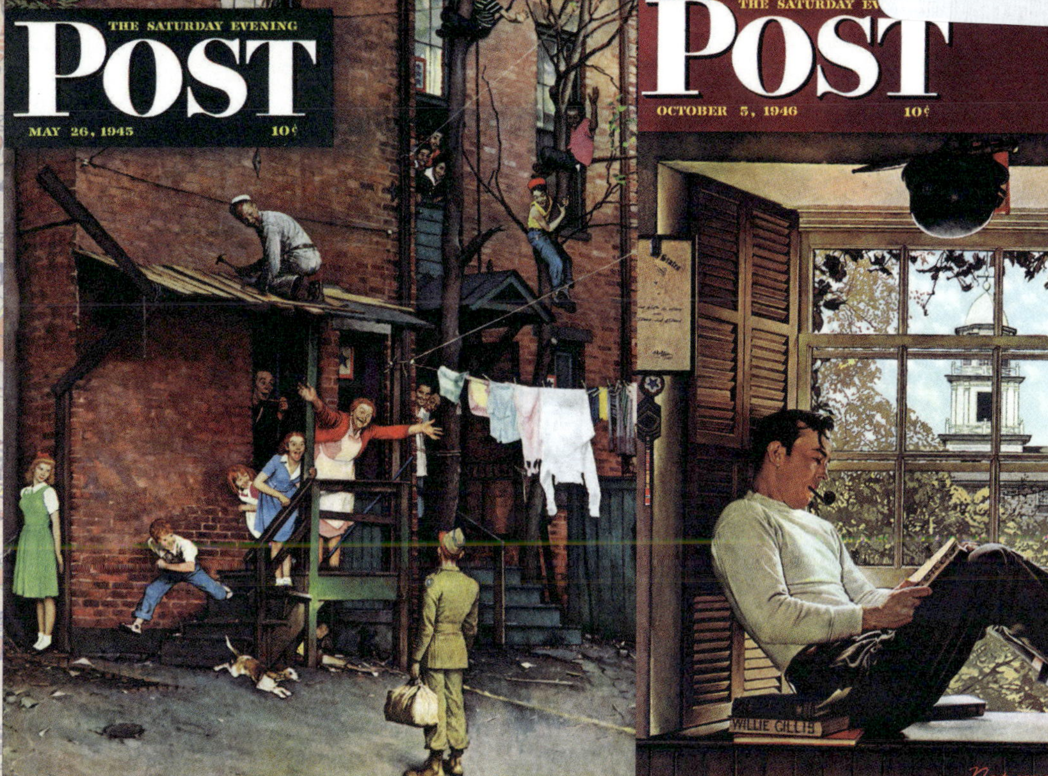
THE SATURDAY EVENING
POST
MAY 26, 1945
10¢
THE SATURDAY EVENING
POST
OCTOBER 5, 1946
10¢
Norman Rockwell

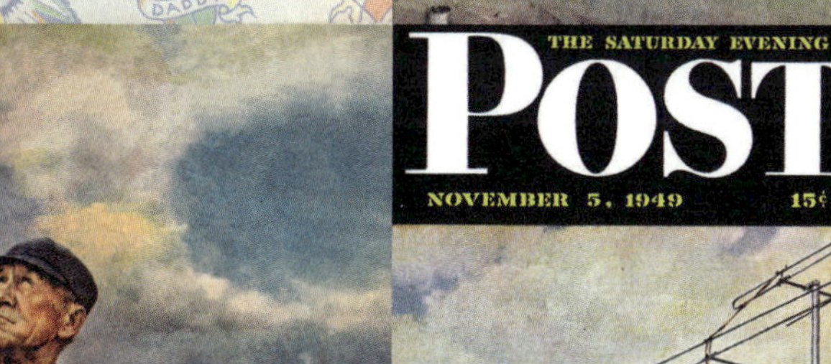
THE SATURDAY EVENING
POST
23, 1949
15¢
THE SATURDAY EVENING
POST
NOVEMBER 5, 1949
15¢

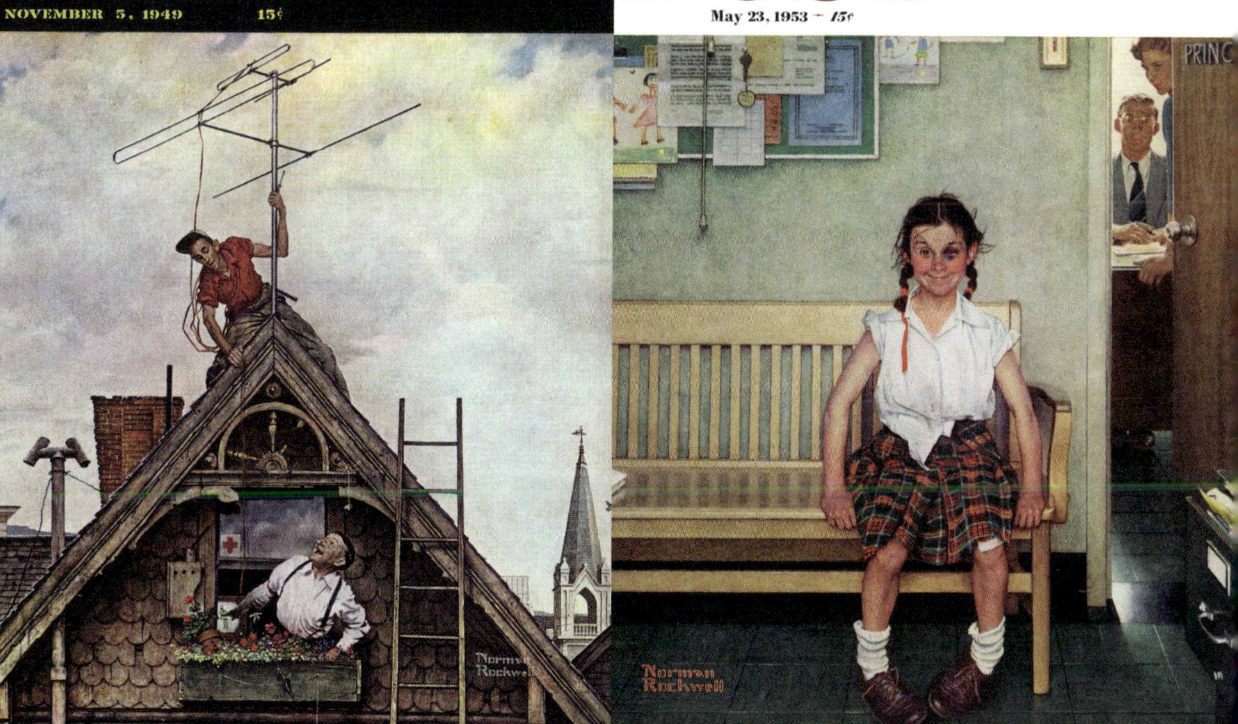
The Saturday Evening
POST
May 23, 1953 ~ 15¢
Norman Rockwell

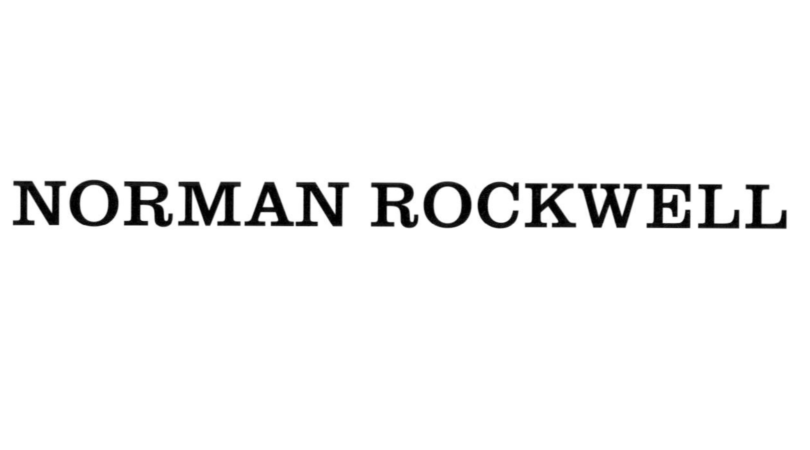

NORMAN ROCKWELL

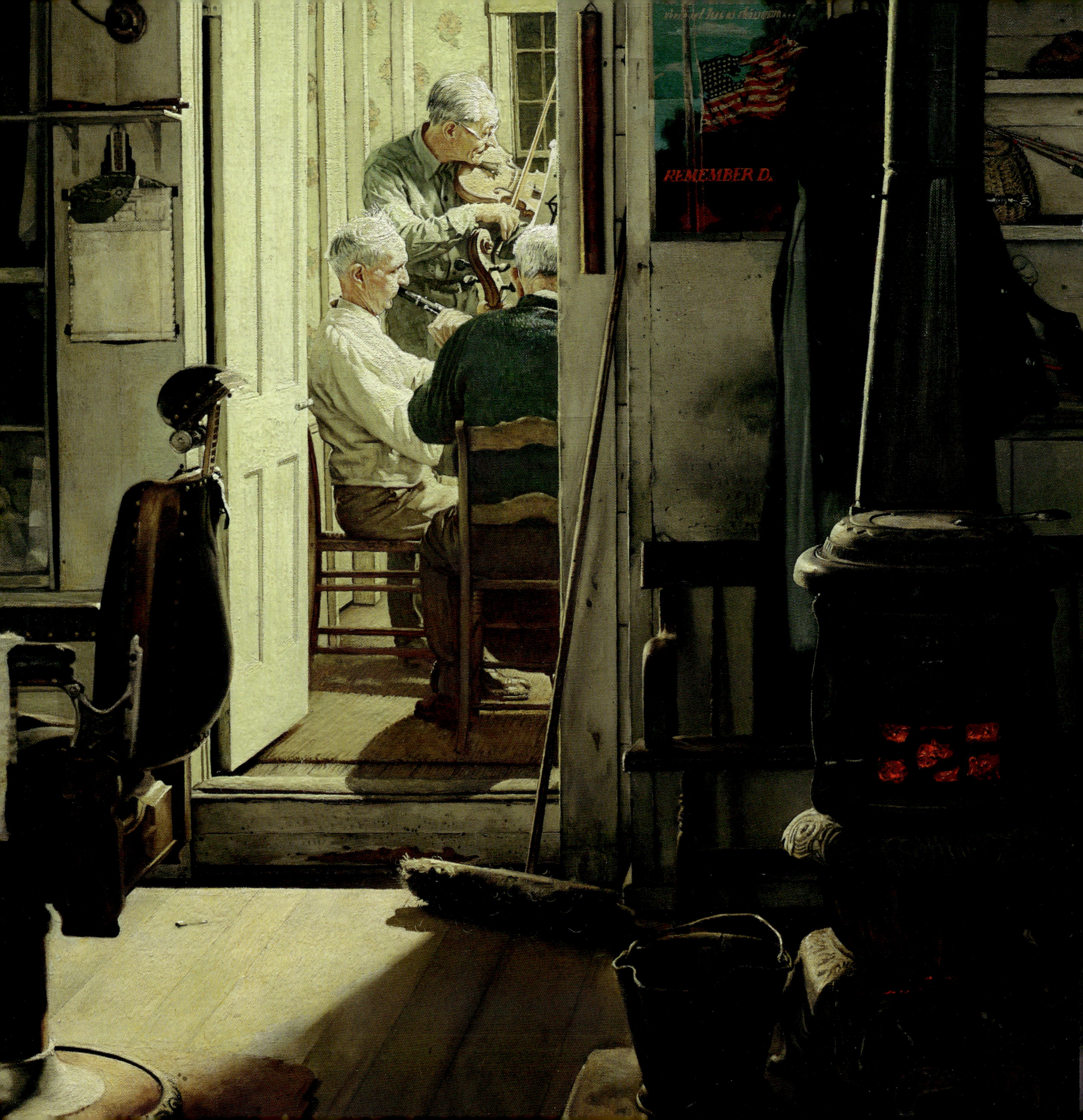
REMEMBER D.

NORMAN ROCKWELL

AT HOME IN VERMONT

Edited by Carolyn Bauer

With essays by Carolyn Bauer, Thomas Denenberg, and Alexander Nemerov

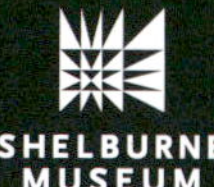

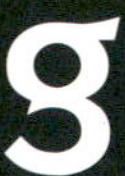

Shelburne Museum, Shelburne, Vermont, in association with D Giles Limited

Norman Rockwell: At Home in Vermont is made possible by the generous support of the Judith and James Pizzagalli American Paintings Endowment, Donna and Marvin Schwartz, Todd R. Lockwood, the Frelinghuysen Foundation, the M&T Charitable Foundation, and Maplefields.

The **M&T** Charitable Foundation

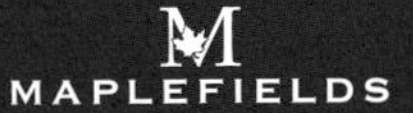

Shelburne Museum exhibitions are also generously supported by our Members and donors to the Annual Fund.

First published in 2026 by GILES
An imprint of D Giles Limited
66 High Street,
Lewes, BN7 1XG, UK
https://gilesltd.com/

EU GPSR authorised representative
LOGOS EUROPE, 9 rue Nicolas Poussin, 17000,
La Rochelle, France
E-mail: contact@logoseurope.eu

ISBN: 978-1-917273-35-0

For Shelburne Museum
Thomas Denenberg, John Wilmerding
Director and CEO
Carolyn Bauer, Marna and Chuck Davis
Curator of American Art
Allison Harig, Archivist & Digital Asset Manager

For D Giles Limited
Copy-edited and proofread by Jodi Simpson
Designed by Alfonso Iacurci
Produced by GILES, an imprint of D Giles Limited
Printed and bound in Europe

All measurements are in inches; height precedes width precedes depth.

Shelburne Museum
PO Box 10
5555 Shelburne Road
Shelburne, Vermont 05482
https://shelburnemuseum.org/

Front cover: Norman Rockwell, *The Craftsman* (detail), 1963. Oil on canvas, 47¼ × 38¼ in. Collection of Shelburne Museum, gift of Polycor and Rock of Ages Corporation. 2024-12.1.
Back cover: Unidentified photographer, *Untitled* [Norman Rockwell painting *The Craftsman*], ca. 1963. Photograph, 10 × 8⅛ in. Vermont Granite Museum. 2021.74.512.
Frontispiece: Norman Rockwell, *Shuffleton's Barbershop* (detail), 1950. Cover illustration for *The Saturday Evening Post*, April 29, 1950. Oil on canvas, 46¼ × 43¼ in. Lucas Museum of Narrative Art, Los Angeles. 2018.10.1. Artwork Approved by the Norman Rockwell Family Agency.

CONTENTS

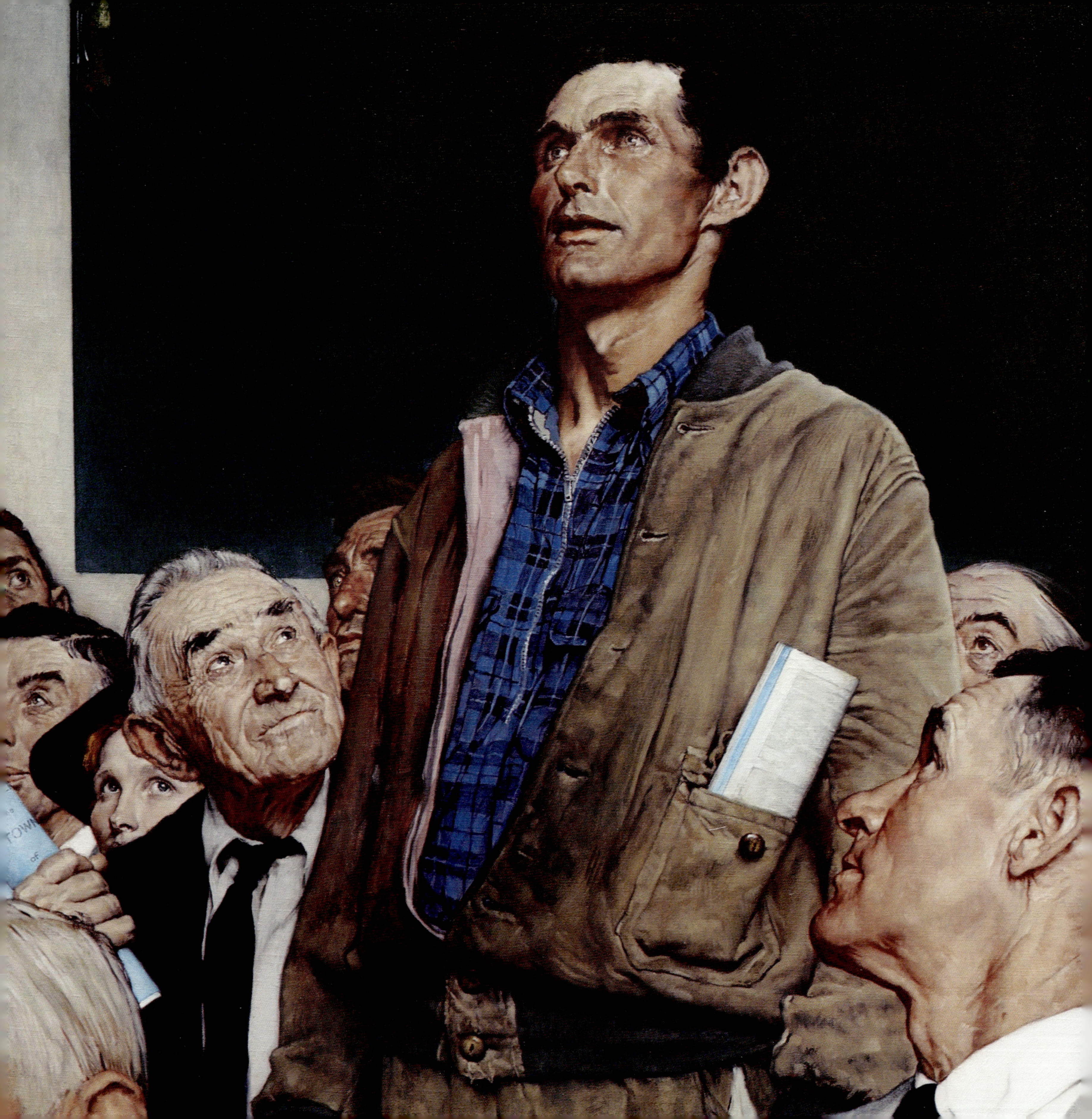

FOREWORD AND ACKNOWLEDGMENTS

Norman Rockwell's paintings are among the most recognizable and beloved images in American visual culture, yet their deep ties to place—particularly Arlington, Vermont, where Rockwell lived from 1939 to 1953—remain less well understood. *Norman Rockwell: At Home in Vermont* explores the remarkable story of how Arlington, a quintessential New England community, became the backdrop for some of Rockwell's most iconic works and, more broadly, how Vermont itself came to embody American ideals in the national imagination.

Rockwell's move from suburban New York to rural Arlington marked a period of tremendous creative growth and professional success. While he produced more than three hundred covers for *The Saturday Evening Post* during his tenure from 1916 and 1963, nearly 175 were painted during his Vermont years. Many of his most celebrated works—including the "Willie Gillis" series (1941–46), *Rosie the Riveter* (1943), *The Gossips* (1948), *Saying Grace* (1951), and *The Young Lady with the Shiner* (1953)—were born of this period, alongside advertising commissions, such as those for Coca-Cola and Hallmark, and the deeply patriotic and popular "Four Freedoms" series (1943), painted during the darkest days of World War II.

Norman Rockwell: At Home in Vermont not only examines this extraordinarily productive chapter in Rockwell's career but also situates the artist within the vibrant social and economic fabric of Vermont as it emerged from the Great Depression and weathered wartime challenges. In Rockwell's hands, Vermont's character—its resilience, civic spirit, and craftsmanship—became synonymous with the nation's own self-image. His paintings reveal how Vermont both inspired and reflected an idealized vision of community at a time when Americans yearned for stability and belonging during the anxious early years of the Cold War.

Accompanied by landmark images from Rockwell's Vermont years, three essays anchor this volume. Carolyn Bauer focuses on the town of Arlington, Vermont, tracing how Rockwell and his fellow illustrators—Mead Schaeffer, John Atherton, Gene Pelham, and others—drew upon the people and landscapes of the community to create a vision of America both nostalgic and enduring. Thomas Denenberg examines Rockwell in the broader context of New England artists and illustrators, charting how images helped crystallize the region as a place of collective memory for the nation. Lastly, Alexander Nemerov considers Shelburne Museum's recent acquisitions: three works by Rockwell that unpack the artist's relationship to questions of mortality, offering new perspectives on the artist and his legacy in creative culture.

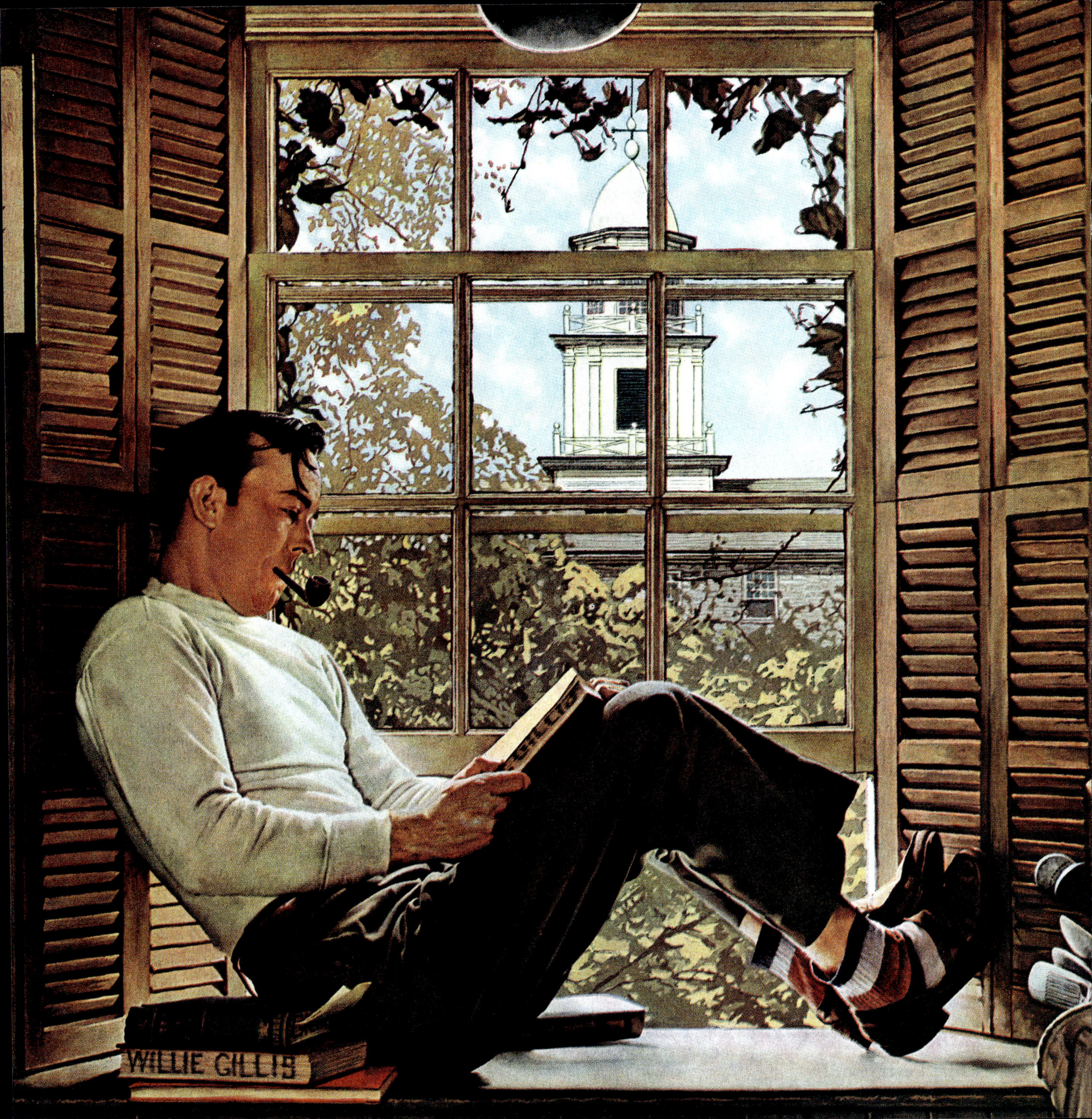
WILLIE GILLIS

As with Rockwell's art, exhibitions and catalogues are the product of community. We would like to thank our colleagues at Bennington Museum, Brooklyn Museum, the Fleming Museum of Art at the University of Vermont, the Hood Museum of Art at Dartmouth College, The Lyman Orton Collection, the Norman Rockwell Museum, the Wadsworth Atheneum Museum of Art, the Whitney Museum of American Art, as well as several private collectors and models for Rockwell for sharing their artworks, archives, and expertise. This catalogue would also not be possible without the assistance of Curtis Licensing and the Norman Rockwell Family Agency.

Special thanks are due to Jodi DeBruyne, Jamie Franklin, Stephan Jost, Russell Lord, Aiden Levy, Laurie Norton Moffatt, Mike Mueller, Alexander Nemerov, Melinda Murphy Pelham, Tom Pelham, Stephanie Plunkett, Margaret Rockwell, and Don Trachte Jr. for their insights, and to the staff at D. Giles Limited for shaping this book into a volume that reflects both Rockwell's artistry and Vermont's lasting place in American art and culture.

At Shelburne Museum, we extend our deep appreciation to Bill Bessette, Alexandra Biss, Marsha Blaisdell, Catie Camp, Keara Cook, Lily Cote, Elena Crites, Devon Davis, Amber Degn, Isa DeMarco, Shaina Driscoll, Giancarlo Filippi, Maria Foley, Sue Hale, Allison Hayes, Deana LaFleche, Rob Landry, Tina LeCours, Arin Lustberg, Kathryn Lynch, Justin Mayo, Bailey Moody, Erin Moore, Reed Nye, Kate Owen, Nancie Ravenel, Kat Redniss, John Rogers, Kory Rogers, Stephen Sperry, Chip Stulen, Sara Turner, Brian Verville, Jason Vrooman, Jackson Walsh, Sara Wolfson, and Leslie Wright, whose collegiality and dedication made this project possible. We would like to especially thank our colleague Allison Harig who worked tirelessly to secure illustrations for the project. The Board of Trustees of Shelburne Museum is remarkable for their vision and support in championing aspirational projects such as *Norman Rockwell: At Home in Vermont*.

Several key individuals, corporations, and foundations supported this endeavor, including Judith and James Pizzagalli, Donna and Marvin Schwartz, Todd R. Lockwood, the Frelinghuysen Foundation, the M&T Charitable Foundation, and Maplefields. We are grateful for your commitment to our community.

Most importantly, we are thankful to Polycor and Rock of Ages Corporation for their remarkable gift of *Kneeling Girl*, *The Craftsman*, and the preparatory sketch for *The Craftsman* to Shelburne Museum, an act of profound generosity that inspired *Norman Rockwell: At Home in Vermont*.

Carolyn Bauer
Marna and Chuck Davis Curator of American Art, Shelburne Museum

Thomas Denenberg
John Wilmerding Director and CEO, Shelburne Museum

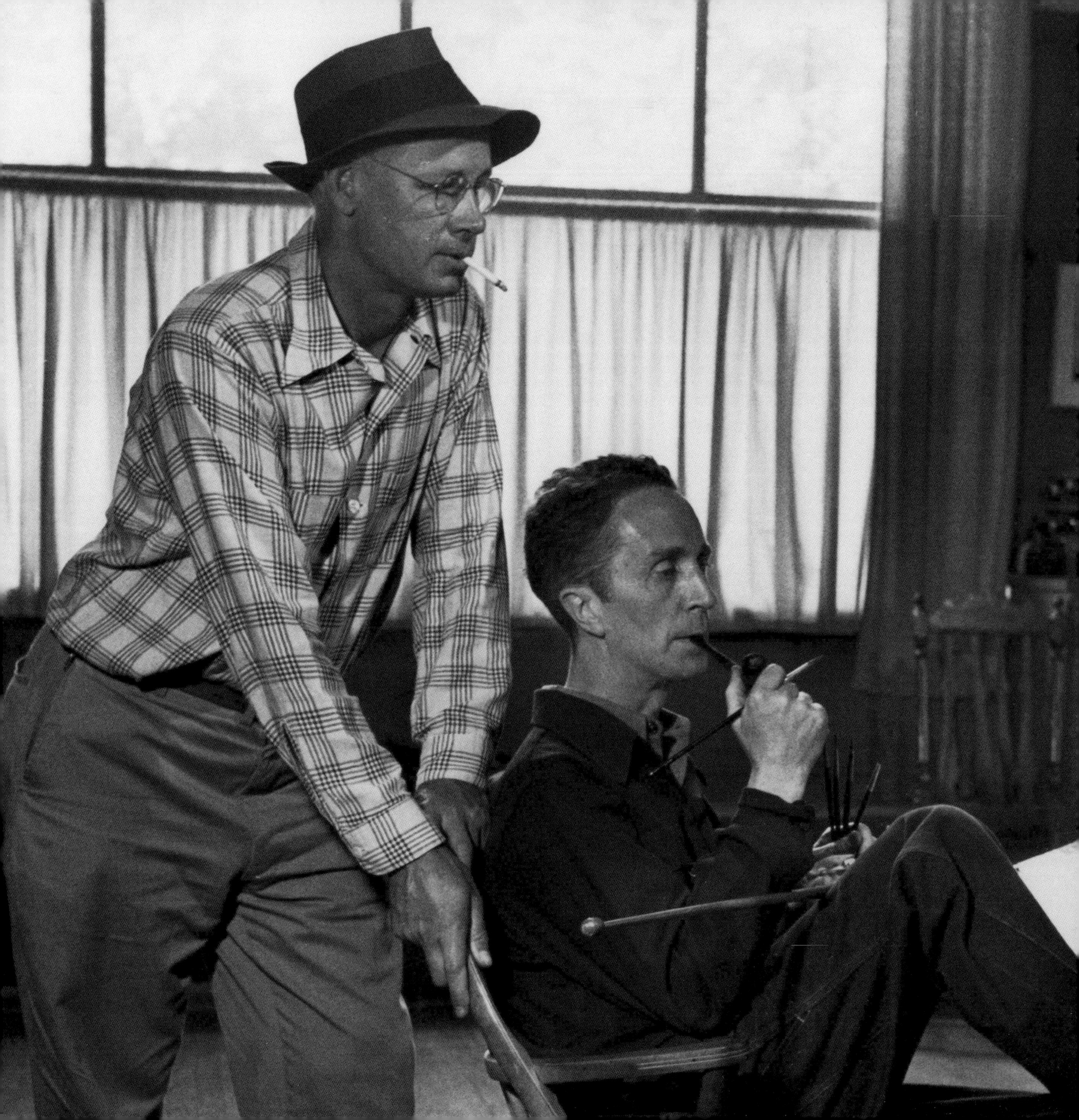

SMALL TOWN, BIG PICTURE

Norman Rockwell and the Arlington Artists

Carolyn Bauer

In the 1937 Vermont guidebook for the Works Progress Administration, best-selling author, education reformer, and arts advocate Dorothy Canfield Fisher (1879–1958) wrote of the Green Mountain state: "When you tell New York saleswomen that you live in Vermont, they say, 'Oh, how nice! I envy you!'"[1] However, this admiration—which would have gone unfounded nearly a decade earlier—ran deeper than surface attraction. It instead reflected the psychological and moral reckoning brought on by the Great Depression, which left many Americans disillusioned about the future and yearning for a steadier past that they believed Vermont embodied. Vermont, she asserted, "represents the past, is a piece of the past in the midst of the present and future."[2] For Norman Rockwell (1894–1978) and a small band of illustrators who gathered in Arlington, Vermont, that past was not simply romanticized, it became the foundation for a powerful visual mythology of American life that they would build.

Despite its modest size and rural character, Arlington and neighboring West Arlington have long drawn people of outsized influence, giving the town a history that far exceeds its scale. In the eighteenth century, Ethan Allen (1738–89), Ira Allen (1751–1814), members of the Green Mountain Boys, and Thomas Chittenden (1730–97)—the state's first governor—made their homes here, and their defiance helped secure Vermont's independence.[3] Nearly two centuries later, this same village, with its white church steeples, rolling farmland, and tight-knit community, would attract celebrated artists and authors seeking inspiration away from urban centers. The appeal lay not in its grandeur but in its authenticity. Arlington offered both a sense of rooted history and an example of core American values—self-reliance, civic spirit, and quiet perseverance—which the authors and artists hoped to capture in their work. It was precisely this blend of unpretentious daily life and symbolic resonance that made the town a magnet for figures intent on shaping how Vermont, and by extension America, was imagined.

The vibrant artistic community that blossomed in mid-century Arlington was anchored by Rockwell and fostered by the intellectual presence of Fisher. These luminaries, along with a group of *Saturday Evening Post* illustrators—Mead Schaeffer (1898–1980), John Atherton (1900–52), Gene Pelham (1909–2004), and George Hughes (1907–90)—used rural Vermont as both backdrop and metaphor, creating a body of work that communicated a reassuring, idealized image of America during some of its most uncertain years.[4] In doing so, they forged a regional artistic identity that ran parallel to the contrasting modernist energies simmering just miles away at Bennington College. Together, these seemingly disparate currents positioned Vermont as both an artistic refuge and a creative catalyst during a pivotal moment in American history when the Green Mountain state was mythologized as democracy's granite-strong refuge.

Rockwell's 1939 move to Arlington, which he called home until 1953, marked a personal and professional turning point. Leaving the previous illustrators'

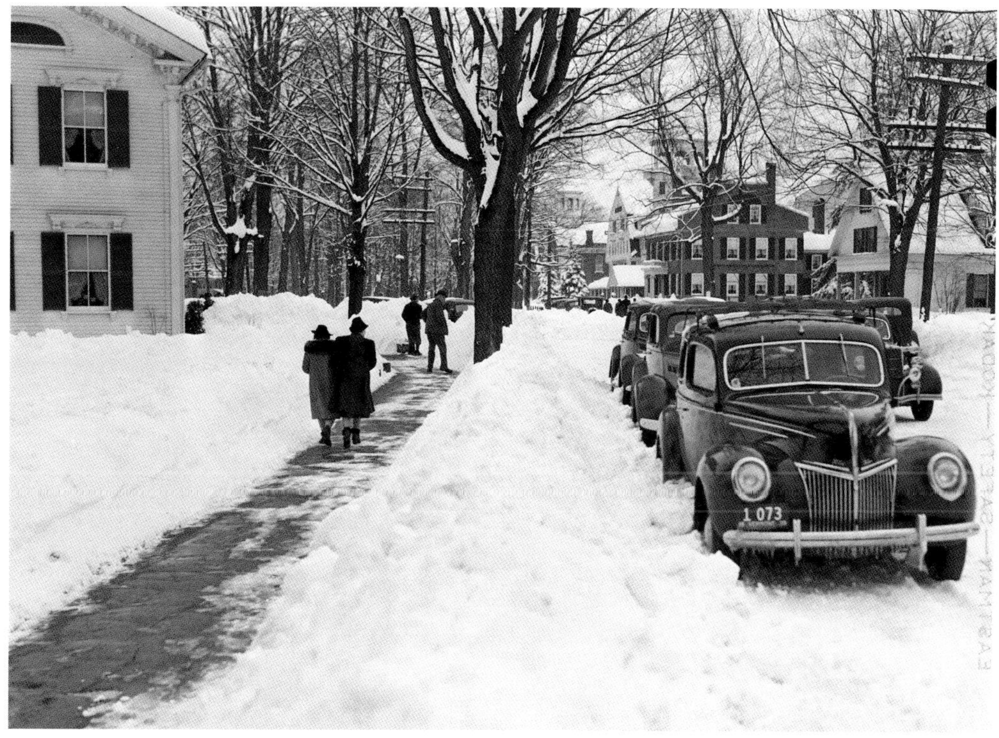

Fig. 1
Marion Post Wolcott, *Street in Woodstock, Vermont on town meeting day*, March 1940. Negative, 3¼ × 4¼ in. Library of Congress Prints and Photographs Division, Farm Security Administration–Office of War Information Photograph Collection. 2017802587.

community within New Rochelle, New York, and the urban churn of New York City, Rockwell sought not just fresh models and new scenery but a slower pace of life for him and his family, and "a real sense of place."[5] "I never had an 'old homestead' before," he reflected during the year of his arrival to Vermont. "But it's great up here, and I feel like a real guy now." This sensation of feeling more complete with his relocation coincided with a national moment of soul-searching: amid the lingering trauma of the Great Depression and the stirrings of a second world war, Americans were rethinking the future by reassessing the past. For Rockwell, there was no better place to retreat to the days of yesteryear than Vermont, a state that in the early twentieth century was seen as too rural and uncivilized but later became a refuge from rapid industrialization (Fig. 1).[6]

In the fall of 1938, Rockwell and his wife Mary (1907–59) made their way to Arlington somewhat by happenstance. They were feeling restless in the increasingly busy suburban New Rochelle, and began touring farms in Bennington, Vermont. After finding this town, and nearby Dorset, a little too posh for their taste, they landed serendipitously in the small village of Arlington for the night. From the Colonial Inn in Arlington (Fig. 2), they got a sense of the town, which

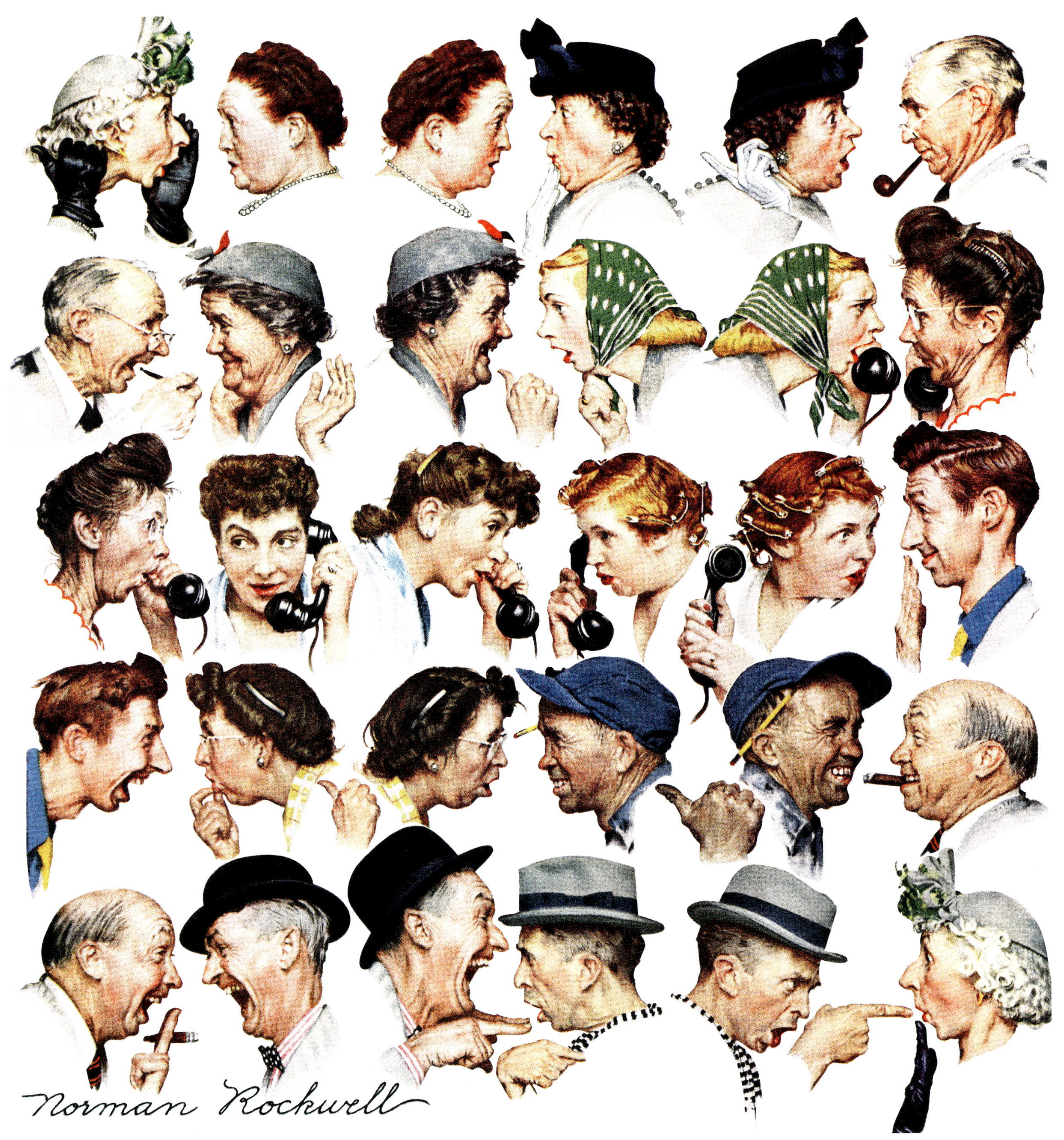
Norman Rockwell

Pl. 1
Norman Rockwell, *The Gossips*, 1948. Cover illustration for *The Saturday Evening Post*, March 6, 1948. Oil on canvas, 33 × 31 in. Private Collection. Illustration provided by SEPS through Curtis Licensing. Artwork Approved by the Norman Rockwell Family Agency.

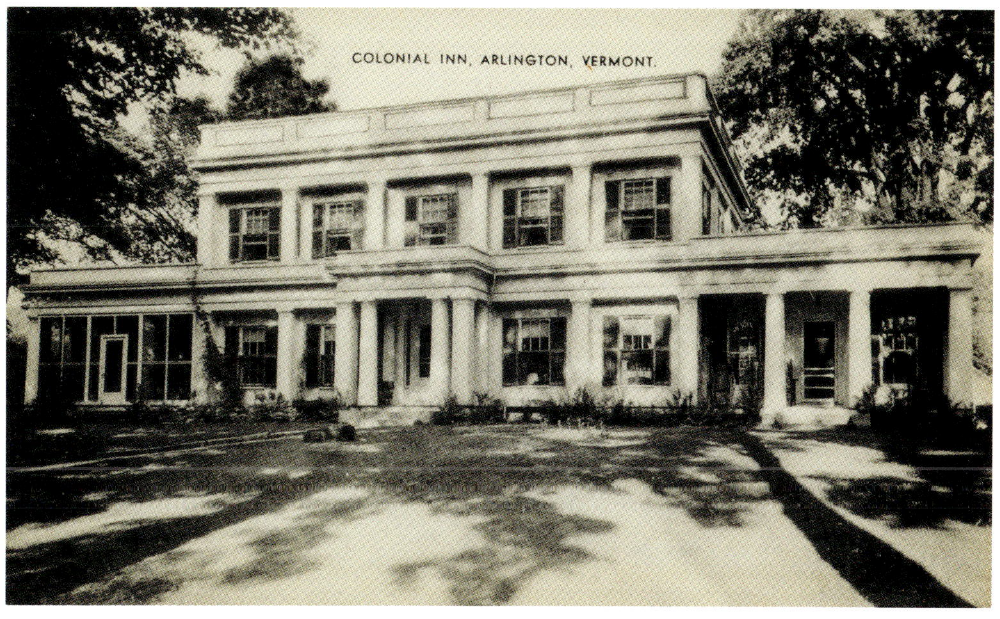

Fig. 2
Published by Artvue Post Card Company, *Colonial Inn, Arlington, Vermont*, 1948–63. Ink on paper, 3½ × 5½ in. Collection of Shelburne Museum Archives. PC7.A.8.

included a library, town hall, and general store. Within twenty-four hours of their stay, the Rockwells had purchased a farmhouse with sixty acres of land.[7] Before they moved into the property later that summer, a studio had been constructed on site out of a preexisting barn.[8] It was in this studio, and his subsequent second property in nearby West Arlington, that Rockwell got to know many of his new neighbors intimately as they posed for his pictures, often with cold Coca-Colas at the ready and five dollars for their time.[9]

Local farmers, doctors, mailmen, and schoolchildren became Rockwell's models, serving as authentic representations of common New Englanders and Vermonters in his nostalgia-riddled illustrations. Perhaps based on real events, Rockwell's *The Gossips* (Plate 1) is a masterclass in visual storytelling, capturing the infectious and cyclical nature of rumor in small-town life through a sequence of expressive cropped portraits. Structured almost like a comic strip, the painting begins with whispered gossip from an elderly woman and ends, humorously, with the original gossiper being confronted by Rockwell, the presumed subject of the piece of gossip. But beyond its clever composition and comic timing, *The Gossips* is a vivid testament to Rockwell's deep connection to Arlington, and his commitment to using its residents as models to embody what he considered authentic American life.

Nearly every figure in *The Gossips* was drawn from Rockwell's Arlington community. He photographed neighbors and friends in his studio, directing them

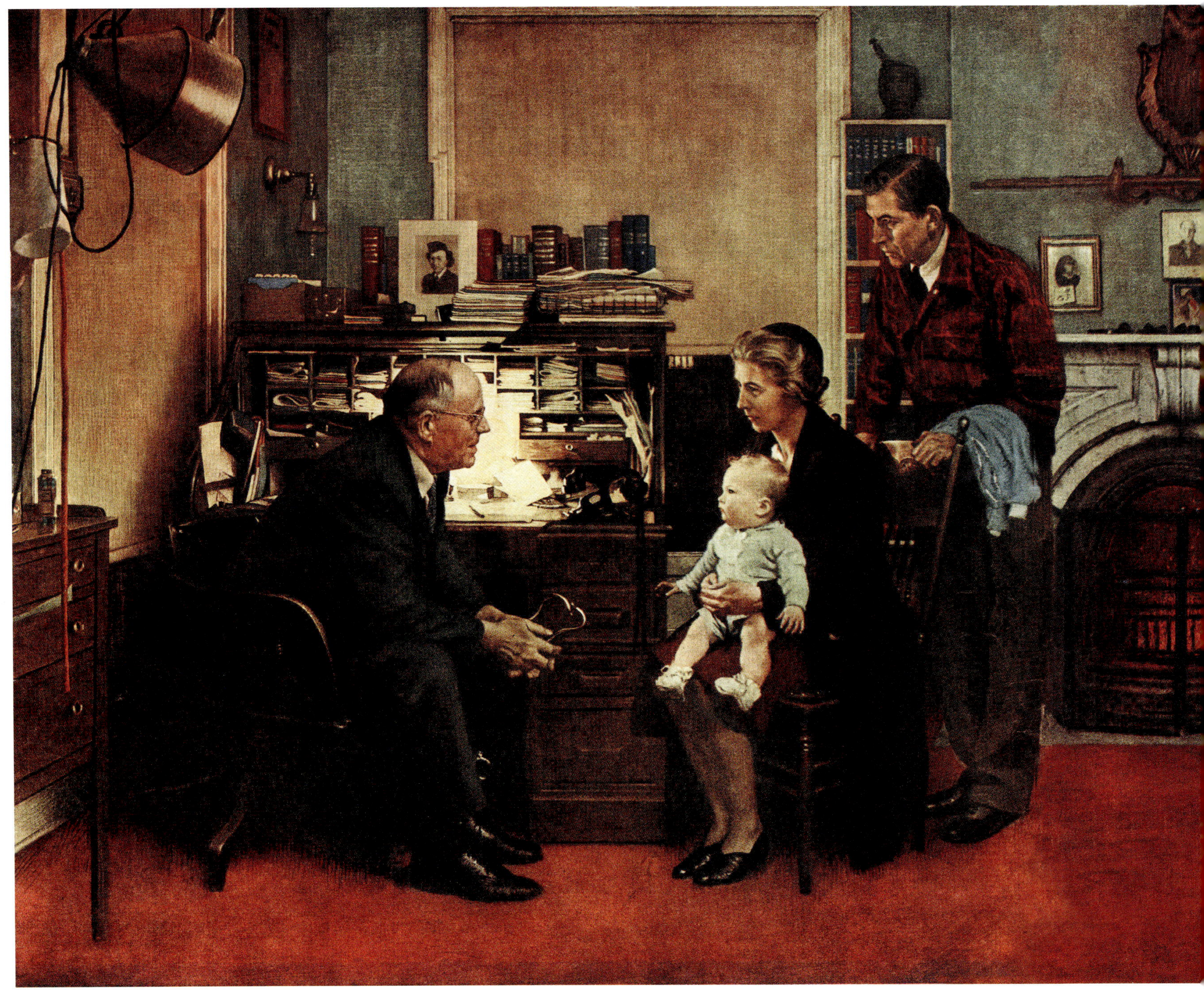

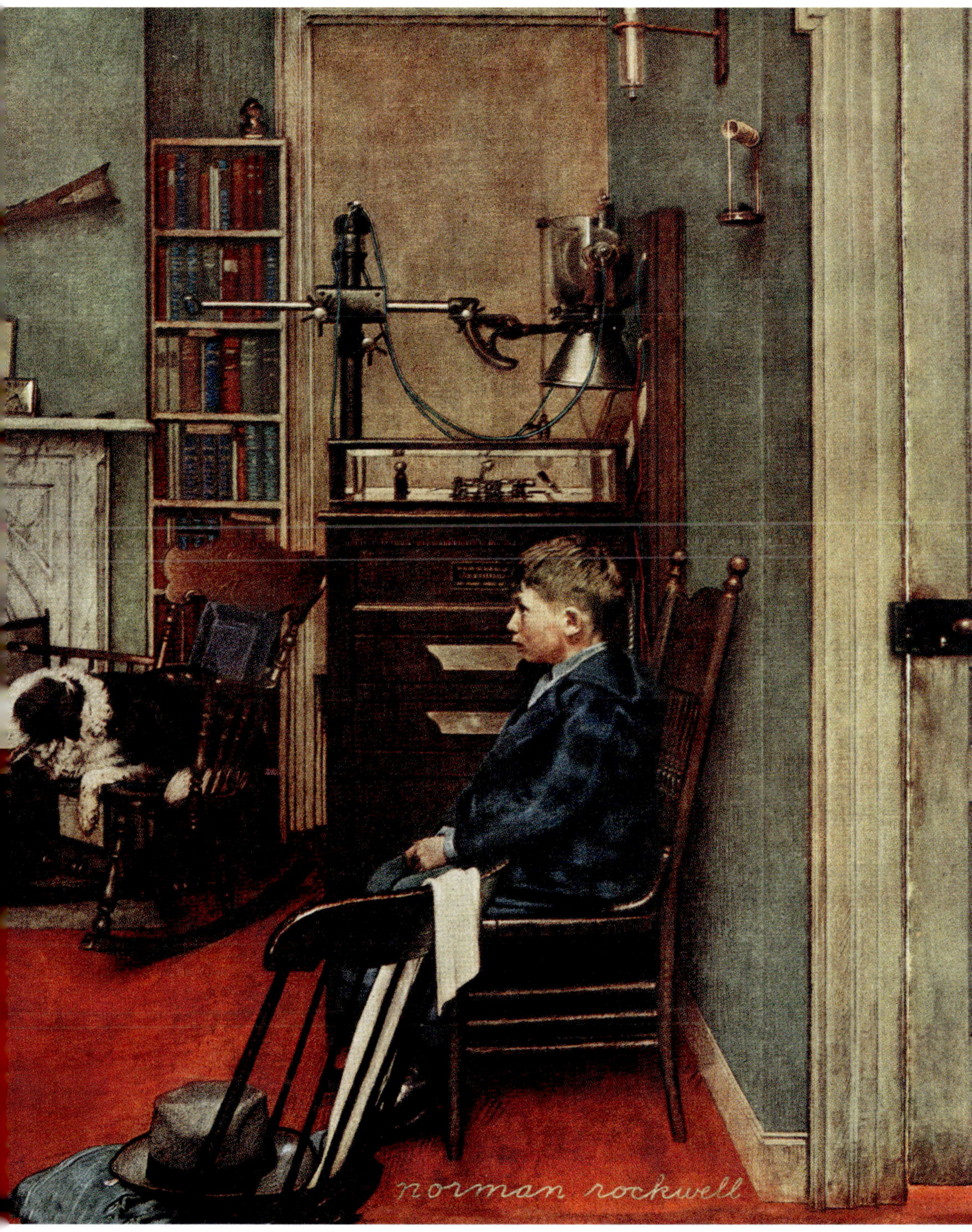

Pl. 2

Norman Rockwell, *Norman Rockwell Visits a Family Doctor*, 1947. Illustration for *The Saturday Evening Post*, April 12, 1947. Oil on canvas, 29⅜ × 59½ in. Norman Rockwell Museum Collection. NRM.1980.01. Illustration provided by SEPS through Curtis Licensing. Artwork Approved by the Norman Rockwell Family Agency.

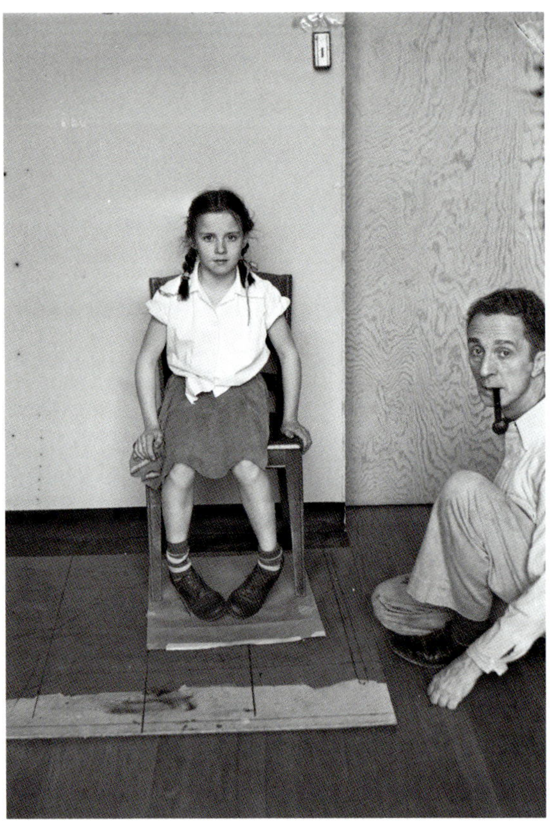

Fig. 3
Gene Pelham, *Reference Photo for The Young Lady with a Shiner*, 1953. Cover illustration for *The Saturday Evening Post*, May 23, 1953. Photographic negative, 3¼ × 4¼ in. Norman Rockwell Museum Collection, Norman Rockwell Art Collection Trust, Studio Collection. ST.1976.8661. Artwork Approved by the Norman Rockwell Family Agency.

to perform exaggerated reactions—shock, indignation, delight—as the imagined secret makes its way through the town. Rockwell and his wife Mary appear in the final panel, making the work both self-aware and unmistakably local. This was not a matter of convenience; it was integral to his artistic philosophy. Rockwell believed that to truly portray the American experience, he needed to draw from real people with their own lived experiences. "In New York," he once lamented, "the models I've had to depend on . . . are all washed-out and unhealthy. Up here [in Arlington], I not only encounter practically every type of American I'll ever have to use, but they look healthy!"[10]

For Rockwell, Vermonters were not just models but partners in storytelling. Their rugged self-possession, naturalistic expressions, and unvarnished individuality inspired him with their emotional truth. "The commonplaces of America are to me the richest subjects in art," he wrote in 1939, and it was in Arlington's town hall, schoolhouses, and post offices that he found the raw material for those "commonplaces."[11] *Norman Rockwell Visits a Family Doctor*

Pl. 3
Norman Rockwell, *The Young Lady with the Shiner*, 1953. Cover illustration for *The Saturday Evening Post*, May 23, 1953. Oil on canvas, 34 × 32¼ in. Wadsworth Atheneum Museum of Art, Gift of Kenneth Stuart. 1973.112. Artwork Approved by the Norman Rockwell Family Agency.

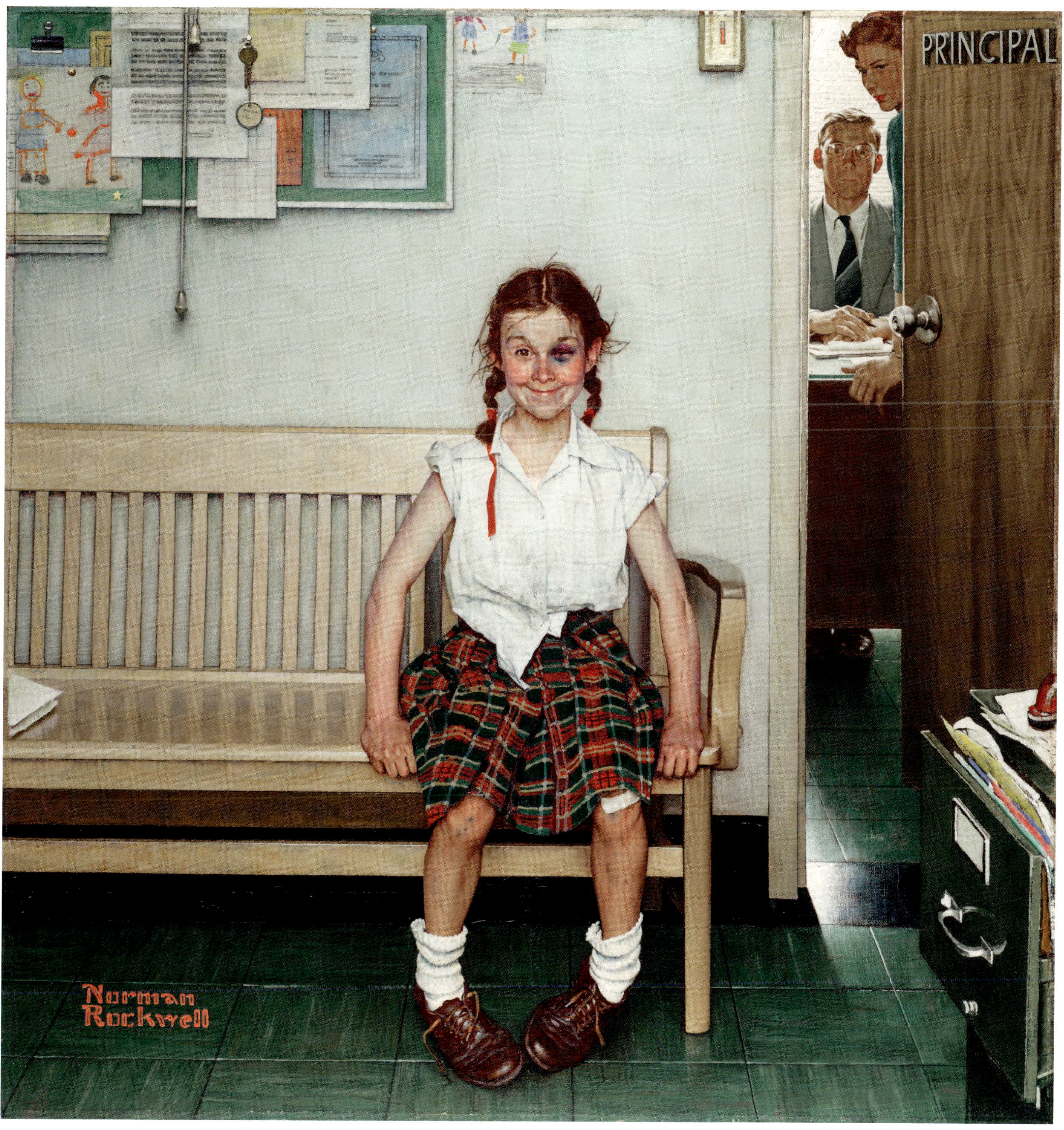
PRINCIPAL
Norman Rockwell

(Plate 2), for example, depicts Arlington's own Dr. George Russell tending to a young family in his home office. By showing his physician in an authentic setting for a national audience, Rockwell elevated his rural, local life.

Children in the community were often his most memorable models. For *The Young Lady with a Shiner* (Plate 3), Rockwell turned to ten-year-old Mary Whalen (b. 1942), a favorite of the artist, who sat for several carefully staged photographs taken by Gene Pelham for this work (Fig. 3).[12] The composition captures her triumphant grin as she sits outside the principal's office, legs crossed and head held high, proudly sporting a black eye that tells its own mischievous story. Rockwell, however, struggled with the bruise itself. Charcoal and makeup failed to capture the varied hues of the actual injury, so he placed an ad in the local *Berkshire Eagle* newspaper requesting photographs of fresh black eyes.[13] Dozens of images arrived, but the most convincing came from a two-and-a-half-year-old who had fallen downstairs and earned himself a spectacular pair of bruises. Rockwell paid the boy twenty-five dollars and translated the photograph into paint.[14] The result is one of Rockwell's most endearing and humorous portraits of childhood resilience that captures a quintessentially American scene.

That same spirit of authenticity extended beyond Rockwell's canvas and into his personal life. While the artist maintained social connections in major cities across the nation, he became an active member of the Arlington community. He joined the local Battenkill Grange—a community service organization—was a regular fixture at the town's square dances, regularly spoke about his work at Rotary clubs and PTA meetings, participated and served as judge in nearby art fairs, acted in one of Fisher's plays, and even became a partial owner of Battenkill Cemetery Inc. of West Arlington.[15] His immersion in the small town fueled his creative pursuits, no doubt providing inspiration and authenticity for his illustrations, the majority of which featured narrative genre scenes from pastoral New England.

Rockwell was not alone in his pursuit of "the commonplaces of America." Other artists—like *Post* artists Schaeffer, Atherton, Pelham, and Hughes—were all informally enticed to the Arlington area. Other relocated artists that joined their circle included cartoonist Don Trachte (1915–2005) and composer and painter Carl Ruggles (1876–1971). What began as a quiet retreat evolved into an informal, synergistic collective. Like Rockwell, these artists straddled the worlds of fine art and commercial illustration, and they all left increasingly crowded and expensive cities and suburbs to embrace the slower pace and clean living in rural Vermont. While many illustrators during this period moved to new artist colonies—for example, leaving New Rochelle, New York, for Westport, Connecticut—it is unique that these illustrators avoided other suburban towns in favor of embracing Vermont's countryside.[16]

However, the Arlington artists continued to work in a similar fashion to the collaborative methods they had used in the city. Working together, they posed

Fig. 4
Unidentified photographer, *Norman Rockwell and John Atherton*, date unknown. Silver gelatin print, $7\frac{5}{8} \times 7\frac{5}{8}$ in. Norman Rockwell Museum Collection, Famous Artists School Collection, gift of Magdalen & Robert Livesey. RC.2013.11.6.246. Artwork Approved by the Norman Rockwell Family Agency.

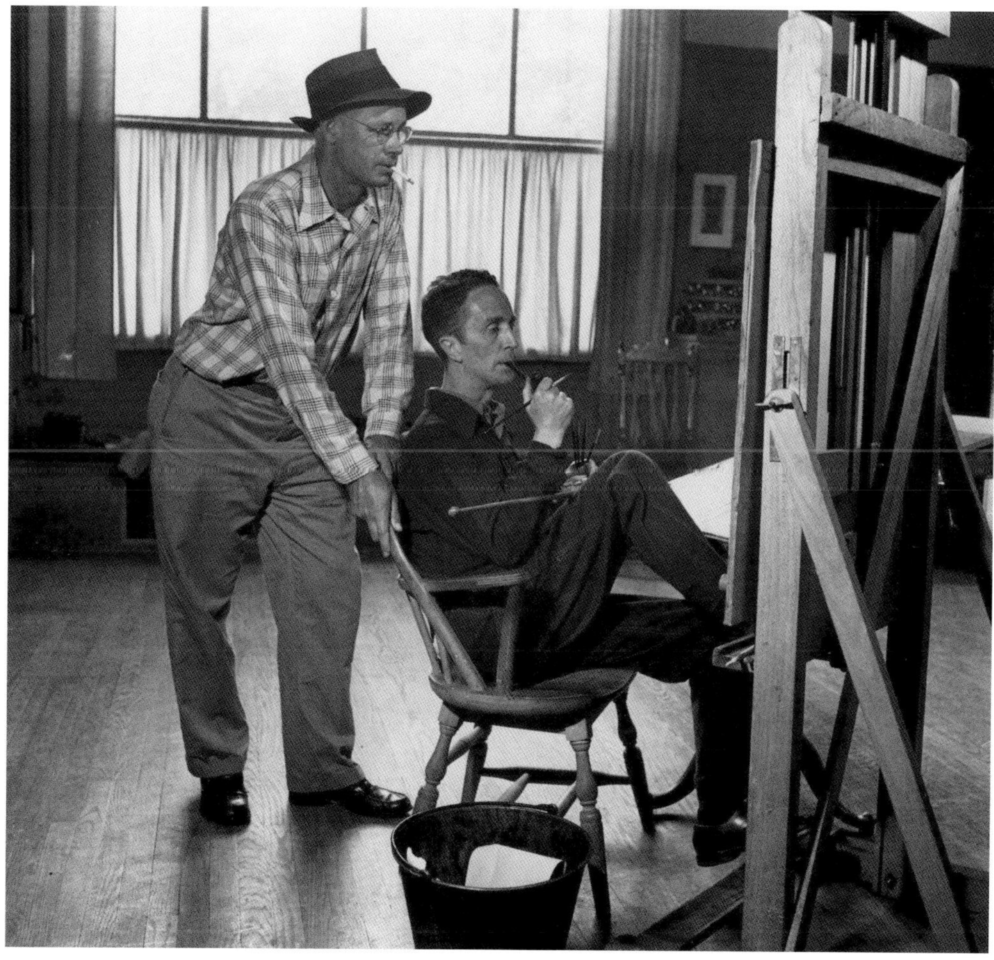

in photographs for one another's works, inspired each other, socialized, consulted each other on their projects, and on rare occasions even collaborated on projects together (Fig. 4).[17] "[In Arlington] we were going to bring back the golden age of illustration," Rockwell wrote in his autobiography, "the glorious days of Howard Pyle, Remington, Abbey."[18] Even in their differences—such as Schaeffer's more muscular figures versus Rockwell's sentimental narratives—their works embodied a shared aesthetic rooted in the ethos of Vermont and nostalgia for simpler times, which resonated across the nation, thanks to the *Post*'s vast readership. Even Atherton's fine art paintings, which more often verged on dystopic landscapes than his other Arlington counterparts, yearned for the preservation of yesteryear, an idealized version of the nation.

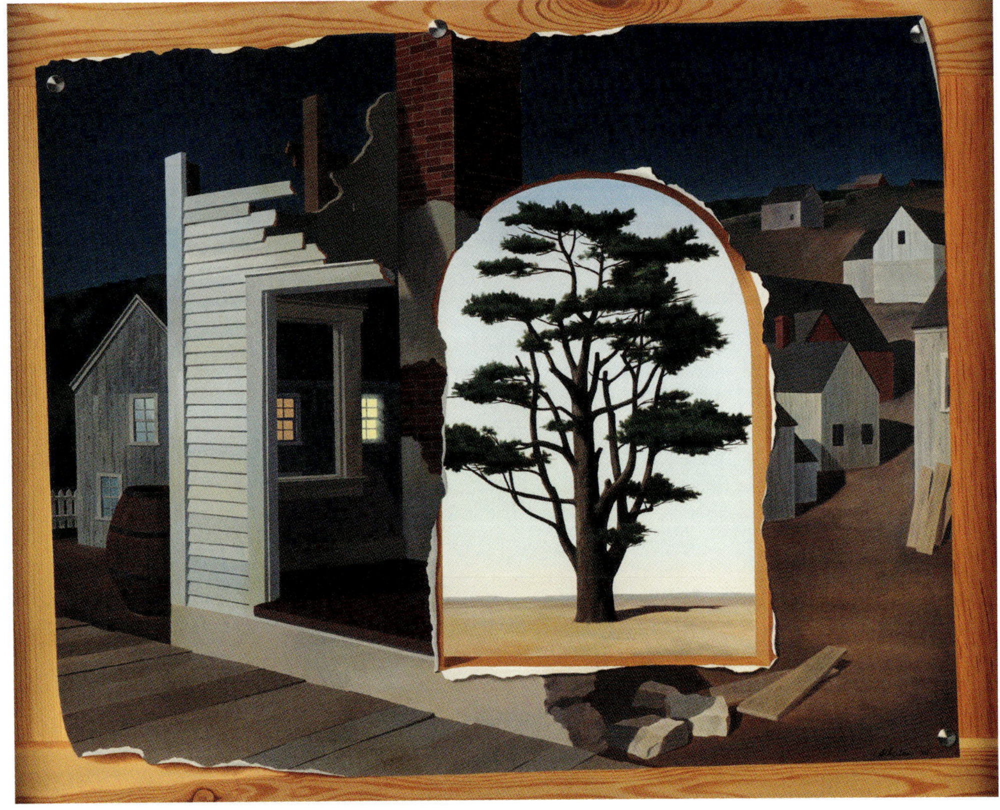

Fig. 5
John Atherton, *Pine Tree*, 1938. Oil on canvas, 24 × 30 in. Collection of Shelburne Museum, museum purchase. 2023-6.

Pl. 4
Norman Rockwell, *Shuffleton's Barbershop*, 1950. Cover illustration for *The Saturday Evening Post*, April 29, 1950. Oil on canvas, 46¼ × 43¼ in. Lucas Museum of Narrative Art, Los Angeles. 2018.10.1. Artwork Approved by the Norman Rockwell Family Agency.

For example, Atherton's *Pine Tree* (Fig. 5) blends surrealism, magic realism, and trompe l'oeil to evoke a haunting sense of unease. A grid of shadowed, uniform houses under a nocturnal sky contrasts with a single illuminated window, while a fragmented foreground and a mysterious arched opening reveals a daytime landscape with an evergreen. The composition resists easy interpretation—an effect Atherton embraced, once stating of his work that "in the end the painting must be felt, not analyzed."[19]

While Rockwell's subject matter offered more hopeful undertones, reaffirming the values of neighborliness, modesty, and humor, these were not naive works. Though Rockwell famously distanced himself from abstraction—"I am the direct opposite of an abstractionist," he declared—his work occasionally flirted with modernist aesthetics.[20] As art historian Jennifer Greenhill notes, *Shuffleton's Barbershop* (Plate 4) reveals Rockwell's "savvy acknowledgment of art-historical precedent," blending seventeenth-century Dutch genre painting with formal geometric abstraction in the grid-like framing of the foregrounded

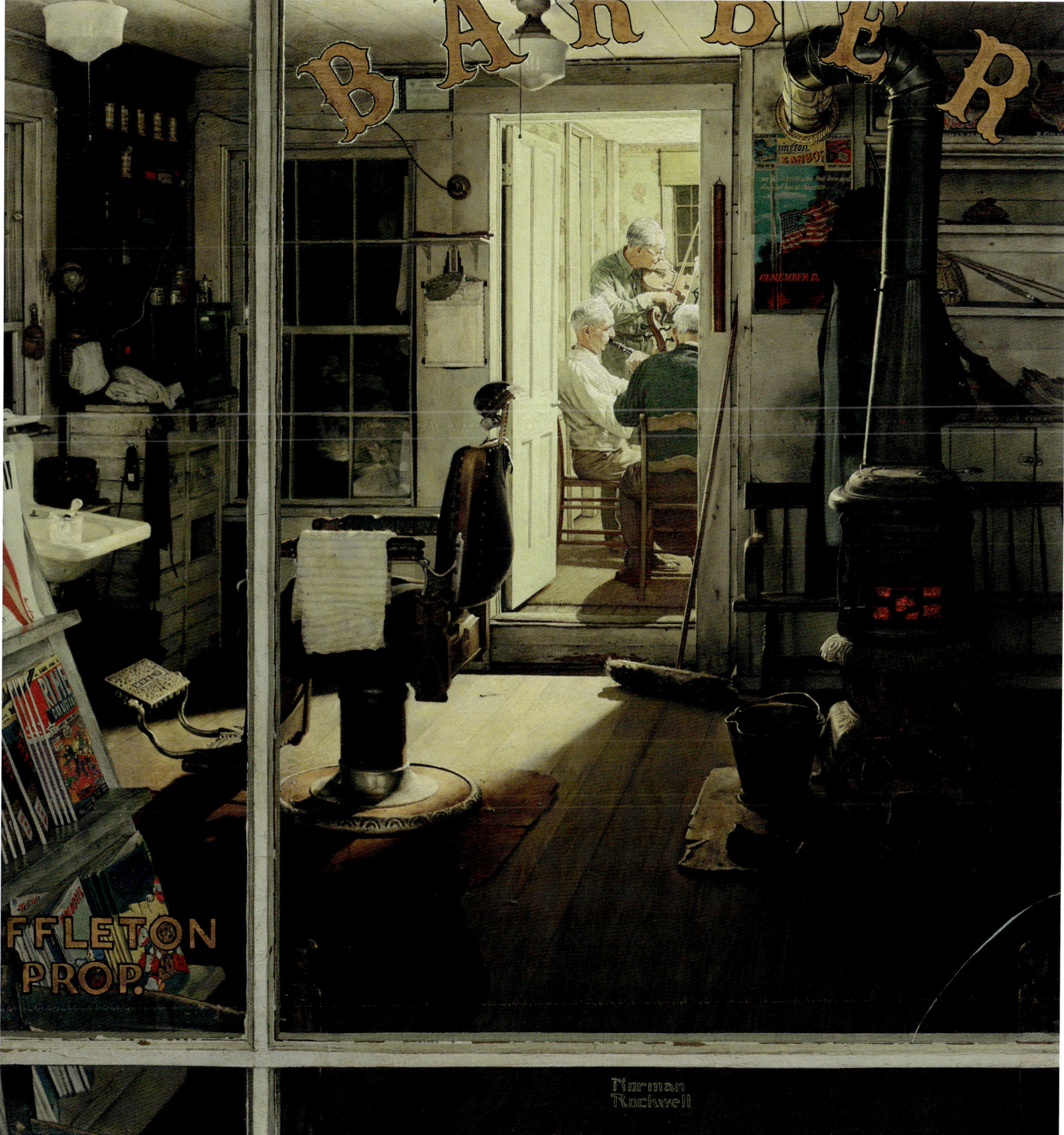
BARBER
FFLETON
PROP.
Norman
Rockwell

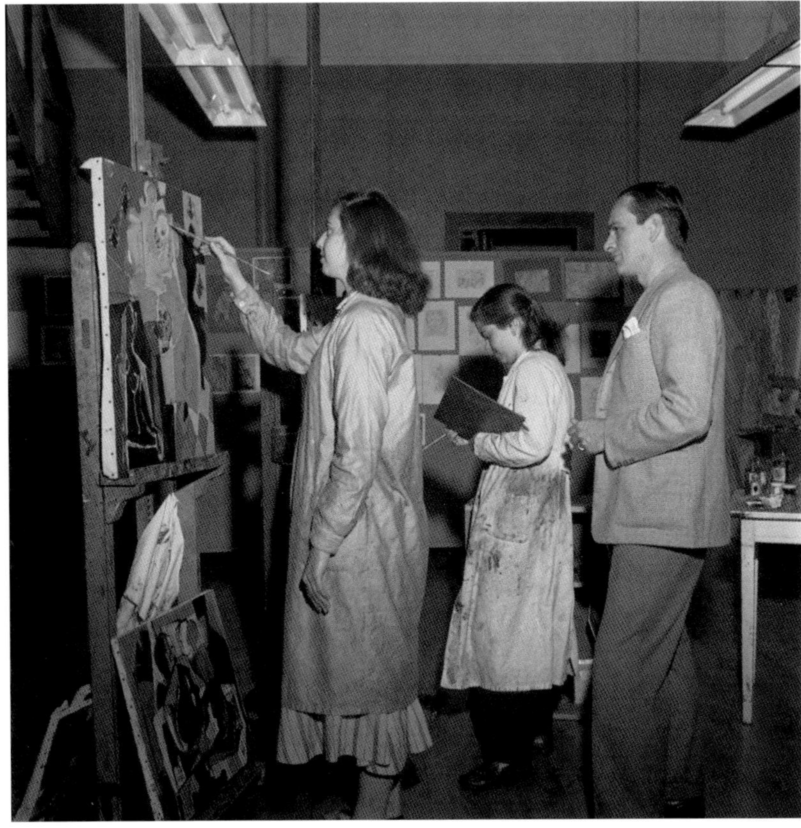

Fig. 6
Unidentified photographer, *Helen Frankenthaler, Ruth Lyford, and Paul Feeley at Bennington College, Vermont*, ca. 1949. Photograph. Bennington College Archives.

windowpanes.[21] Rockwell's admiration of this later movement was quiet, perhaps even self-deprecating, but it was real: "You can learn a tremendous lot from the abstractionists and so forth," he once said, "but I like to please people and they don't."[22]

While Rockwell left abstraction to others, he could not escape its growing influence even in Vermont. Just a short drive from Arlington to Bennington, Bennington College had become a hub of modernist innovation. Founded in 1932, the college's art department, led by Paul Feeley (1910–66), nurtured rising talents like Helen Frankenthaler (1928–2011), who studied there from 1946 to 1949 (Fig. 6).[23] By the 1950s and '60s, prominent artists such as David Smith (1906–65) and Jules Olitski (1922–2007) taught at Bennington, while exhibitions featured major figures like Joan Mitchell (1925–92), Larry Rivers (1923–2002), and Hedda Sterne (1910–2011)—clear evidence that the avant-garde had taken root in the Green Mountains.[24] Whereas Bennington's

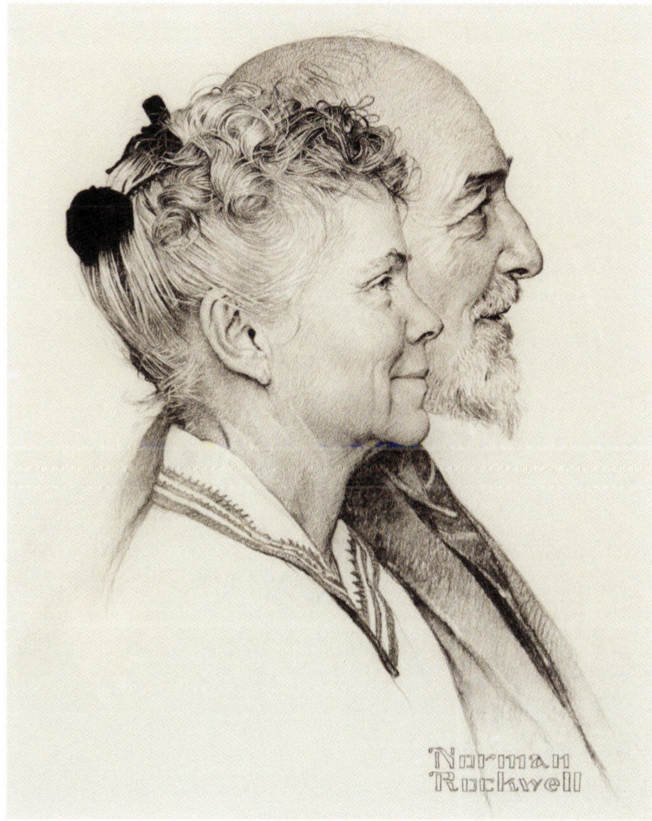

Fig. 7
Norman Rockwell, *Dorothy Canfield and John Fisher*, ca. 1950. Charcoal on paper, 11 × 14 in. Bennington Museum, Funds for purchase provided by exchange from the Colyer Collection, in Memory of Joseph H. Colyer, Sr. 2018.3. Artwork Approved by the Norman Rockwell Family Agency.

modern artists deconstructed form and color, Arlington's illustrators constructed meaning with memories. Yet both movements and colonies reveal Vermont as a creative sanctuary with national reach.

If Bennington fostered the new, Arlington honored the enduring—and no one shaped that vision more than Fisher, the town's cultural matriarch and a driving force behind its strong artistic community (Fig. 7). A celebrated author, social reformer, and public intellectual, Fisher positioned Vermont as a haven of old-fashioned values at a time when Americans were turning away from modernity's promises. In 1942, she described Vermonters as uniquely equipped to weather hard times, steeped in thrift and self-sufficiency. "Much of what we call 'Vermontism,'" she wrote, "is nothing but good 'old-Americanism' surviving in an out-of-the-main-current community, which has not been so beaten upon as communities elsewhere by the storms of modern life."[25] Like the Arlington artists, Fisher did more than observe; she actively cultivated this identity for

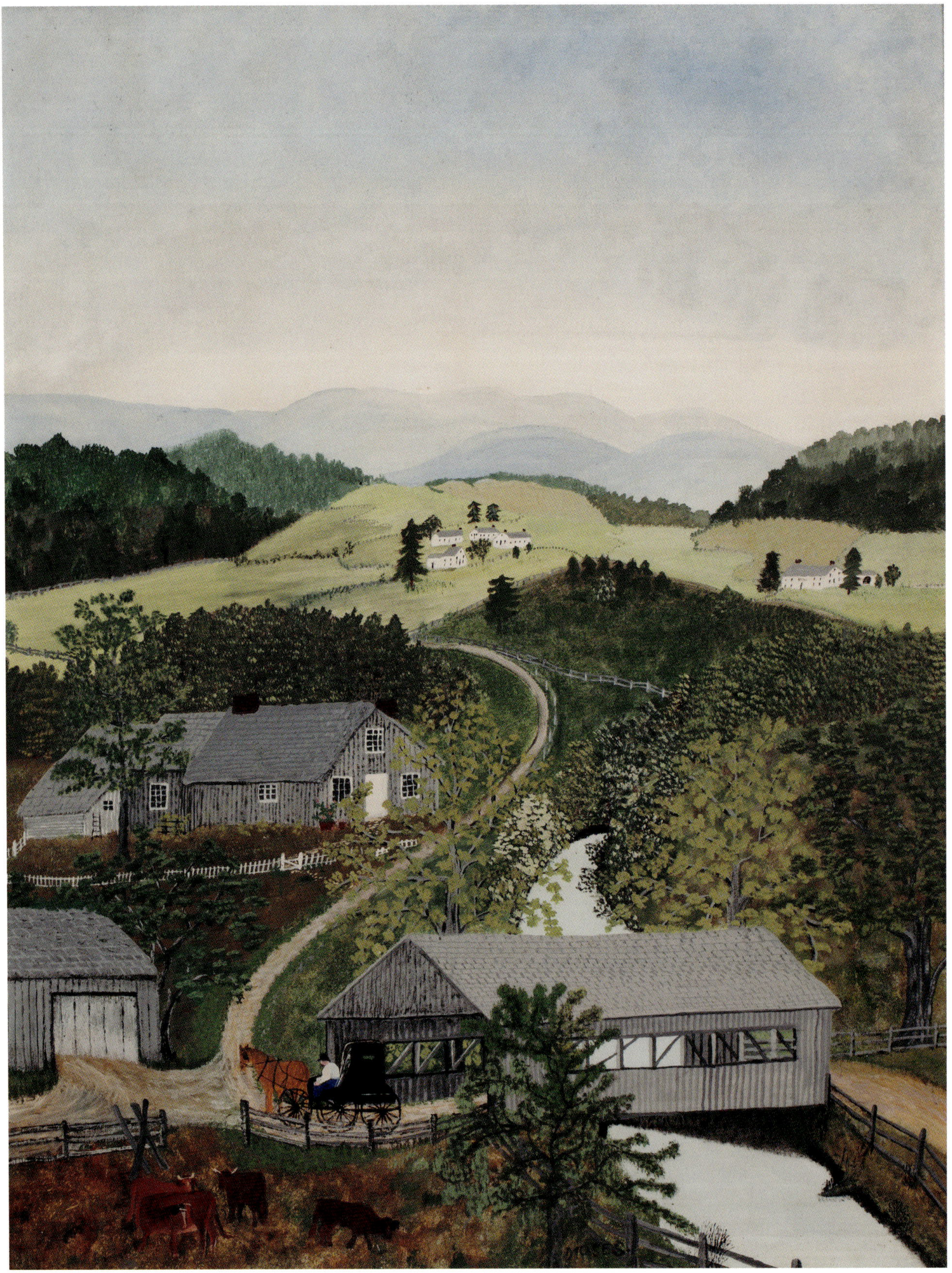

Fig. 8
Anna Mary Robertson "Grandma" Moses, *Covered Bridge with Carriage or Black Buggy*, 1946. Oil on Masonite, 29 × 22⅜ in. Collection of Shelburne Museum, museum purchase, 1961, acquired from Otto Kallir. 1961-210.3. © Estate of Grandma Moses (Bridgeman Copyright).

Vermont. As historian Dona Brown notes, Fisher worked "tirelessly throughout her life to attract professionals as visitors and migrants to the state," believing they would help sustain Vermont's values.[26] Rockwell and the other artists in town were no exception. Fisher helped lay the cultural and ideological groundwork for Arlington's modern creative community, collaborating with local artists and nationally amplifying Vermont's steadfast anti-materialist, self-reliant ethos.

While unique, Arlington was not, however, an isolated phenomenon in the state but part of a larger trend: artists across the state were turning to Vermont's pastoral landscapes as antidotes to modern dislocation. Nearby, Anna Mary Robertson "Grandma" Moses (1860–1961), who befriended Rockwell in her later years, painted her childhood memories with charming directness, refusing to be swayed by fashion or technique (Fig. 8).[27] Luigi Lucioni (1900–88) captured the

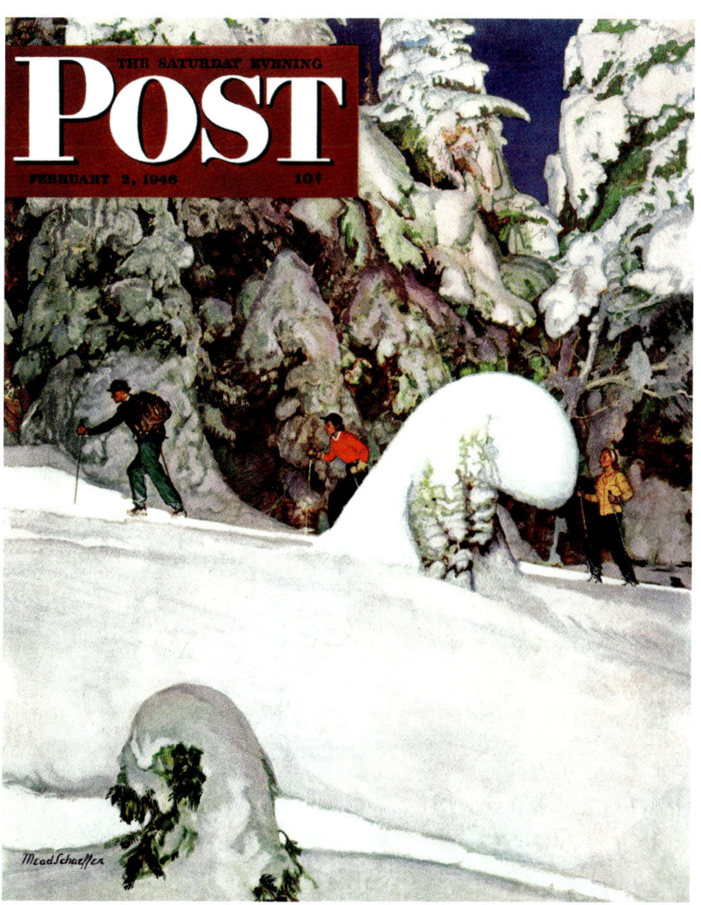

Fig. 9
Designed by Mead Schaeffer, *Cross Country Skiers*, *The Saturday Evening Post*, February 2, 1946. Cover illustration tear sheet, 14¼ × 11¼ in. Illustration © SEPS licensed by Curtis Licensing.

sharp light and topographical clarity of the Vermont landscape. Likewise, Rockwell Kent (1882–1971) and Paul Sample (1896–1974) drew on the state's mythic qualities, painting both its tranquility and its tenacity.

Even in its imagined form, Vermont became a national ideal. To outsiders disillusioned by economic collapse and global conflict, Vermont's self-sufficiency, town-hall approach to democracy, and community-mindedness offered a kind of secular salvation. While Vermont "is not Utopia," as the popular historian Bernard DeVoto put it, "it is a citizenship, and it glances toward the almost-perfect state."[28] Rockwell and the Arlington illustrators were instrumental in shaping this national perception of Vermont as the bedrock of American ideals. Their scenes of civic engagement, family dinners, and outdoor recreation are more than quaint Americana—they are reflections of values born in hardship, sustained through community, and rooted in a very real place. A striking example is Schaeffer's *Saturday Evening Post* cover of 1942, which portrays three figures climbing Bromley Mountain, just outside Arlington, on Nordic skis (Fig. 9).[29] The illustration, with its fresh snowfall and vigorous figures with their sense of shared activity, recasts Vermont's rugged landscape as a wholesome winter playground. In doing so, it not only reflects the state's natural beauty, but it also reinforces the growing popular image of Vermont as a tourist destination for outdoor recreation.

Arlington was not merely a setting; it was a nexus for creatives. Here, artists collaborated and critiqued. They relied on neighbors for modeling, advice, and inspiration. Rockwell attended the local square dances and served as deputy commander of Civil Defense.[30] The Arlington artists all contributed to the annual Community Club art exhibition.[31] Fisher wrote and spoke publicly, advocating for Vermont tourism, mentoring newcomers who would fuel the arts sectors, and assisting in establishing the state's symphony orchestra.[32] Together, they forged an artistic identity that still informs how we see Vermont and how we imagine America.

During Rockwell's years in Vermont, as the nation was searching for direction, these artists looked backward and inward, to the granitic virtues of a small town in Vermont. What they created was not escapism but aspiration. "Illustration is the principal pictorial form of conveying ideas and emotions and telling funny stories," Rockwell shared in an interview. Postulating on his own life's work, he said he "feels that I am doing something when I paint a picture that appeals to most people."[33] Rockwell's legacy endures, reminding us that art, at its best, does not just reflect a place but builds community.

Pl. 5

Norman Rockwell, *Marble Champion (Girl Playing Marbles),* 1939. Cover illustration for *The Saturday Evening Post,* September 2, 1939. Oil on canvas, 28 × 22 in. Private Collection. Illustration provided by SEPS through Curtis Licensing. Artwork Approved by the Norman Rockwell Family Agency.

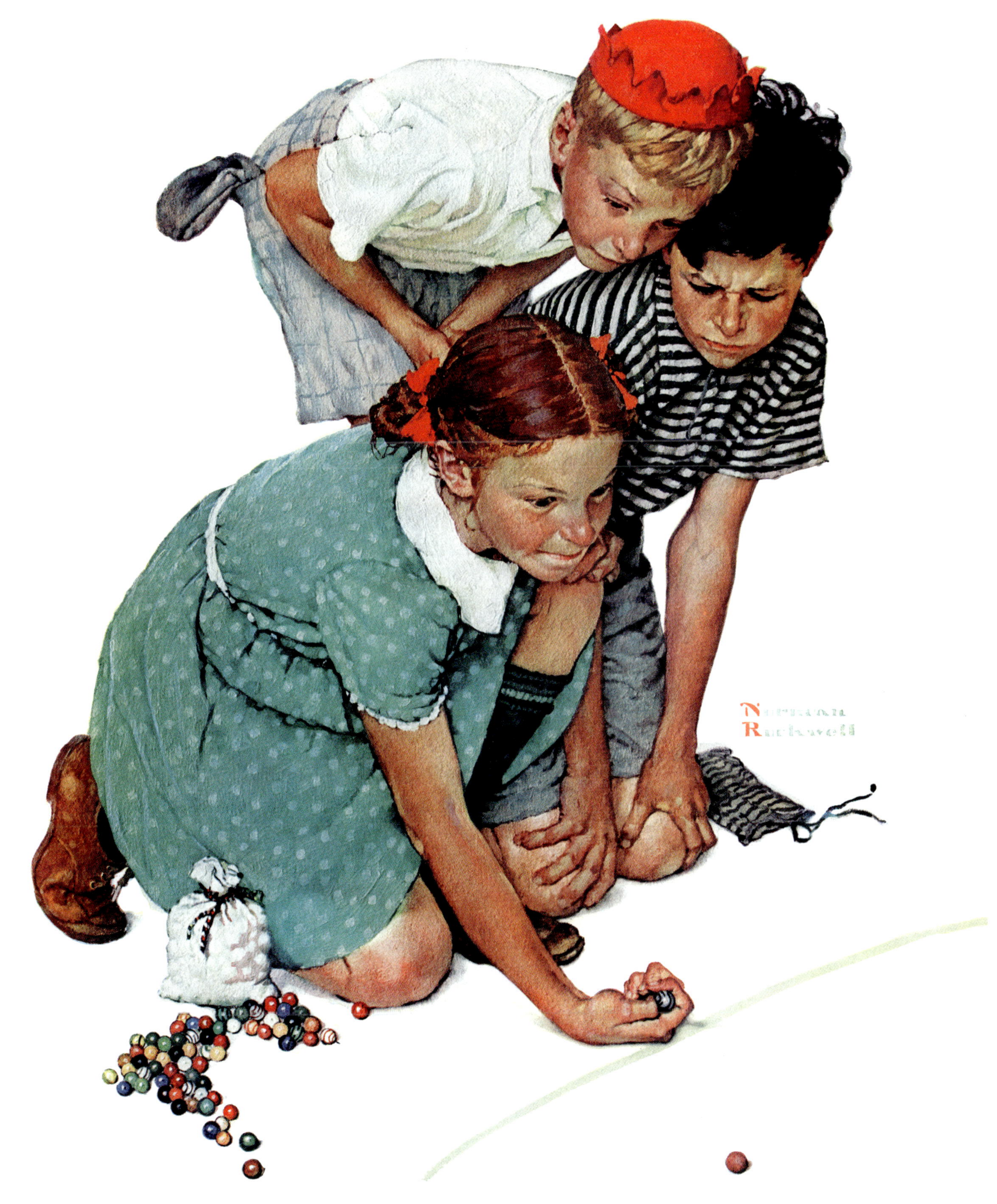

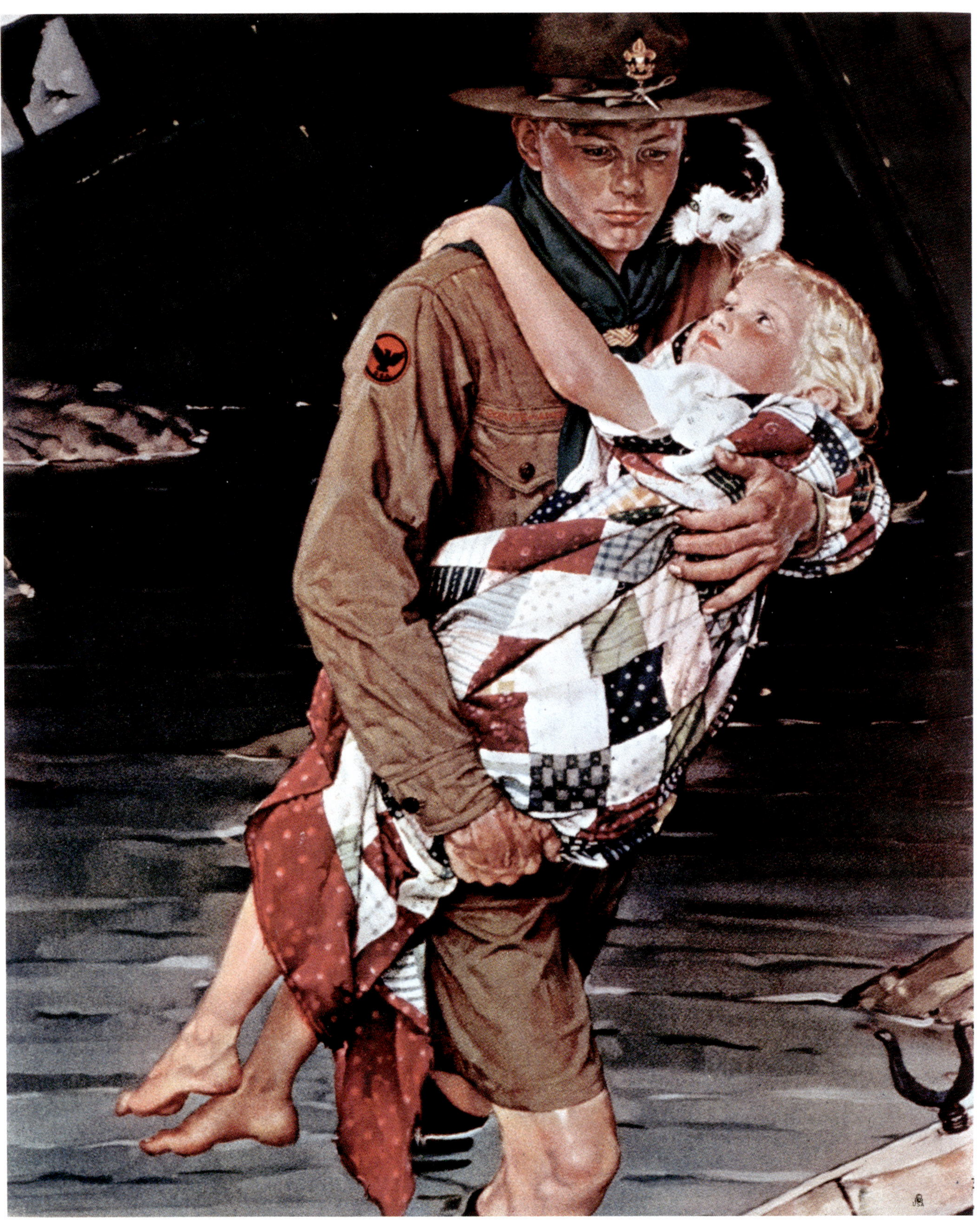

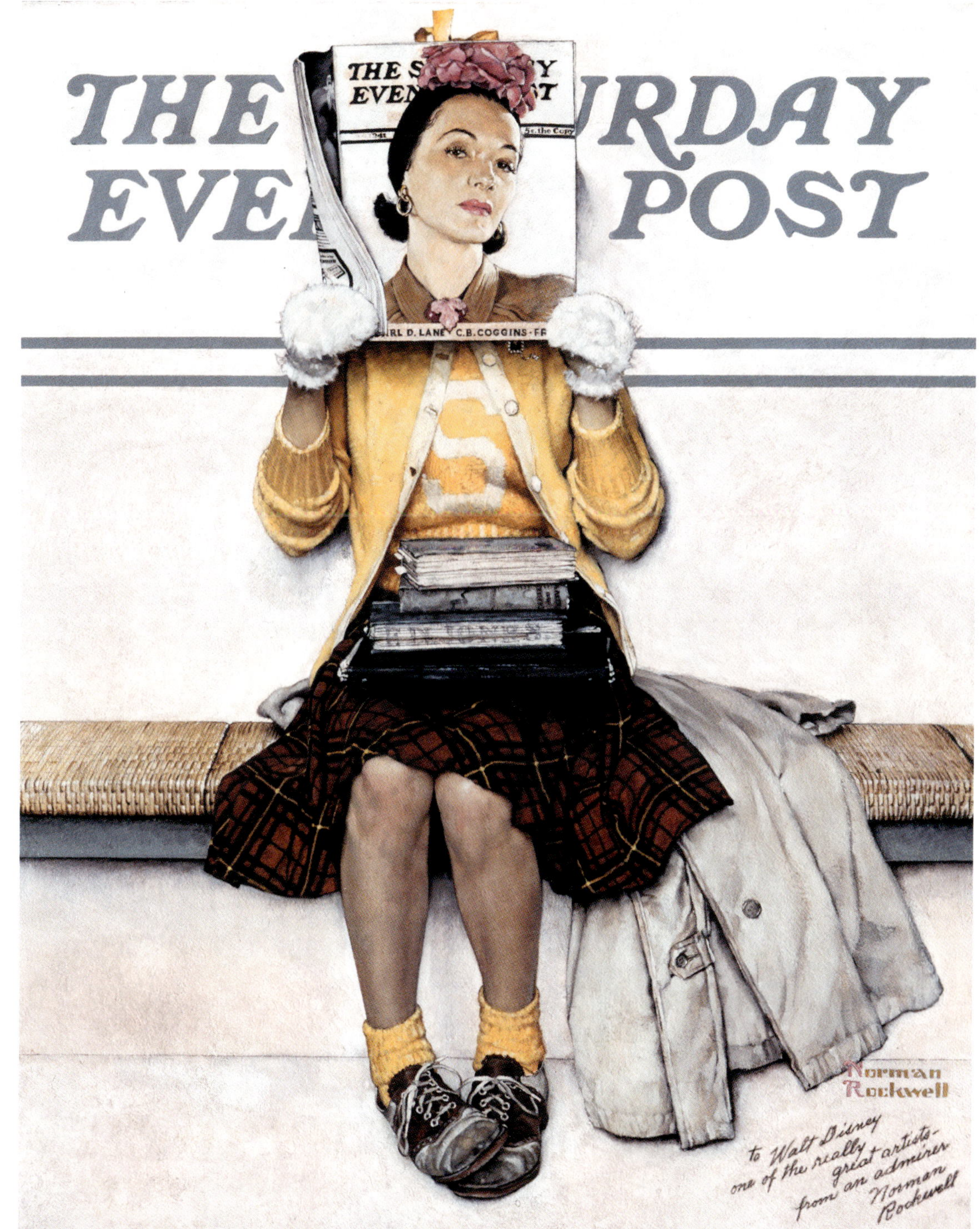

Pl. 6
Norman Rockwell, *A Scout is Helpful*, 1941. Calendar illustration for *Boy Scouts of America*. Oil on canvas, 34 × 24 in. Norman Rockwell Museum Collection, Museum purchase. NRM.1988.10. © 1941 Brown & Bigelow Licensing. All rights reserved. Artwork Approved by the Norman Rockwell Family Agency.

Pl. 7
Norman Rockwell, *Girl Reading the Post*, 1941. Cover illustration for *The Saturday Evening Post*, March 1, 1941. Oil on canvas, 32¼ × 27¼ in. Norman Rockwell Museum Collection, Gift of the Walt Disney Family. NRM.1999.03. © 1941 SEPS: Curtis Licensing, Indianapolis, IN. All rights reserved. Artwork Approved by the Norman Rockwell Family Agency.

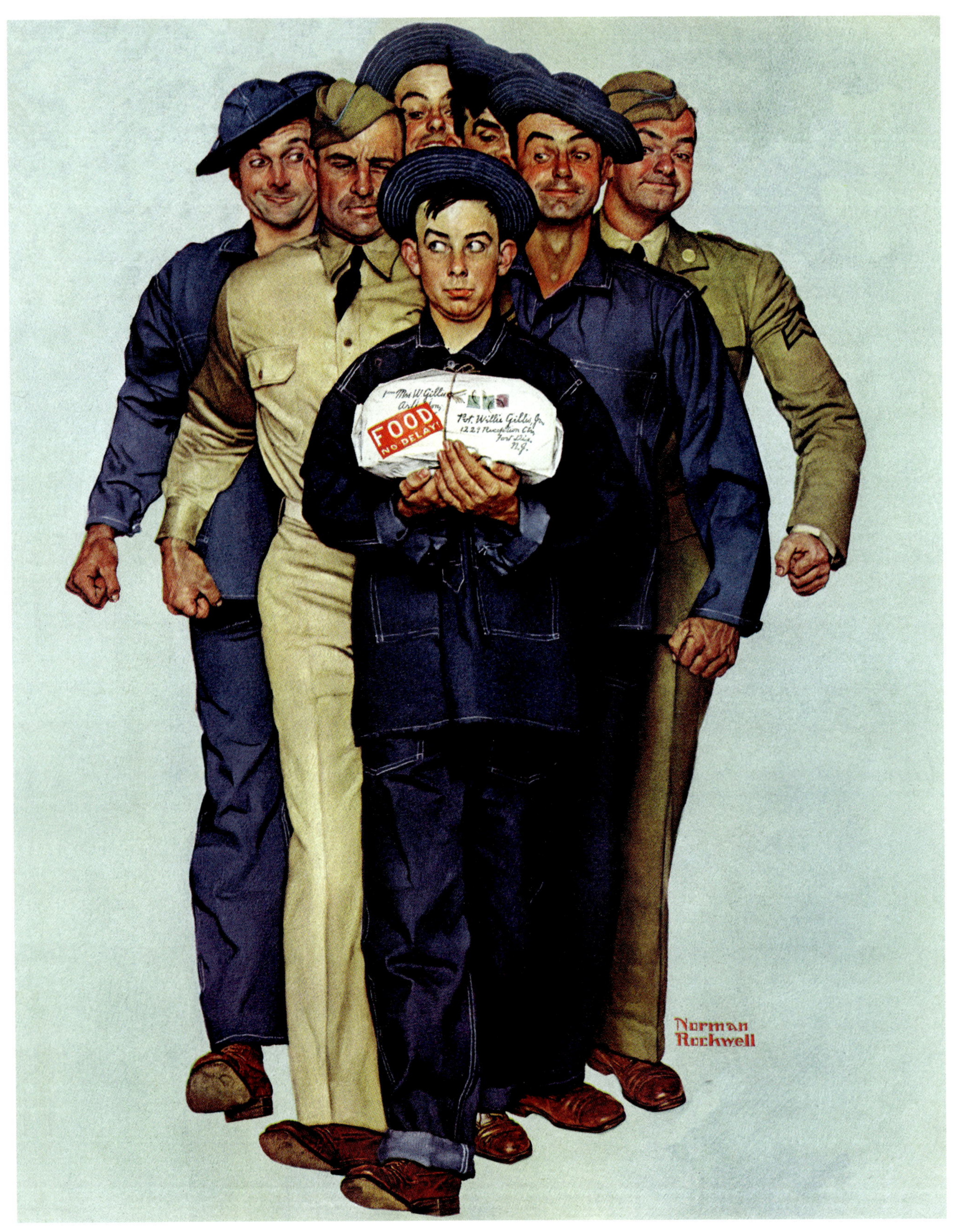
FOOD
NO DELAY!
Pvt. Willie Gillis, Jr.
N.J.
Norman
Rockwell

Pl. 8

Norman Rockwell, *Willie Gillis: Food Package*, 1941. Cover illustration for *The Saturday Evening Post*, October 4, 1941. Oil on canvas, 38 × 50 in. Private Collection. Illustration provided by SEPS through Curtis Licensing. Artwork Approved by the Norman Rockwell Family Agency.

Pl. 9
Norman Rockwell, *Willie Gillis: Home Sweet Home*, 1941. Cover illustration for *The Saturday Evening Post*, November 29, 1941. Oil on canvas, 44 × 35 1/16 in. Private Collection. Illustration provided by SEPS through Curtis Licensing. Artwork Approved by the Norman Rockwell Family Agency.

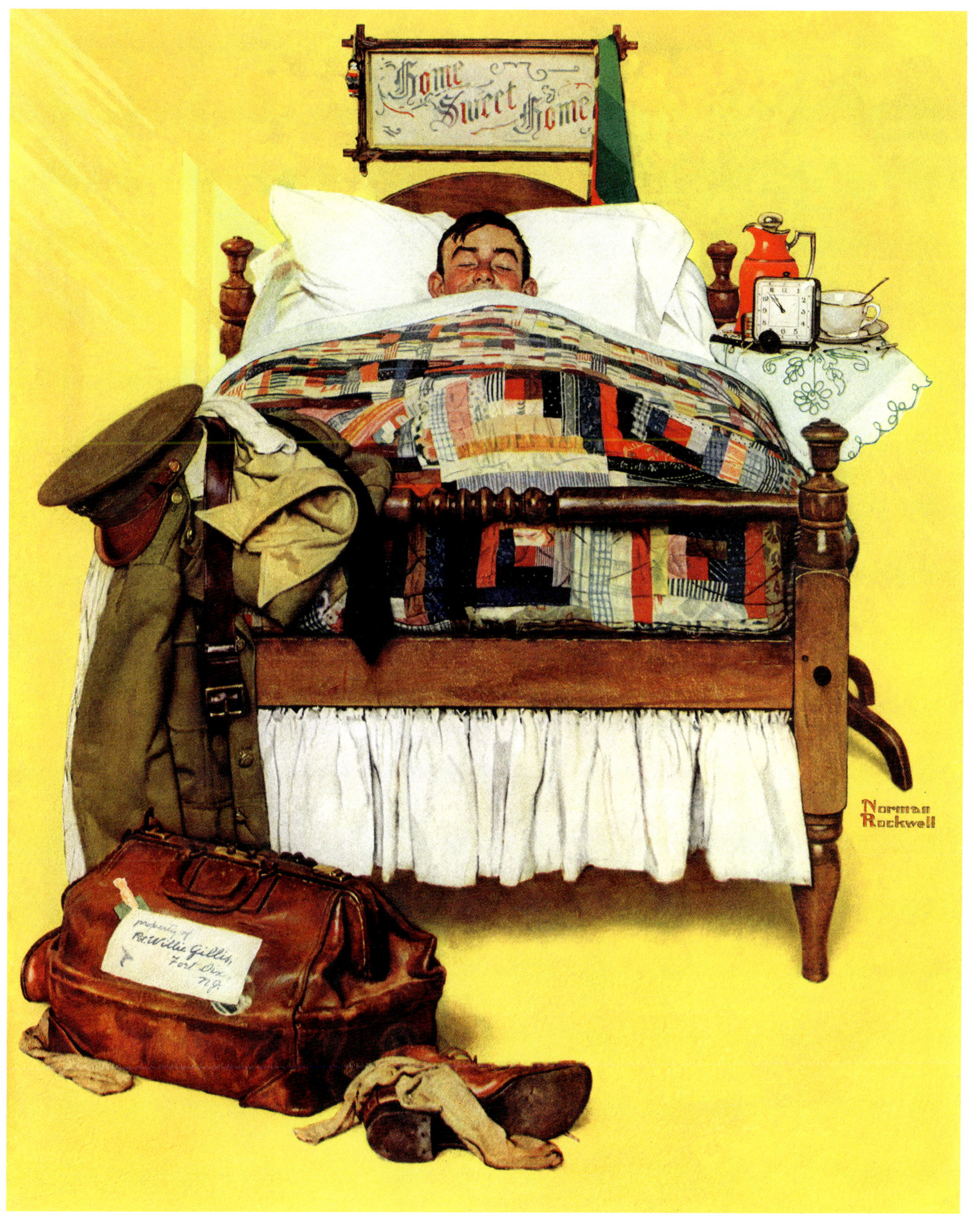
Home Sweet Home
property of
Pvt. Willie Gillis,
Fort Dix,
N.J.
Norman
Rockwell

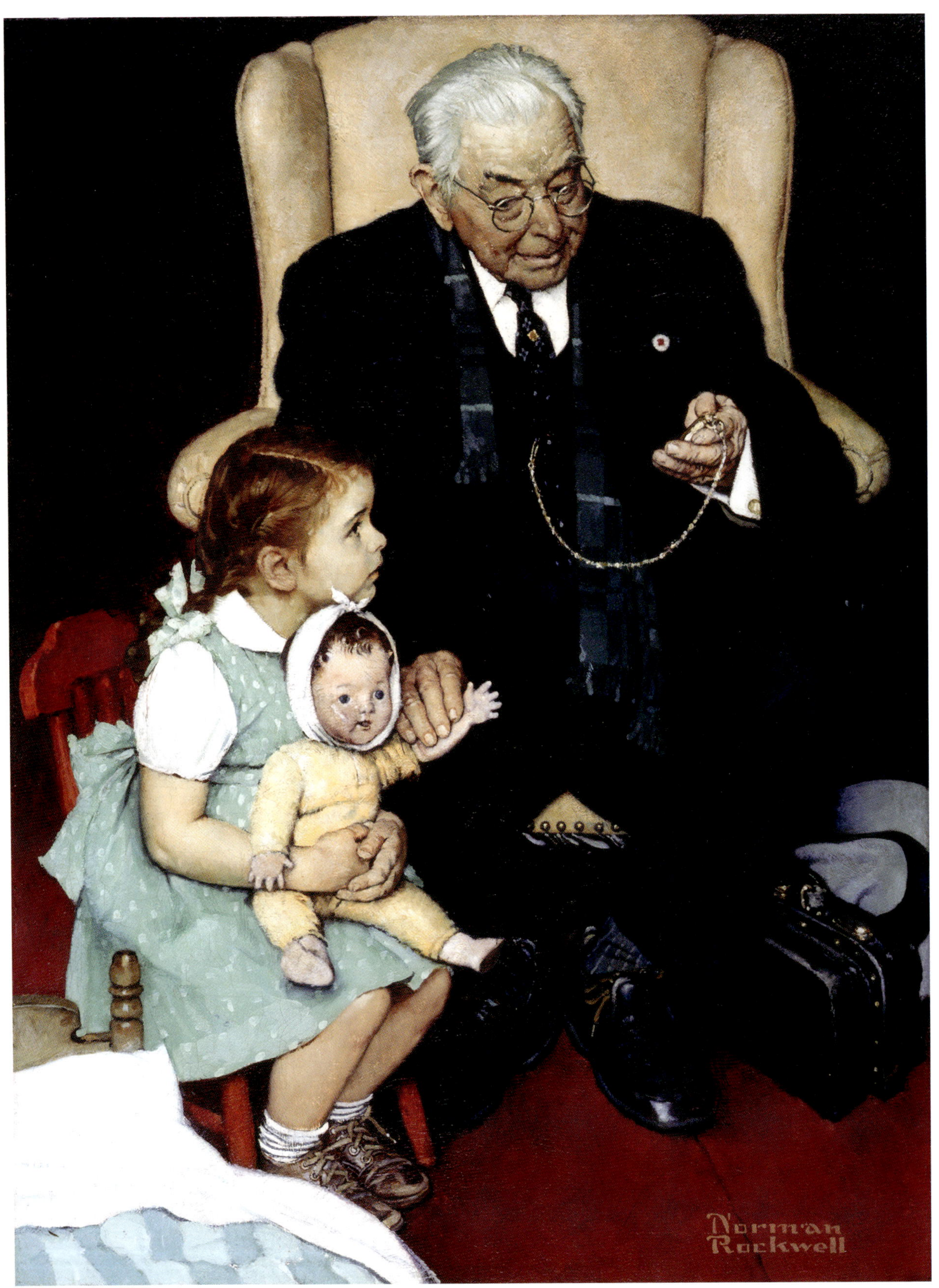

Pl. 10

Norman Rockwell, *Doctor and Doll*, 1942. Oil on canvas, $32\frac{5}{8} \times 23\frac{5}{8}$ in. Private Collection. Illustration provided by SEPS through Curtis Licensing. Artwork Approved by the Norman Rockwell Family Agency.

Pl. 11

Norman Rockwell, *Willie Gillis: USO*, 1942. Cover illustration for *The Saturday Evening Post*, February 7, 1942. Oil on canvas. Private Collection. Illustration provided by SEPS through Curtis Licensing. Artwork Approved by the Norman Rockwell Family Agency.

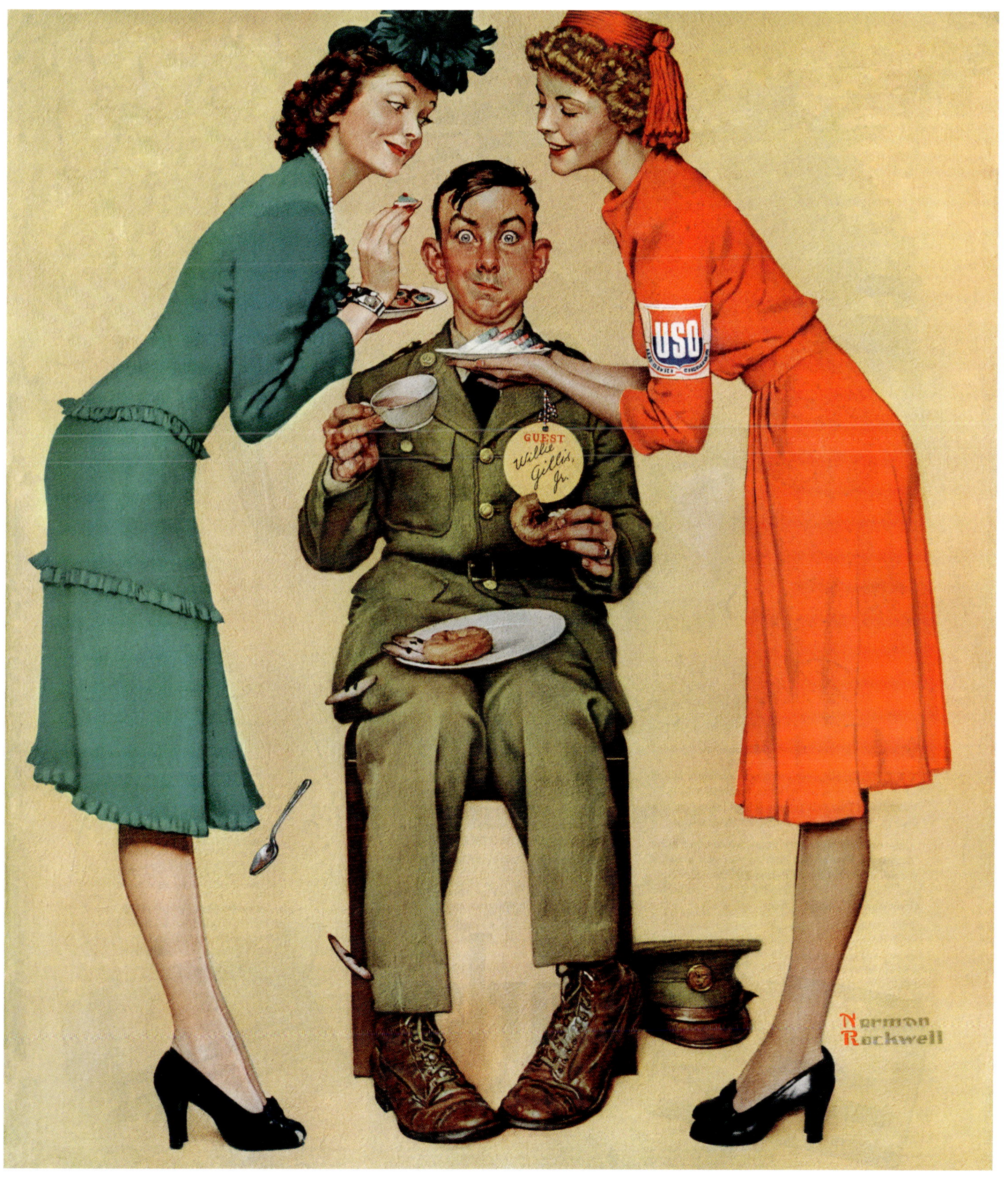
USO
GUEST
Willie Gillis, Jr.
Norman Rockwell

Pl. 12
Norman Rockwell, *Willie Gillis: Hometown News*, 1942. Cover illustration for *The Saturday Evening Post*, April 11, 1942. Oil on canvas, 38 × 30 in. Private Collection. Illustration provided by SEPS through Curtis Licensing. Artwork Approved by the Norman Rockwell Family Agency.

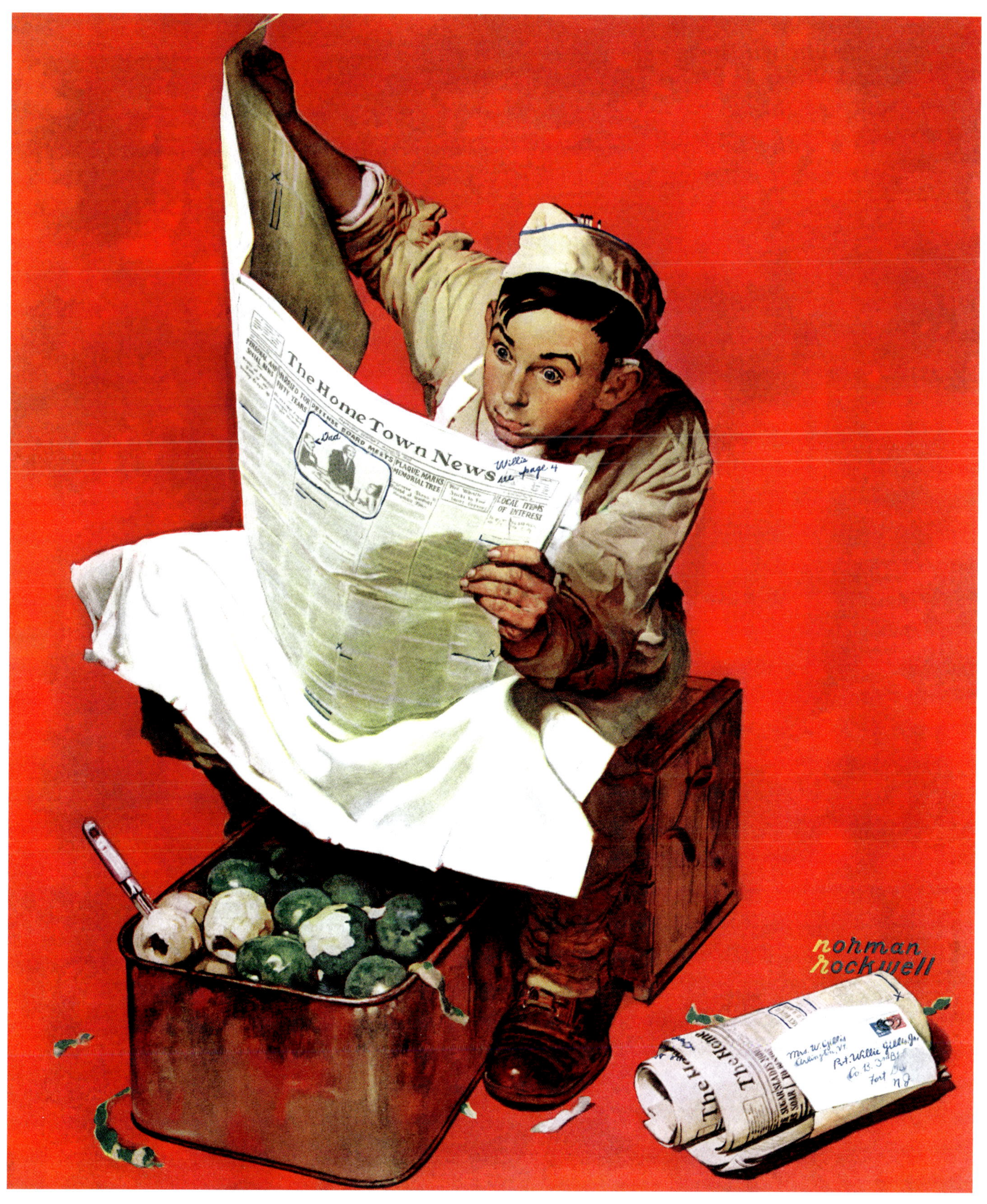
The Home Town News
DEFENSE BOARD MEETS
PLAQUE MARKS MEMORIAL TREE
LOCAL ITEMS OF INTEREST
Dad
norman rockwell

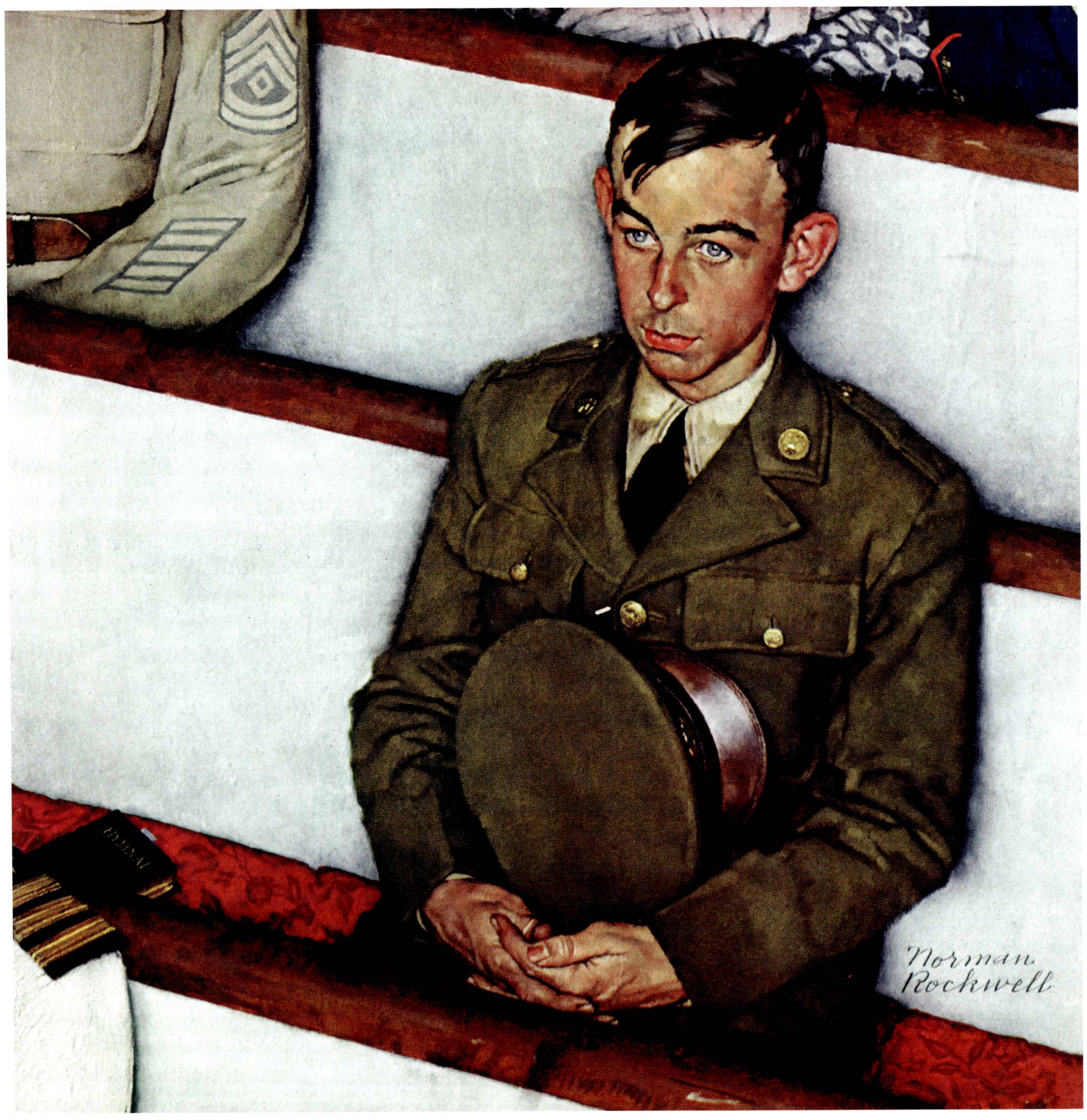
Norman
Rockwell

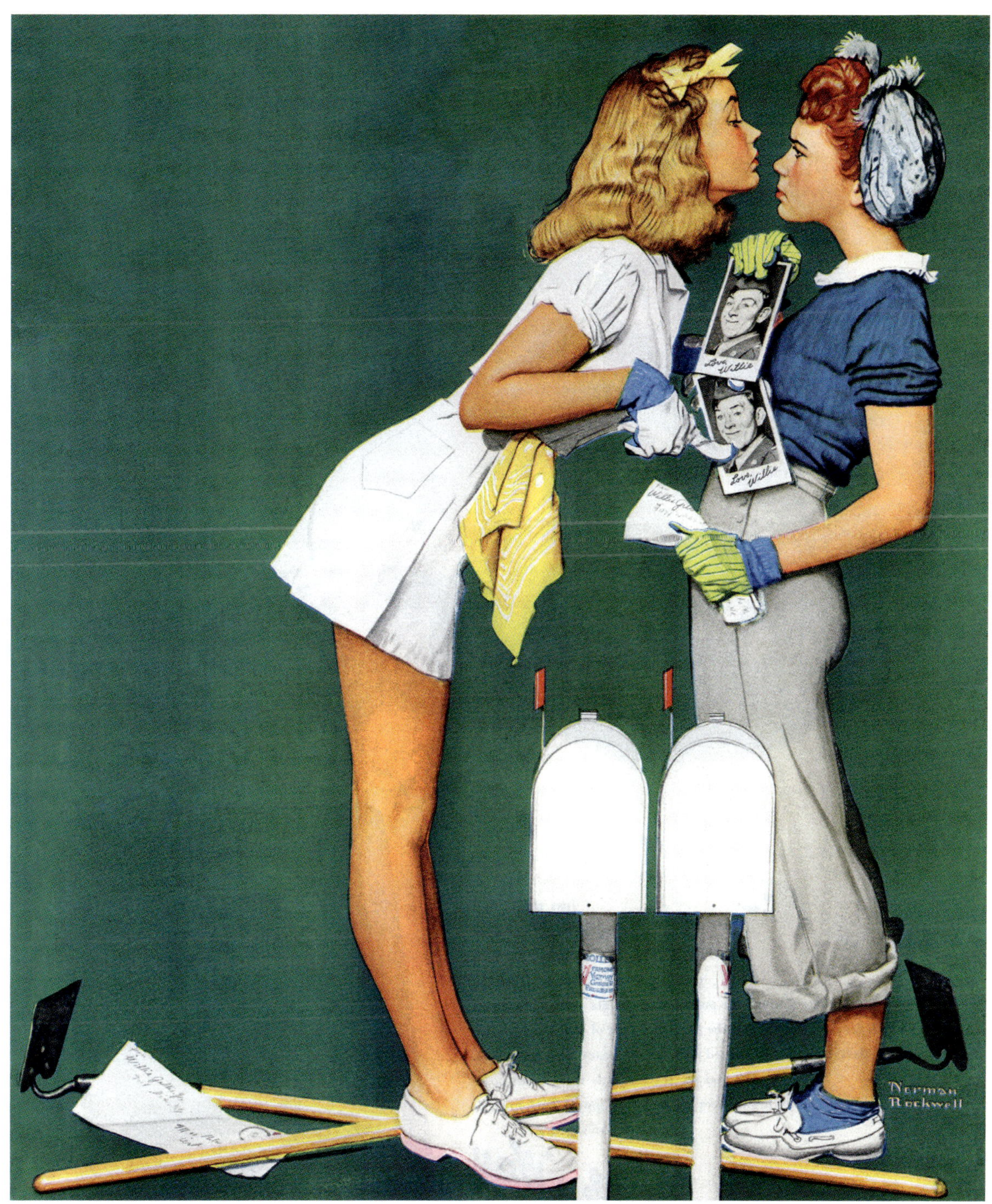

Pl. 13

Norman Rockwell, *Willie Gillis in Church*, 1942. Cover illustration for *The Saturday Evening Post*, July 25, 1942. Oil on canvas. Private Collection. Illustration provided by SEPS through Curtis Licensing. Artwork Approved by the Norman Rockwell Family Agency.

Pl. 14

Norman Rockwell, *Willie Gillis: Girls with Letters*, 1942. Cover illustration for *The Saturday Evening Post*, September 5, 1942. Oil on canvas. Private Collection. Illustration provided by SEPS through Curtis Licensing. Artwork Approved by the Norman Rockwell Family Agency.

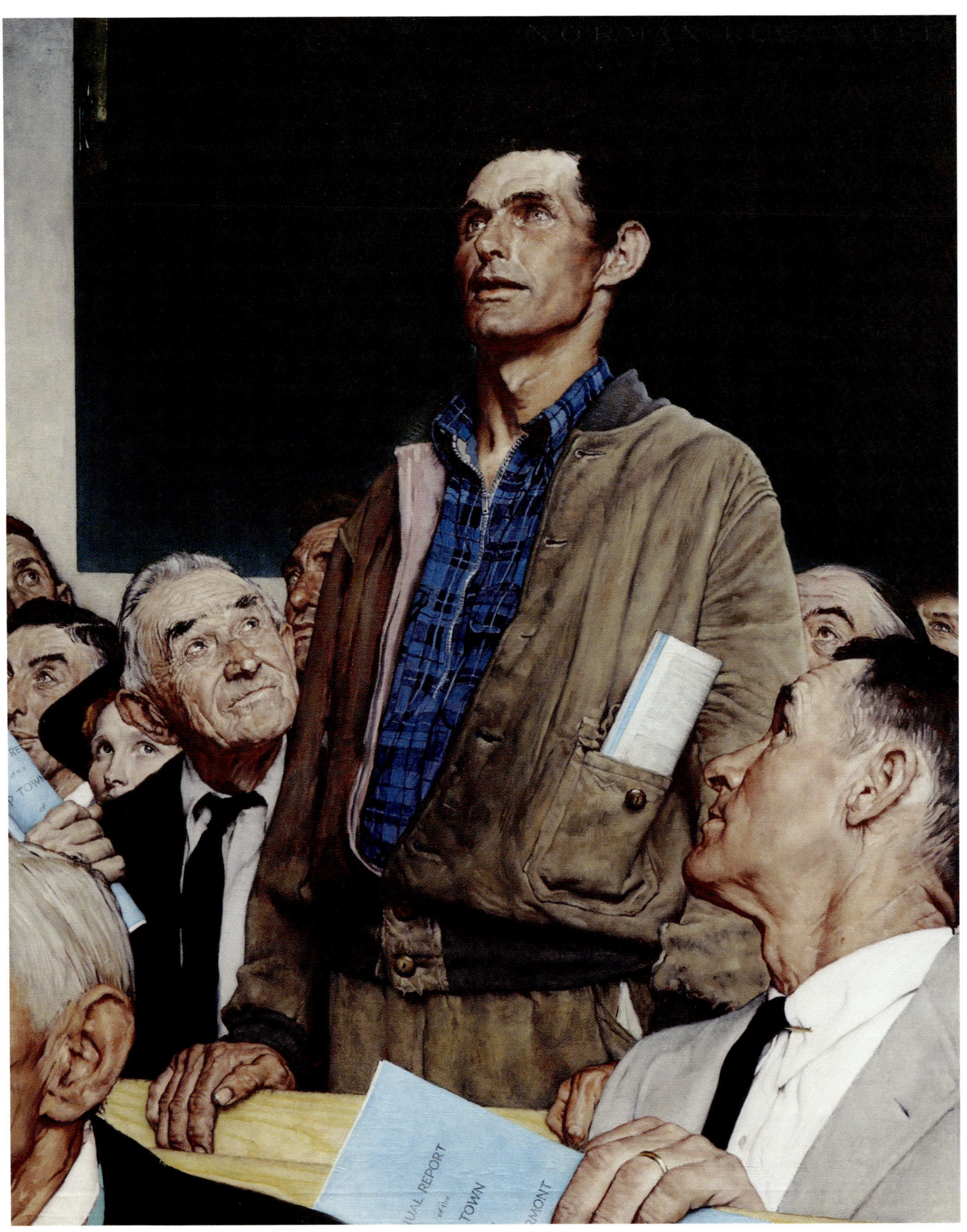
REPORT
of the
TOWN

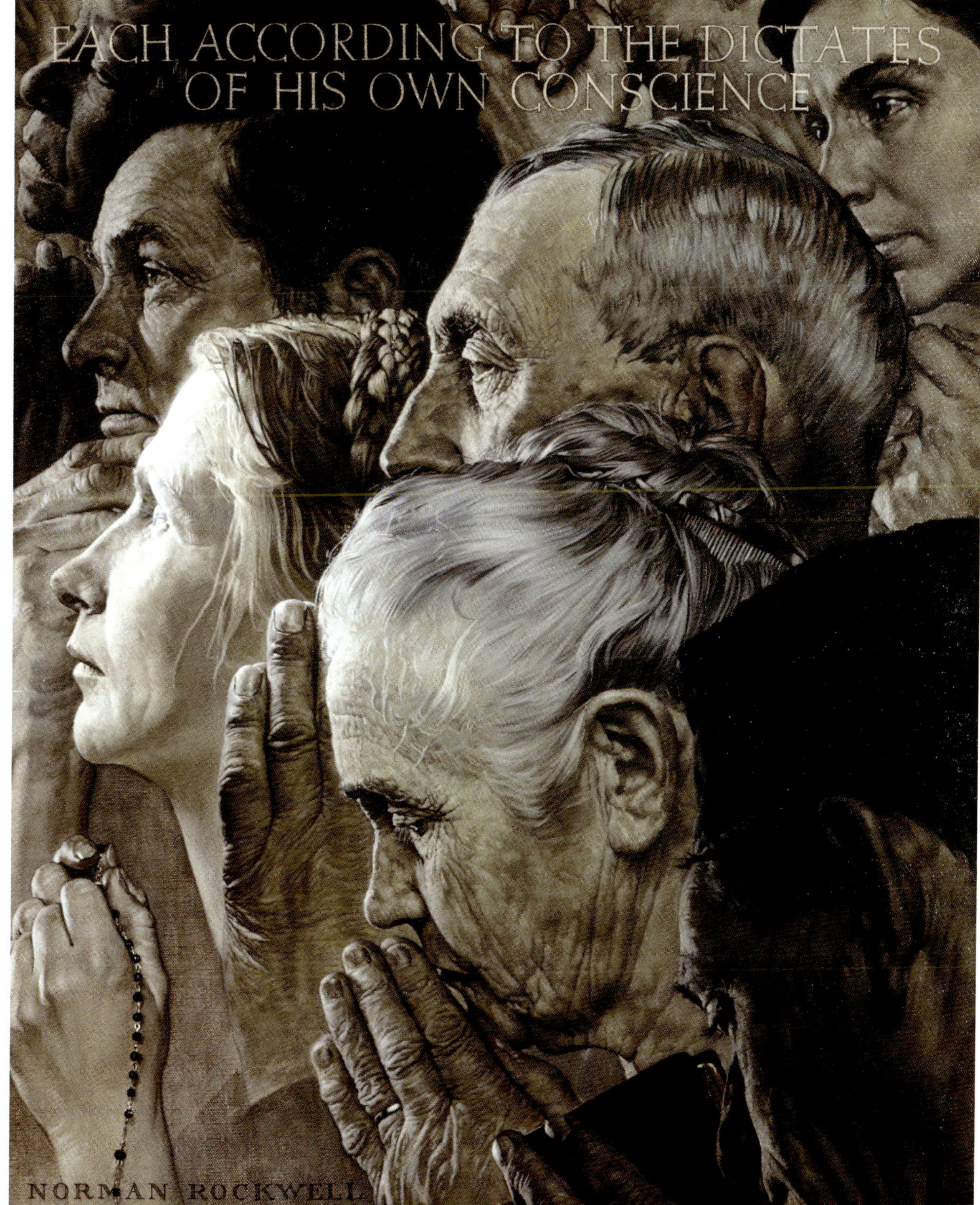

Pl. 15

Norman Rockwell, *Freedom of Speech*, 1943. Illustration for *The Saturday Evening Post*, February 20, 1943, p. 13. Oil on canvas, 45¾ × 35½ in. Norman Rockwell Museum Collection, Norman Rockwell Art Collection Trust. NRACT.1973.021. © 1943 SEPS: Licensed by Curtis Licensing, Indianapolis, IN. All rights reserved. Artwork Approved by the Norman Rockwell Family Agency.

Pl. 16

Norman Rockwell, *Freedom of Worship*, 1943. Illustration for *The Saturday Evening Post*, February 27, 1943, p. 13. Oil on canvas, 46 × 35½ in. Norman Rockwell Museum Collection, Norman Rockwell Art Collection Trust. NRACT.1973.023. © 1943 SEPS: Licensed by Curtis Licensing, Indianapolis, IN. All rights reserved. Artwork Approved by the Norman Rockwell Family Agency.

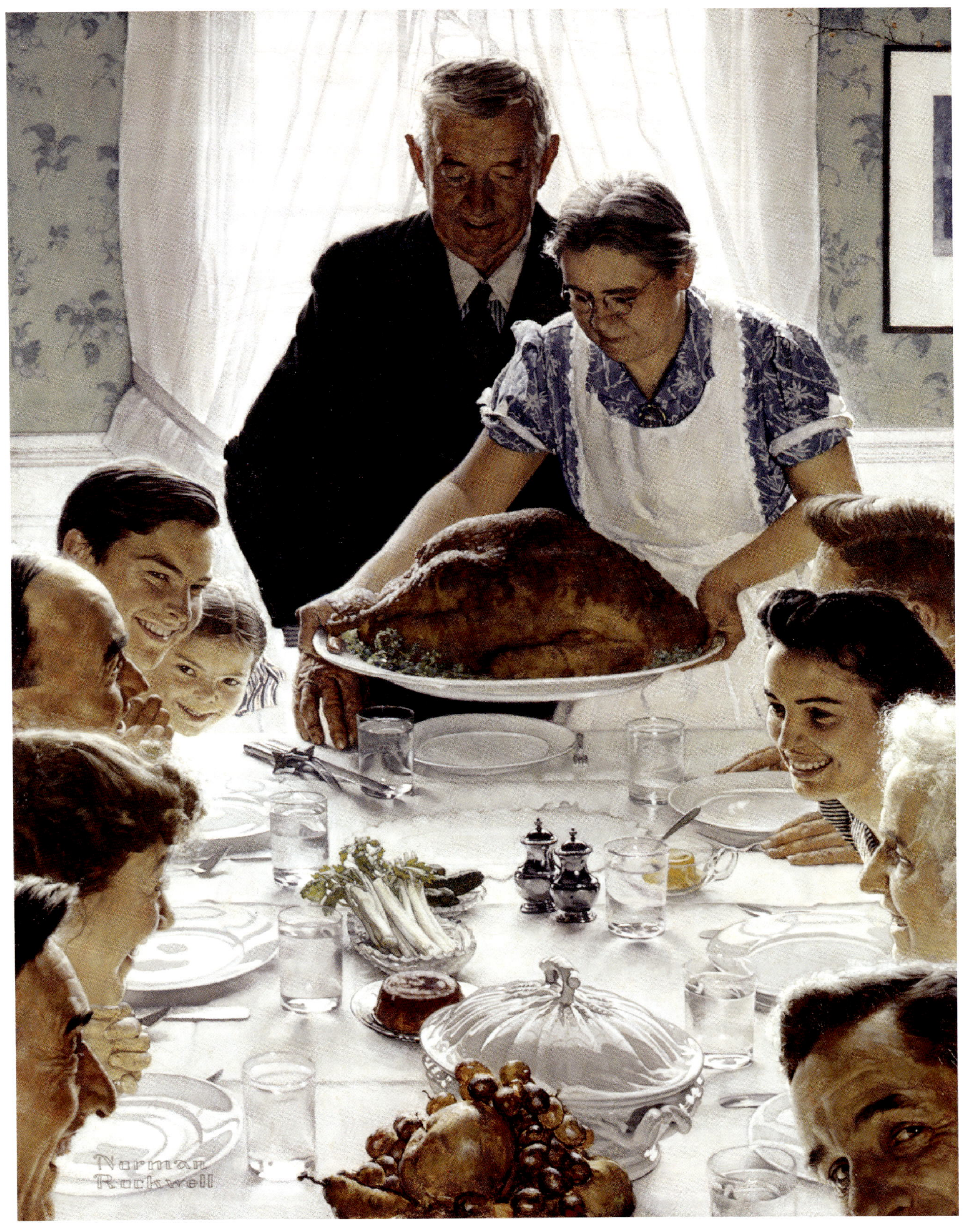
Norman
Rockwell

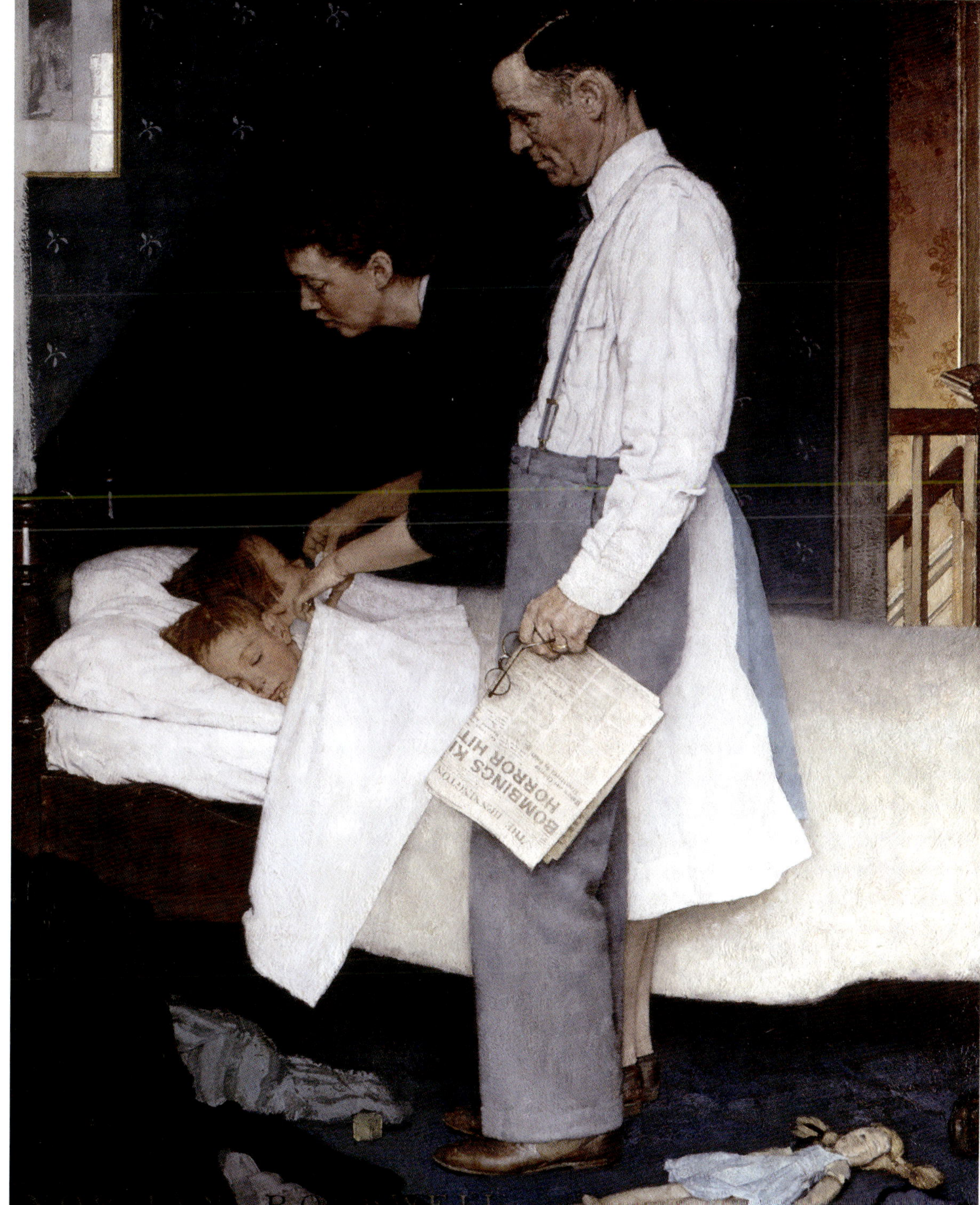

Pl. 17

Norman Rockwell, *Freedom from Want*, 1943. Illustration for *The Saturday Evening Post*, March 6, 1943, p. 13. Oil on canvas, 45¾ × 35½ in. Norman Rockwell Museum Collection, Norman Rockwell Art Collection Trust. NRACT.1973.022.

Pl. 18

Norman Rockwell, *Freedom from Fear*, 1943. Illustration for *The Saturday Evening Post*, March 13, 1943, p. 13. Oil on canvas, 45¾ × 35½ in. Norman Rockwell Museum Collection, Norman Rockwell Art Collection Trust. NRACT.1973.020.

Pl. 19

Norman Rockwell, *April Fool (Checkers)*, 1943. Cover illustration for *The Saturday Evening Post*, April 3, 1943. Oil on board, 11½ × 11½ in. Private Collection. Illustration provided by SEPS through Curtis Licensing. Artwork Approved by the Norman Rockwell Family Agency.

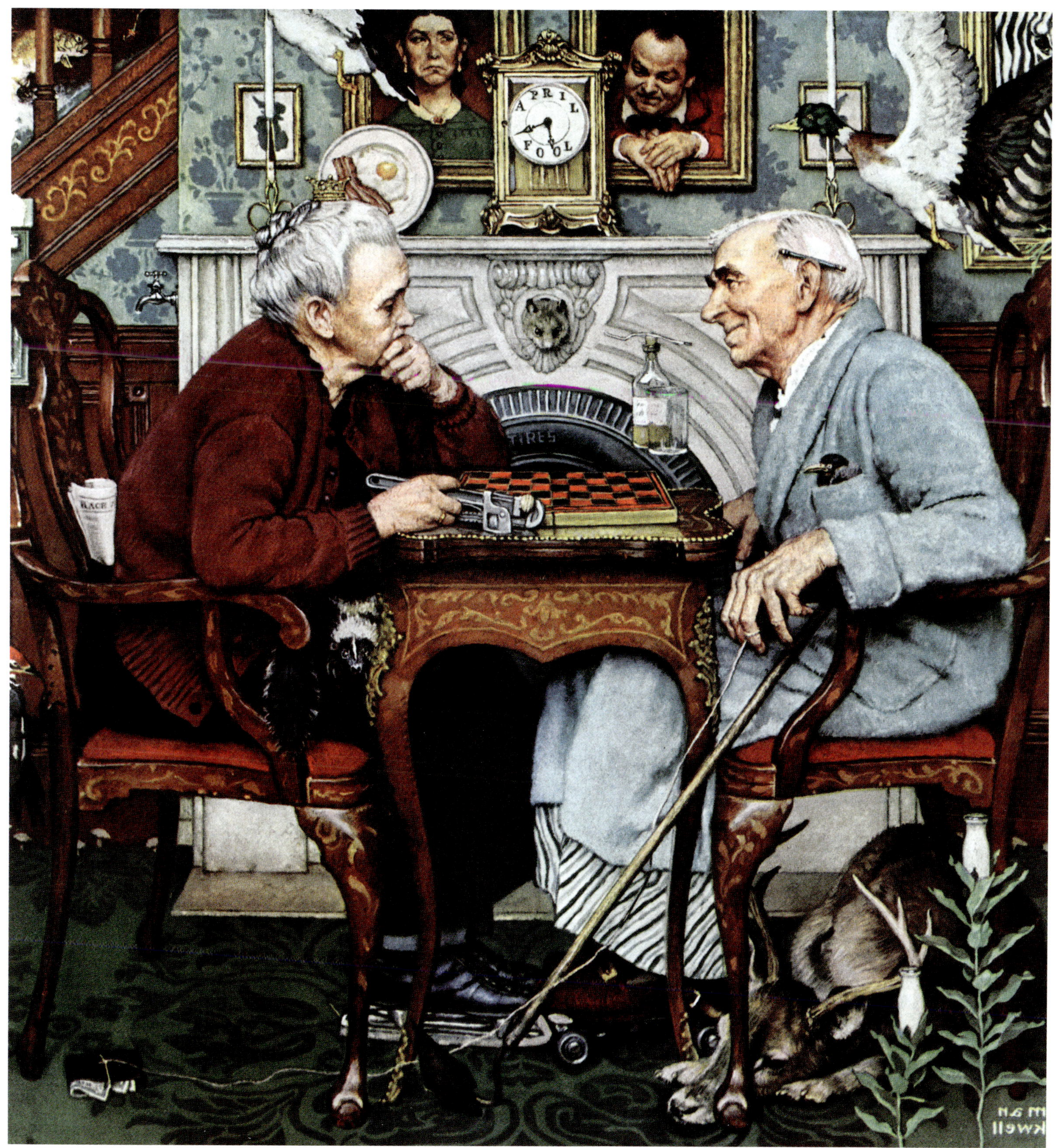
APRIL
FOOL
TIRES

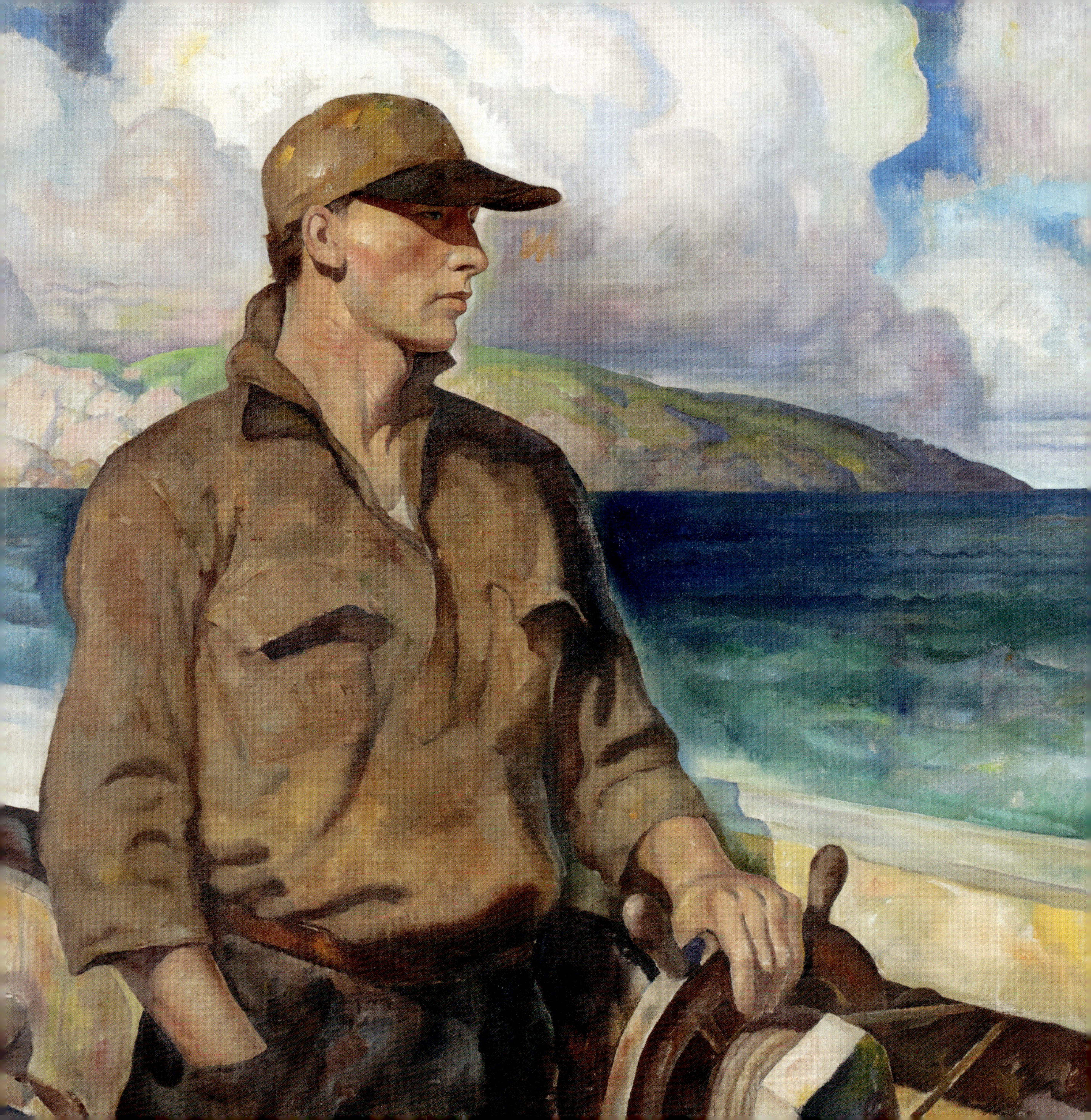

LOOKING NORTH

Illustration, Art, and the Places in Between

Thomas Denenberg

By the time Normal Rockwell moved with his family to Arlington, Vermont, in 1939, he was already a household name. Rockwell's images had graced the cover of *The Saturday Evening Post* since 1916 and had appeared in countless other books, magazines, calendars, and advertising campaigns for corporations such as Coca-Cola, Jell-O, and General Motors. Such work, however, carried baggage. Illustration, on the surface a respectable profession in an era that witnessed widespread economic growth, remained stigmatized in fashionable circles. The illustrator was seen by society as a commercial operator, a "businessman with a brush" in league with the "ad man," rather than an individual creative practitioner or a heroic modern artist.[1] As Rockwell navigated the early stages of his life and career, commuting to Manhattan from suburban Mamaroneck and New Rochelle, two notions coalesced in the popular imagination: that art for art's sake trumped the more mercenary business of illustration, and that the place to measure oneself as an artist surprisingly came not in New York City but in the small towns of northern New England.

A LITERARY INDUSTRIAL COMPLEX

Rockwell followed a well-worn path to Vermont, as New England had long enjoyed great cultural currency.[2] In the mid-nineteenth century, authors such as Harriet Beecher Stowe and the popular "fireside poets"—Henry Wadsworth Longfellow, John Greenleaf Whittier, and James Russell Lowell—spun sentimental narratives by the yard, creating the trope of the New England village populated by Yankee characters displaying steady habits.[3] Cultural topography, however, is seldom static for long. As the historian Stephen Nissenbaum has written, throughout the 1930s the "real" New England moved north as writers and artists sought the authenticity of lived experience rusticating "North of Boston" while following Robert Frost's well-known literary Baedeker. Images of genteel Connecticut and Massachusetts gave way as scenes of rugged Maine, Vermont, and New Hampshire emerged as a landscape of the mind for the fast-growing and increasingly heterogeneous United States.[4] The apogee of this northern prospect came in 1938 when Thornton Wilder's play *Our Town* opened on Broadway, quickly winning a Pulitzer Prize.[5] Set in the fictional town of Grover's Corners, New Hampshire, *Our Town* fixed the popular view of the region as populated by strong-minded, independent people immune to the vicissitudes of contemporary society. Adolph Dehn's advertisement for the play's tour concretizes Wilder's setting (Fig. 10). Tidy and white-washed, replete with four church spires and a village barber shop, Dehn's town is informed by a long line of illustrators who imagined New England, a narrative tradition amplified by Winslow Homer, archetype of the illustrator-turned-artist.

Fig. 10
Designed by Adolf Dehn, published by the National Theatre, *Flyer for the Play "Our Town" by Thornton Wilder*, 1938. Lithograph, 10½ × 6⅝ in. Private Collection. © Estate of Adolf Dehn, courtesy of D. Wigmore Fine Art, Inc.

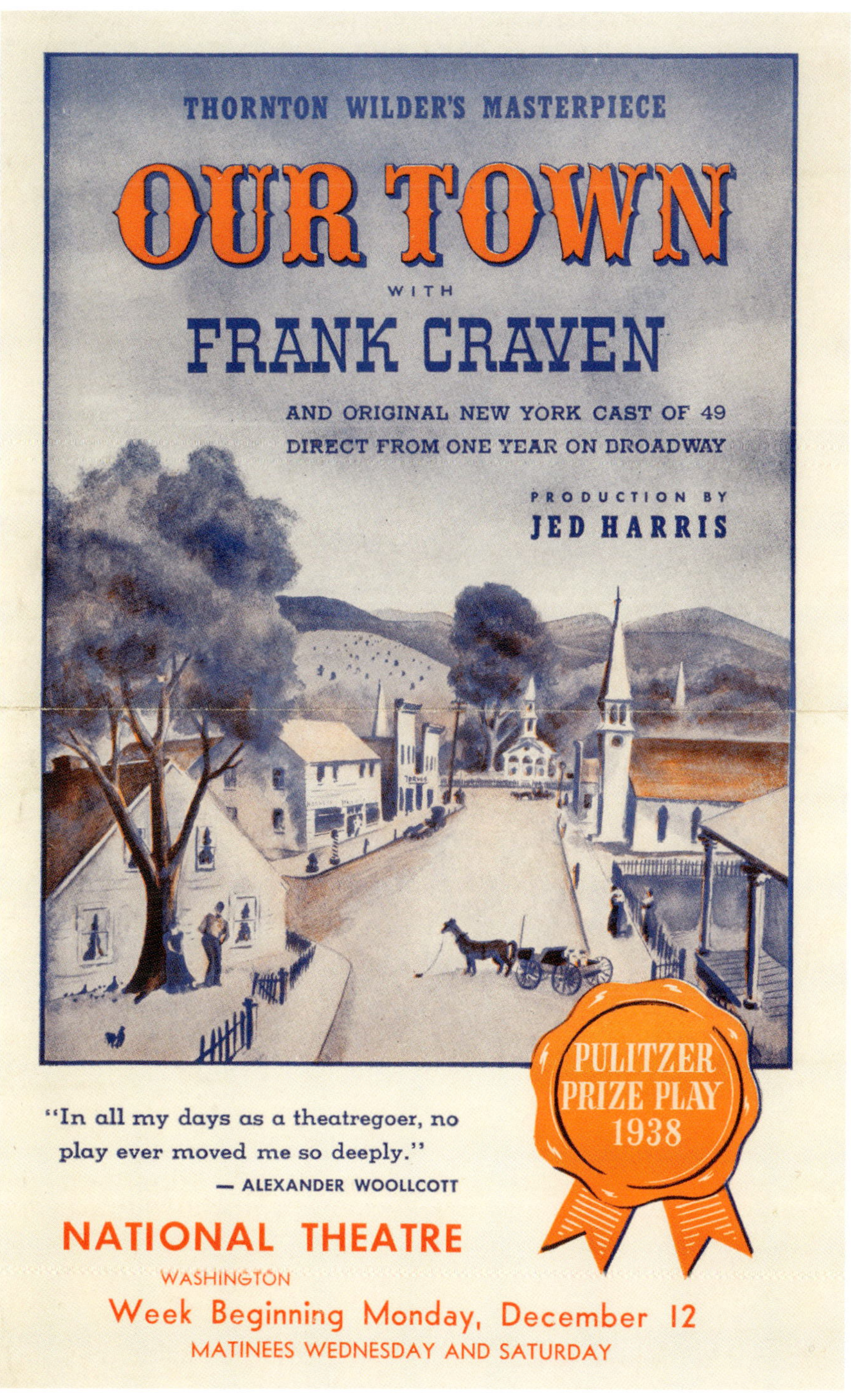

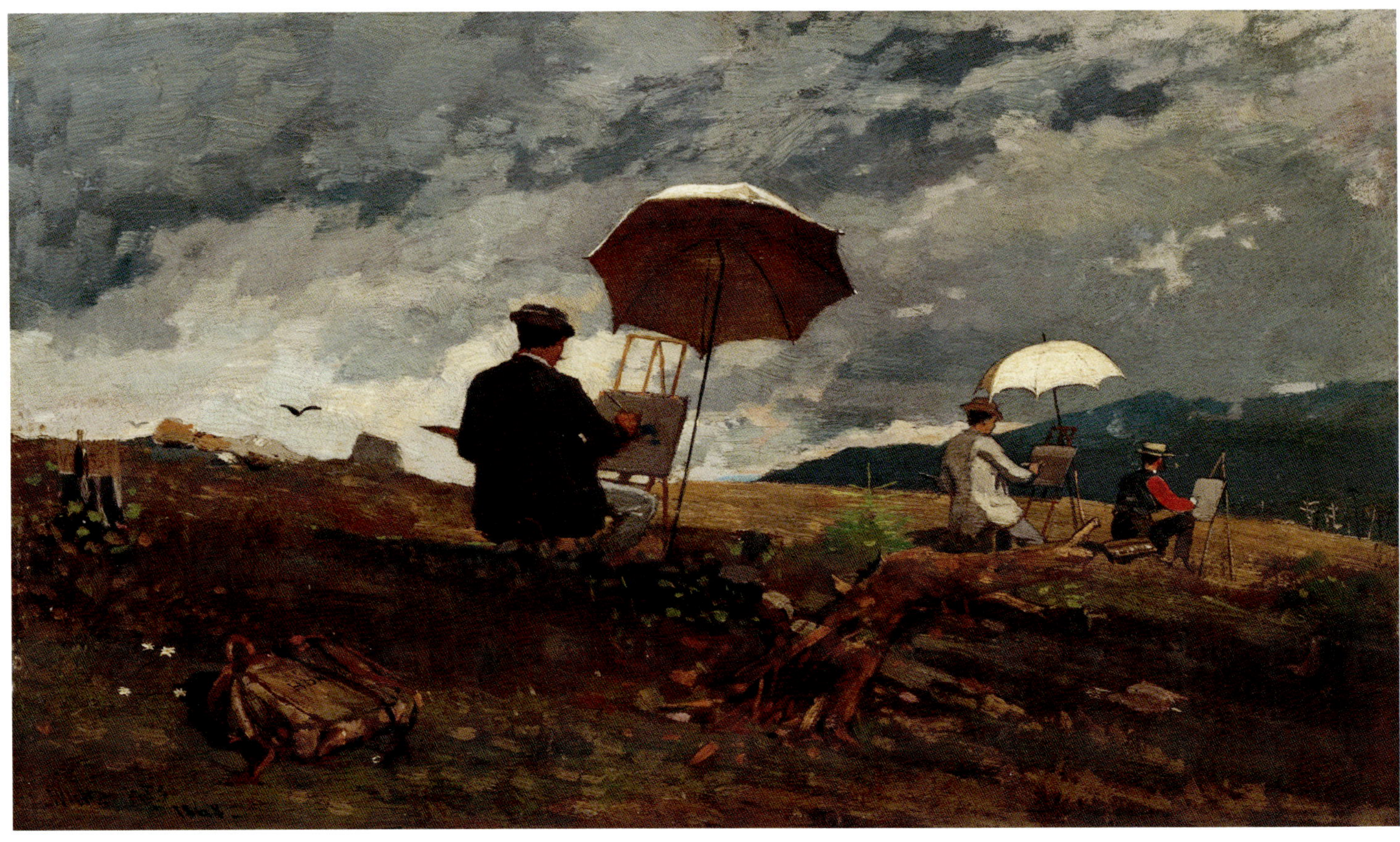

Fig. 11
Winslow Homer, *Artists Sketching in the White Mountains*, 1868. Oil on panel, 9 7⁄16 × 15 13⁄16 in. Portland Museum of Art, Maine, bequest of Charles Shipman Payson. 1988.55.4.

ARTISTS SKETCHING

Winslow Homer (1836–1910) is a paradigm for any discussion of illustration, art, and the hegemony of an idealized New England. Homer, born in 1836, began his career as a journeyman chromolithographer with the Boston firm of J. H. Bufford, prior to signing up as a sketch artist for the popular *Harper's Weekly* during the Civil War. Moved by experiences at the seat of conflict, Homer set his sights on becoming a painter, executing between 1863 and 1866 a series of camp and battle scenes remarkable for their elliptical quality. Homer's gift, the ability to tell a story without end, led to a productive career and, eventually, his status as father figure to modernists vexed by sentiment who found inspiration and succor in New England.[6] Throughout the 1860s and '70s, however, Homer carried a dual portfolio, that of illustrator and painter, in what art historian Margaret Conrads has written was "a class alone—at once radical and old guard, controversial and status quo."[7]

Fig. 12
Engraved by John Karst, after Winslow Homer, published by D. Appleton & Co., *The Artist in the Country*, 1869. Cover illustration for *Appletons' Journal*, June 19, 1869. Wood engraving, $11 \times 7\frac{9}{16}$ in. The Metropolitan Museum of Art, Harris Brisbane Dick Fund, 1933. 33.21.1(2).

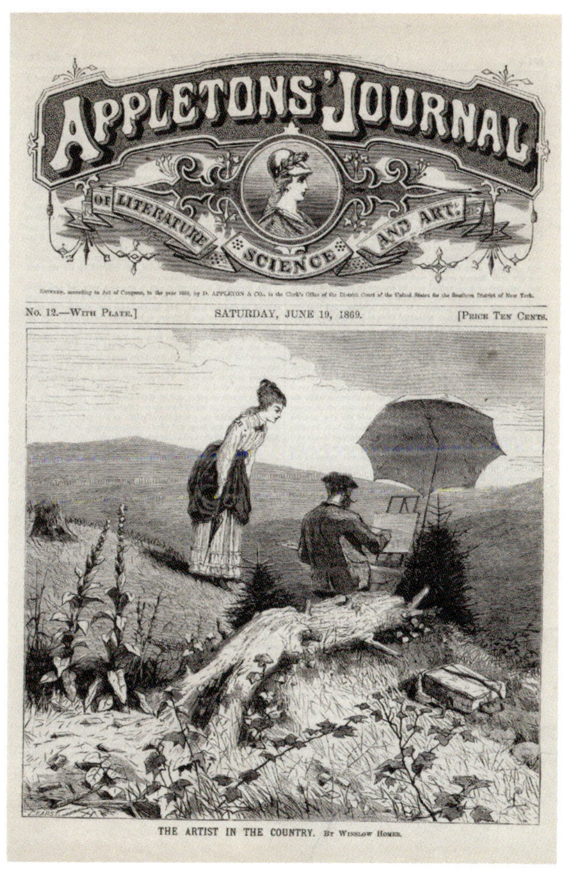

Not only did Homer presage Rockwell as an illustrator of New England people and places, but he also shared a penchant for irony and an arch worldview. Consider Homer's *Artists Sketching in the White Mountains* from 1868 (Fig. 11).[8] At first glance, the painting appears without guile. Identified by art historian Robert McGrath as depicting a spot in the Intervale above North Conway, New Hampshire, on the surface Homer's painting depicts an everyday scene in the White Mountains. The Intervale, long the subject of creative attention, offered sweeping views of the Presidential Range from a unique, low-lying vantage point that heightened the drama of the scene. As early as 1855, a popular journal for artists described the area as "the pet valley of our landscape painters. There are always a dozen or more here during the sketching season, and you can hardly glance over the meadows in any direction, without seeing one of their white umbrellas shining in the sun."[9] By the 1860s, to be taken seriously as an artist required at least one pilgrimage to paint Mount Washington. Thomas Cole, Asher Durand, Benjamin Champney, Alfred Thompson Bricher, Jasper Cropsey, John Frederick Kensett, and Albert Bierstadt are but a handful who made views of the White Mountains their stock in trade.

Artists Sketching, however, was born of economic reasons rather than creative impulse as Homer traveled to New Hampshire in the spring of 1869 on assignment from two fashionable illustrated magazines, *Harper's Weekly* and *Appletons' Journal*. His brief: capture the evolving culture of summer. "What should we do with our vacations?" asked *Appletons'* in an article from that summer. "How could we endure the monotony of professional labors, or of city occupations, in the summer-months every year did not seduce us into the fields and mountains . . . ?"[10] With a wink and a nod, Homer sketched his answer, knowing it would be engraved for publication and, subsequently, widespread distribution (Fig. 12).

Homer's work is a small canvas that takes a large, self-deprecating poke at the general state of American painting. Although the artists in the scene are frequently identified as Homer Dodge Martin, John Fitch, and Homer himself, the painter leaves only his own identity without ambiguity by signing his name on the knapsack in the foreground.[11] Prizing narrative, Homer fills the frame with his three central characters, rendering the subject of their attention a mystery by cropping it out of the composition. As with many of his illustrations, Homer's composition is an inside joke, a send-up, as he places himself at the end of a line of painters queued up to paint the glories of the White Mountains: three swells in the country, well-provisioned with a bottle of wine and protected from too much nature by umbrellas. Art historian Jennifer Greenhill has written perceptively about Homer's deadpan sensibility, a sense of humor that masked his critique of late nineteenth-century American culture—in this case painting himself into the canon of landscape painters but clearly bringing up the rear and too late to capture the scene before it had become a cliché.[12]

Homer moved to Prouts Neck, Maine, in 1883, leaving behind his space in the well-known and highly social Tenth Street Studio Building in New York City. In doing so he also moved on from his career as an illustrator, embodying the carefully constructed persona of a misanthrope so wedded to his muse that he eschewed society to live alone on the rocky coast painting his neighbors, the rugged working class. A newspaper article titled "The Strange Hermitage of Winslow Homer on the Maine Coast" appeared within months of his arrival and established the myth of Homer as the "Hermit of Prouts Neck."[13] So compelling and complete was the performance that acolytes regarded Homer as a creative forebear when they subsequently looked north in the twentieth century. Rockwell Kent (1882–1971), who lived by turns in Maine and Vermont, spoke for many of his generation when he declared "Homer the realist: why

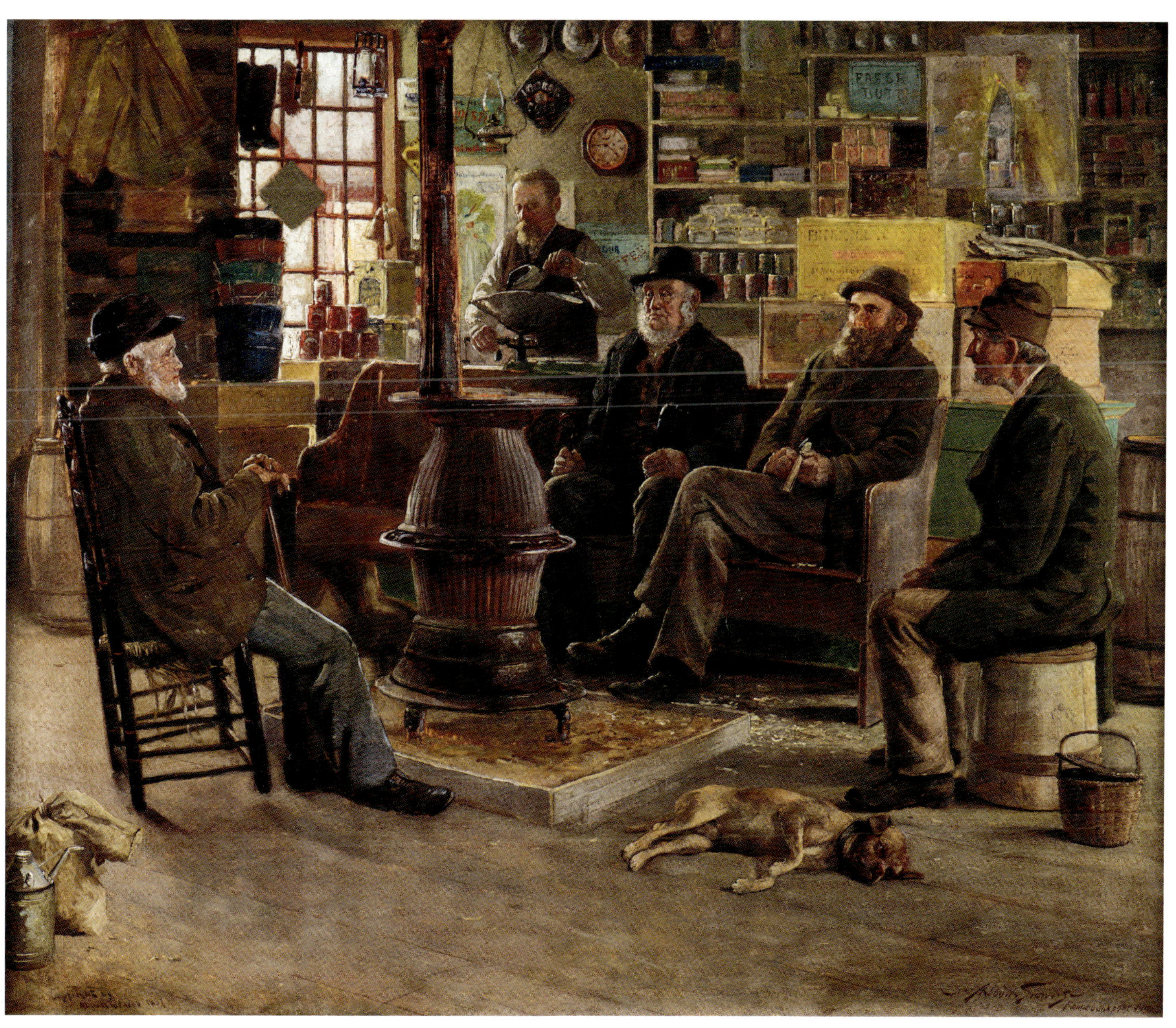

Fig. 13
Abbott Fuller Graves, *A New England Country Grocery*, 1897. Oil on canvas, 36 × 42 in. Collection of Shelburne Museum, donated by the Harper Family Foundation in honor of its Founders, Mr. and Mrs. Charles M. Harper, Omaha, Nebraska. 2017-17.

realism was his job in his youth! Strong, simple, honest, true and by the power of those qualities profoundly moving, we claim him proudly as an exemplar."[14] Homer thus became the artistic standard and measure, though few were as successful and therefore able to renounce the steady, remunerative work of illustration.

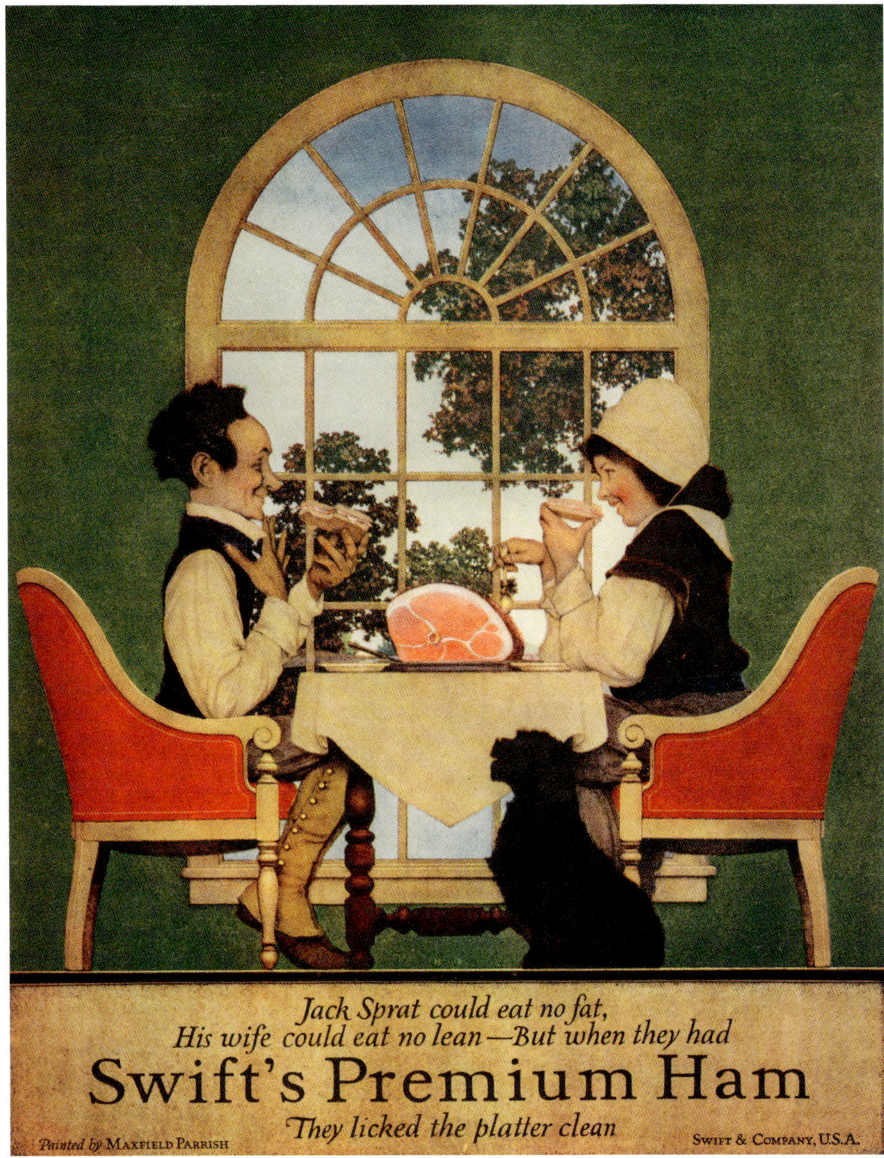

Fig. 14
Designed by Maxfield Parrish, *Swift's Premium Ham*, 1921. Advertisement for Swift & Company in *The Ladies' Home Journal*, November 1921, p. 156. Ink on paper, 10½ × 14 in. Private Collection.

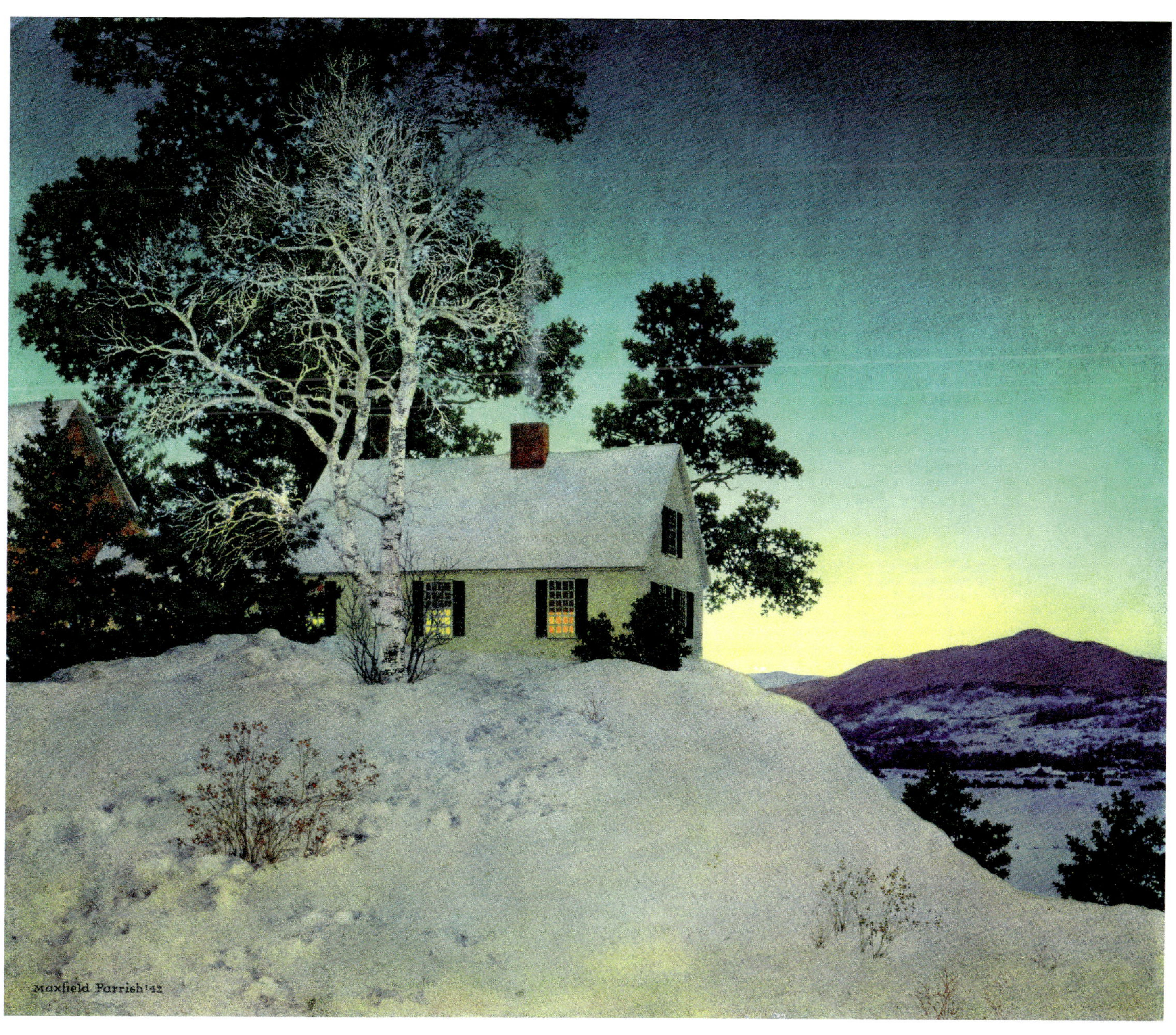

Fig. 15
Maxfield Parrish, *Dusk*, 1942. Oil on Masonite, 13¼ × 15¼ in. New Britain Museum of American Art, Charles F. Smith Fund. 1966.52LIC. © 2025 Maxfield Parrish Family, LLC / Artists Rights Society (ARS), NY.

A CONSUMING PAST

The visual culture of "Old" New England reached maturity in the decades that bracketed the turn of the century, with artist-illustrators such as Abbott Fuller Graves (1859–1936) selling the idea of community with a full measure of sentimental imagery. His large-scale *A New England Country Grocery* of 1897 is one of several scenes he painted in a Kennebunkport, Maine, store, but also the most widely distributed (Fig. 13). Like Rockwell's later efforts, Graves's painting had commercial origins in that it was commissioned by Chase & Sanborn, the first coffee company to sell their product pre-ground in hermetically sealed tins. Trading in clichés, Graves's image proposes a simple narrative progression for consumers: drink Chase & Sanborn and enjoy the warmth of association with old acquaintances sitting by a cast-iron stove, passing the time. It is advertising through and through. Graves gives the viewer a wink, however, with the anthropomorphized dog's countenance, the sly mark of an artist who wants to be taken seriously as a painter while paying the rent by marketing coffee and selling tradition.

In contrast to the comforting warm tones of Graves's patinated country store is the dream-like world conjured by Maxfield Parrish (1870–1966), a wildly popular image maker who successfully straddled the line between art and commerce largely through his fascination with the opportunities offered by new reproductive technologies. A new model artist, Parrish, wrote his biographer Lawrence Alloway, belonged to an "invisible art world . . . unseen and undiscussed by all those concerned with the traditions of fine art."[15] The son of a painter, Parrish attended the Pennsylvania Academy of the Fine Arts and the Drexel Institute of Art, Science & Industry, where he studied under famed illustrator Howard Pyle before moving to Plainfield, New Hampshire, and building an idealized New England cottage, described in the *Architectural Record* as "very local" and "very American."[16] From Plainfield, Parrish produced fanciful, iridescent illustrations for books and popular journals such as *Ladies' Home Journal*, *Harper's Bazaar*, and *The Century Magazine* (Fig. 14). His calendars for corporations such as General Electric could be found from coast to coast, often with plates of ethereal, attractive women painted in iridescent palette.[17] By the 1930s, Parrish, having become wealthy as an illustrator, largely eschewed, in his own words, "girls on rocks," or playful advertisements for ham, in favor of painting the New England landscape as he pleased (Fig. 15).[18] In doing so, he joined the ranks of Winslow Homer and N. C. Wyeth as erstwhile illustrators who sought creative freedom and social status.

YANKEE TYPES

N. C. Wyeth's debt to Winslow Homer is obvious and profound. Wyeth (1882–1945), initially drawn to the established summer art colony of Ogunquit in 1907, began to summer down east in the weathered fishing village of Port Clyde in 1920, soon purchasing a run-down house. Throughout the Great Depression, Wyeth renovated the building to fit his image of life on the coast, even calling the home "Eight Bells" in homage to Homer's famous painting of the same name and hanging a print of the work in his living room. Wyeth admired the scene depicting two sailors shooting the sun with an octant, as did a period critic who proclaimed the figures "men who are dead in earnest, who hate all bunting and shams, and who have taken off their coats in the service of truth and are not ashamed to be found in their shirt sleeves."[19] Wyeth, like Homer, returned to the motifs offered by life on the Atlantic frontier time and time again, with paintings such as *Young Maine Fisherman* of 1933 (Fig. 16), finding their way into popular culture as book illustrations (Fig. 17).

Wyeth, in the same way as Homer and Parrish, saw landscape painting as the road to creative redemption, though unlike the others, he never abandoned narrative or left the figure behind. If anything, he doubled down on storytelling. *Island Funeral* (1939) stands as Wyeth's magnum opus, a meditation on life and death on the coast (Fig. 18). A magisterial bird's-eye view of Teel's Island off Port Clyde, the painting depicts the funeral of Rufus Washington Teel witnessed by the artist some five years earlier.[20] The procession, a time-honored ritual, represents the voyage of a life, with vessels of all stripes standing in for the people and passages one meets and experiences from cradle to grave. In the final reckoning, *Island Funeral* is a story of community, imagined by Wyeth but fervently sought by Americans in the darkest days of the Great Depression on the eve of World War II. It comes as no surprise to note that Wyeth finished the painting the very year Rockwell moved to Vermont.

PLACES IN BETWEEN

If *Island Funeral* distills the anxiety of the Great Depression and foreshadows the darkness to follow, then Norman Rockwell's *Crestwood Commuter Station* is harbinger of a different moment in history, the seismic shift to 1950s America. (Plate 20). The painting, like all of Rockwell's work, is a deceptively simple narrative, one that served as the cover illustration for *The Saturday Evening Post* on November 16, 1946—a short sixteen months after the bombing of Hiroshima and Nagasaki brought an end to World War II and opened the initial chapter of the

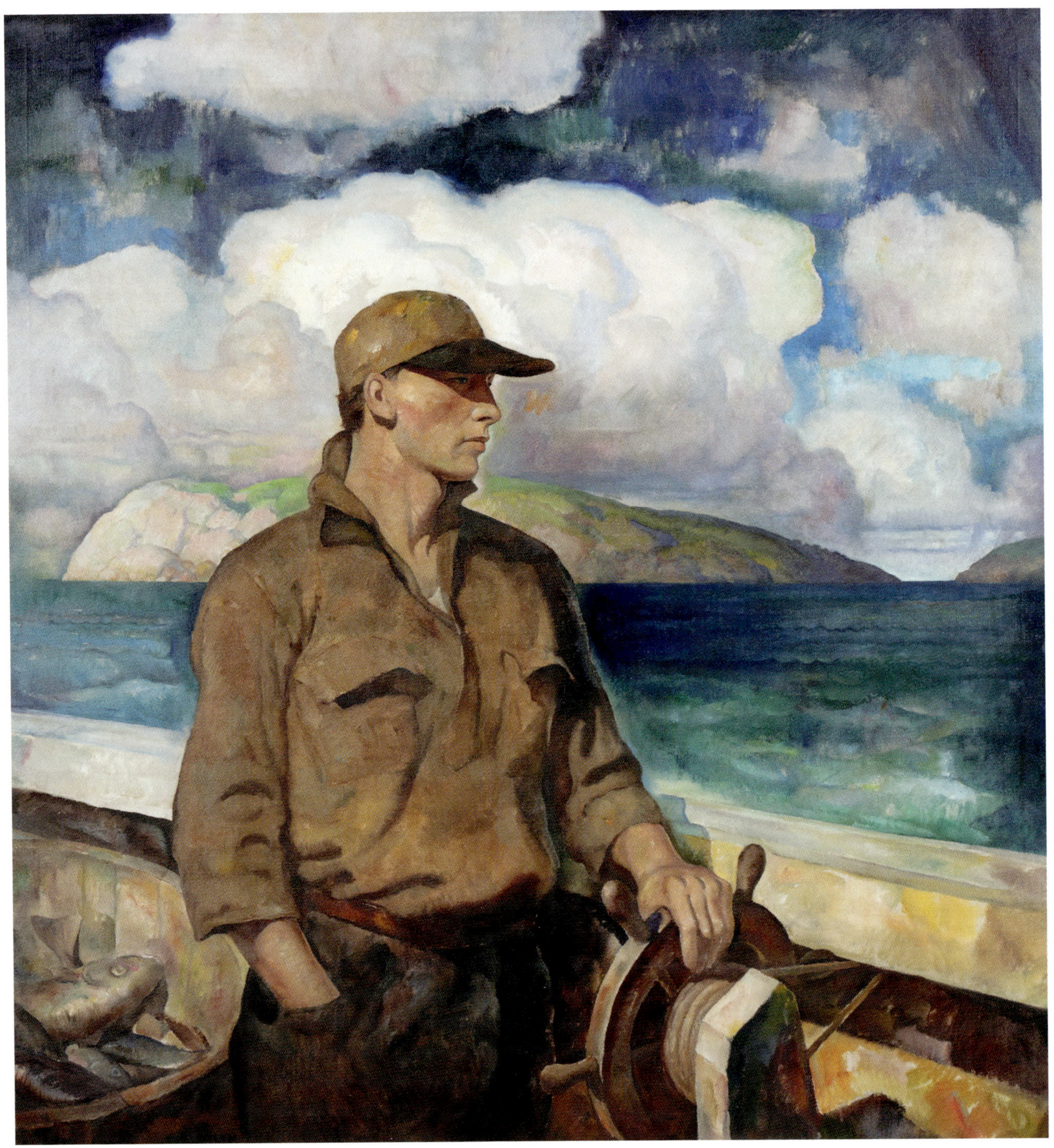

Fig. 16
N. C. Wyeth, *Young Maine Fisherman*, 1933. Oil on canvas, 52⅜ × 48⅛ in. Bank of America Collection. O5106.

Fig. 17
Written by Kenneth Roberts, illustrations by N. C. Wyeth, published by Little, Brown & Company, *Trending into Maine*, 1938. Hardcover book, 9 × 6 × 1½ in. Private Collection.

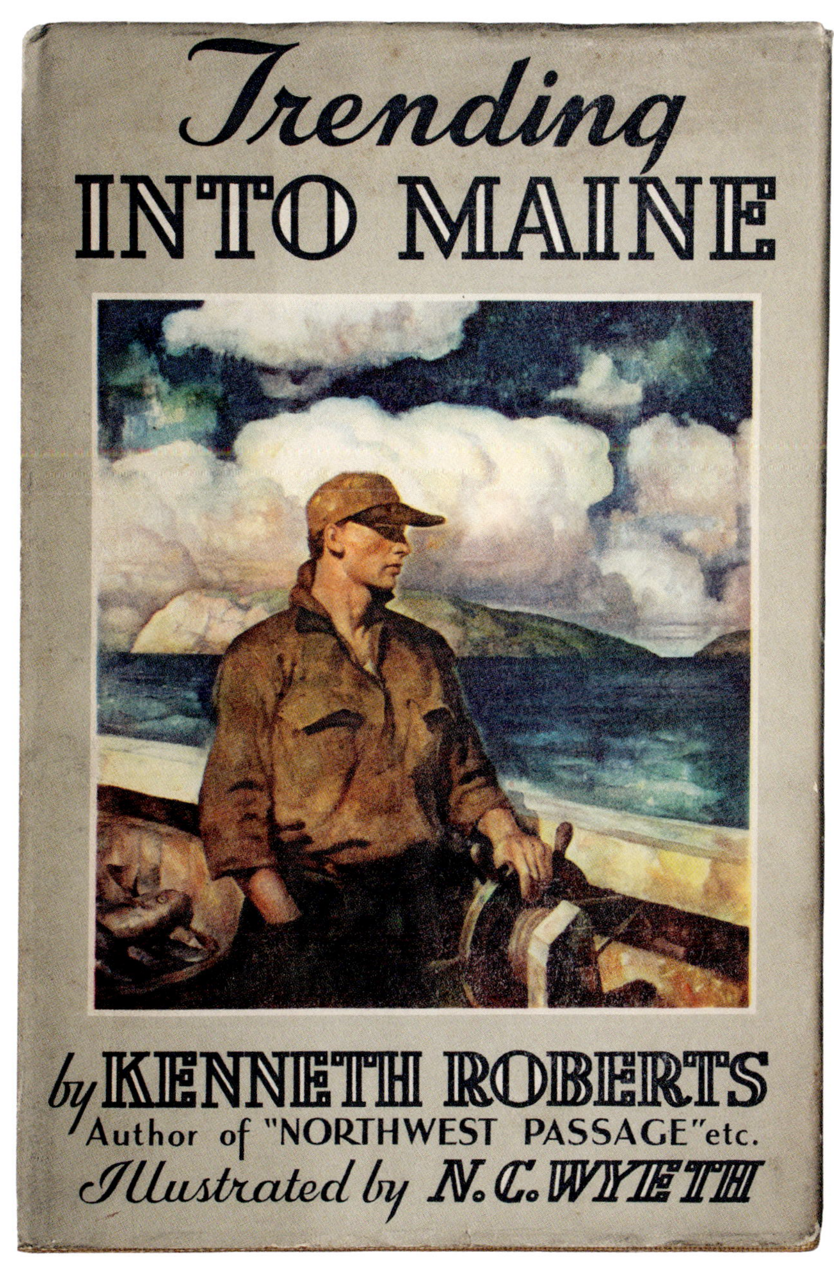

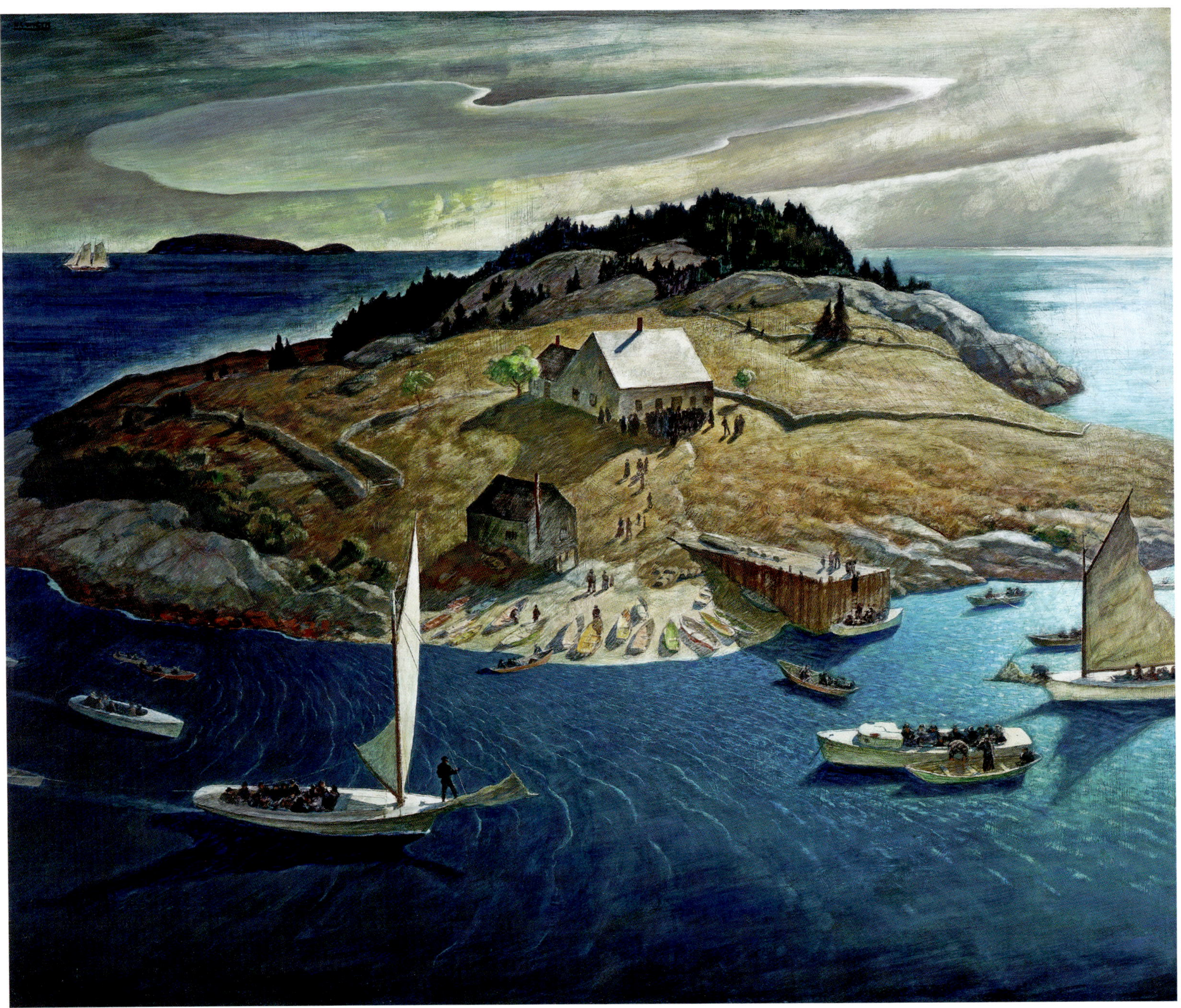

Cold War (Fig. 19). In *Crestwood Commuter Station*, Rockwell offers a soothing view of middle-class life to a nation reckoning still with the trauma of war by essentializing an easily identifiable suburban ritual—the morning migration to work. A row of commuters neatly lines the station in Tuckahoe, New York, a bedroom community adjacent to Rockwell's former home of New Rochelle, ironically engaged in the communal act of reading individual copies of the same newspaper. Latecomers rush to catch the arriving trains, stopping by the newsboy before dashing through a tunnel under the tracks with the hustle and bustle adding a signature humorous touch to the scene.

Crestwood Commuter Station is a master class in formal composition. A white iron fence reinforces the sense of order in an already tidy layout, offering a kind of symbolic protection to the viewer—an express train, after all, could roar through the picture at any moment. The diagonal queue of passengers zigzag through the gate, mirroring a row of quaint Tudor revival houses ascending the hill, leading the viewer offstage from the morning drama. Crestwood served the line to Grand Central Station, indicating the throng is on their way to Manhattan. Despite this geographic specificity, Rockwell conjures a scene repeated every morning throughout the country as men, and a few well-dressed "office" women, are on their way to work in the city. The view is New York, but it could have been Philadelphia, Chicago, Washington, Boston, or a myriad of other urban centers. Ever knowing, with a wink and a nod, Rockwell presents a universal theme and, in the process, reassures us that all is well in postwar America.

Unlike his predecessors, Rockwell only occasionally chafed at the place of the illustrator in society. For the breadth of his storied career, as chronicled by art historian Laurie Norton Moffat, Rockwell himself proudly embraced his role as a storyteller, seeking to reveal humanity in everyday life.[21] Critics will pass judgement, however, and much ink has been spilled locating Rockwell within the large aesthetic movements of the modern era. Rockwell, in typical self-deprecating style, participated himself in the echo chamber that marked twentieth-century art criticism, wryly comparing himself to luminaries such as Jackson Pollock in the 1950s while simultaneously standing to one side. At the end of the day, however, Rockwell's life and work in Vermont raises the question: How useful are the categories of "high" (art) and "low" (illustration) when discussing popular visual culture? To return to Robert Frost, however, the secret sits in the middle and there are places in between.[22]

Rockwell's *The Craftsman* is one such interstitial creative place and the work aptly serves as a coda to New England's role in American visual culture (Fig. 20; Plate 35). Sketched and then fully realized in 1963, almost a decade after the artist and his family decamped from the Green Mountain State to Stockbridge, Massachusetts, it depicts a stonecutter laying out a gravestone in the shed at Rock of Ages, a venerable pillar of Vermont

Fig. 18
N. C. Wyeth, *Island Funeral*, 1939. Egg tempera and oil on hardboard, 44½ × 52 in. Brandywine River Museum of Art, Gift of E. I. du Pont de Nemours and Company in honor of the Brandywine Conservancy and Museum of Art's 50th Anniversary, 2017. Licensed by Bridgeman Images.

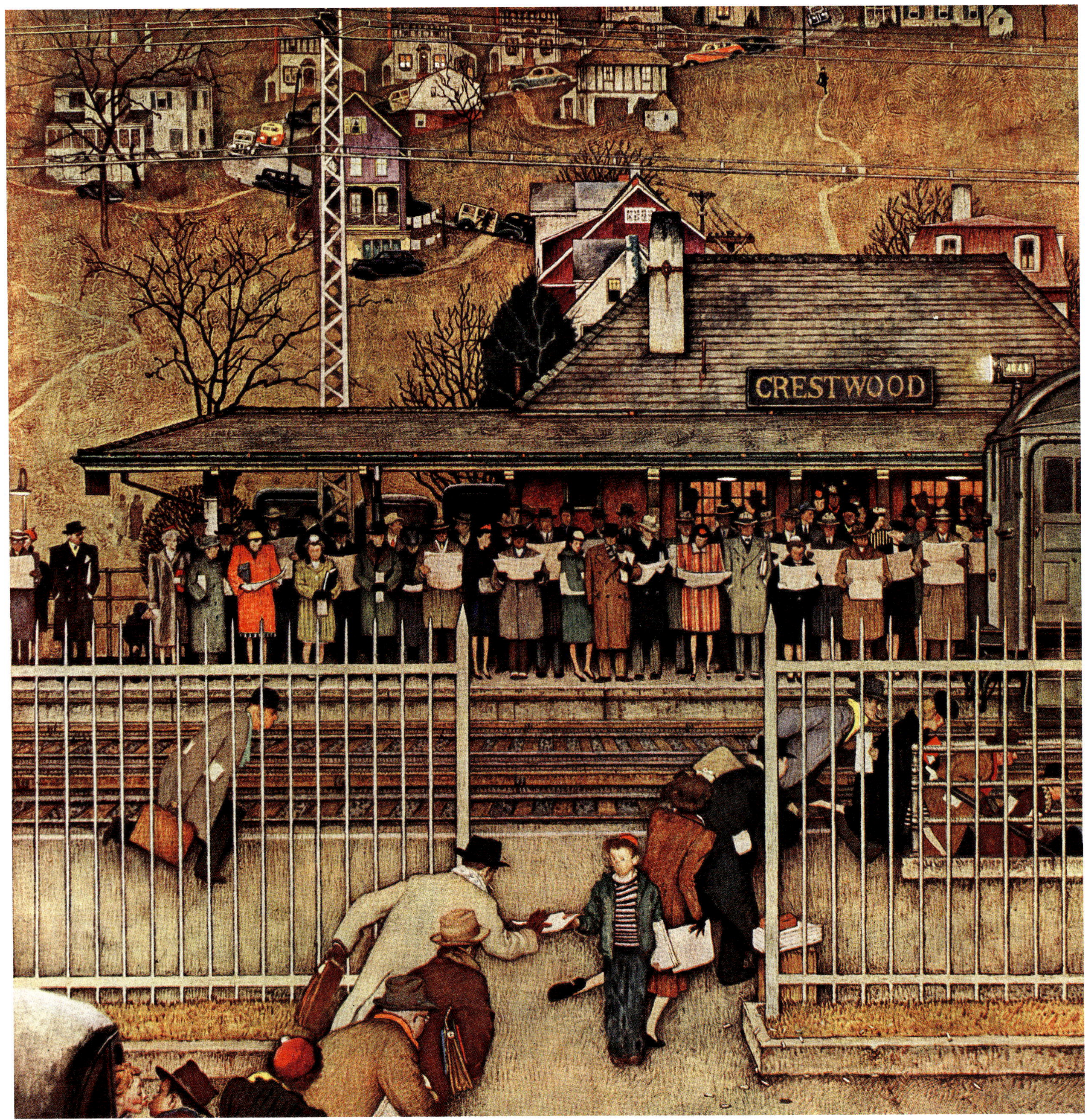
CRESTWOOD

Pl. 20
Norman Rockwell, *Crestwood Commuter Station*, 1946. Cover illustration for *The Saturday Evening Post*, November 16, 1946. Oil on canvas, 22 × 20¾ in. Private Collection. Illustration provided by SEPS through Curtis Licensing. Artwork Approved by the Norman Rockwell Family Agency.

Fig. 19
Designed by Norman Rockwell, *Crestwood Commuter Station*, *The Saturday Evening Post*, November 16, 1946. Cover illustration tear sheet, 14¼ × 11¼ in. Illustration provided by SEPS through Curtis Licensing. Artwork Approved by the Norman Rockwell Family Agency.

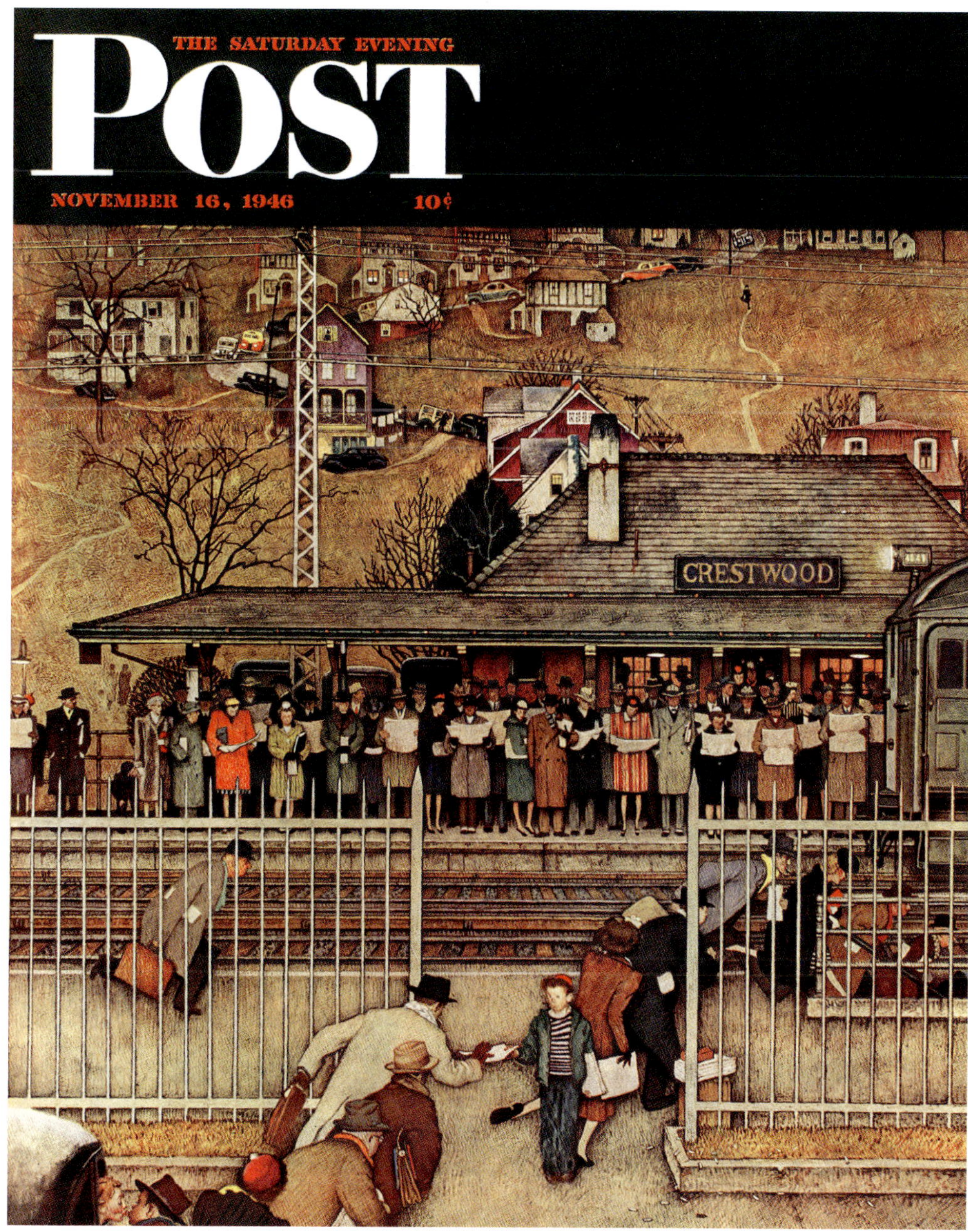

industry. Commissioned by the company as a magazine advertisement, the work celebrates the enduring themes of material, labor, and place by employing time-honored imagery. Indeed, the wise, good man, bathed in light and looked over by an angel, could have been a religious scene from any point in the previous three centuries. An illustration trading in easel traditions, *The Craftsman* is also a contemplation of constancy and a return to a moment when New England stood in for the country writ large in the popular imagination. Born in an era that preferred abstraction, Rockwell conjured a narrative that served as capstone and harbinger, an image that encapsulates the mythic, sentimental culture of the region while foreshadowing all that it will become.

Fig. 20
Norman Rockwell, *The Craftsman* [sketch], 1961–62. Oil on board, 47⅞ × 38⅞ in. Collection of Shelburne Museum, gift of Polycor and Rock of Ages Corporation. 2024-12.2. © Rock of Ages Corporation.

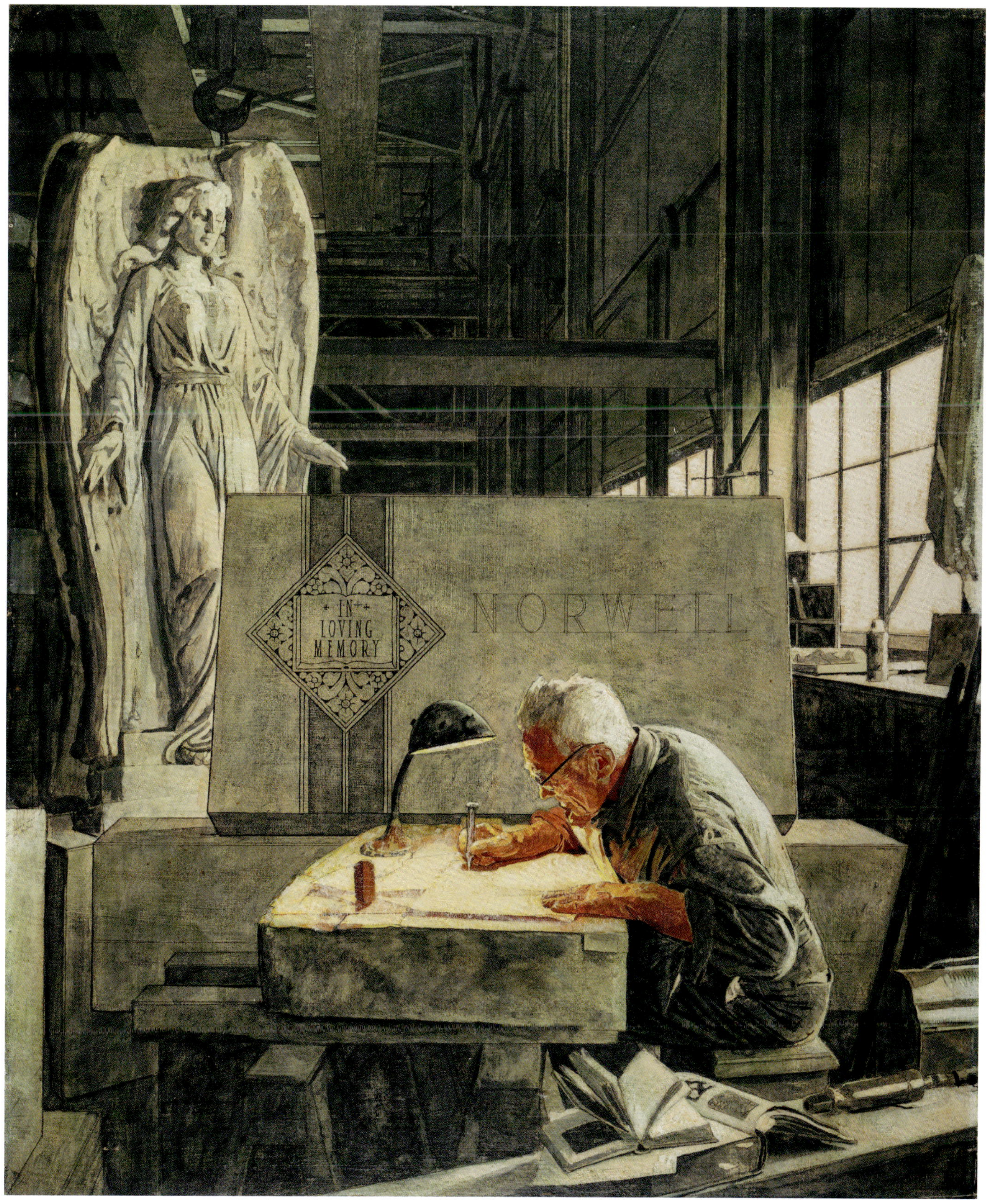

IN
LOVING
MEMORY
NORWELL

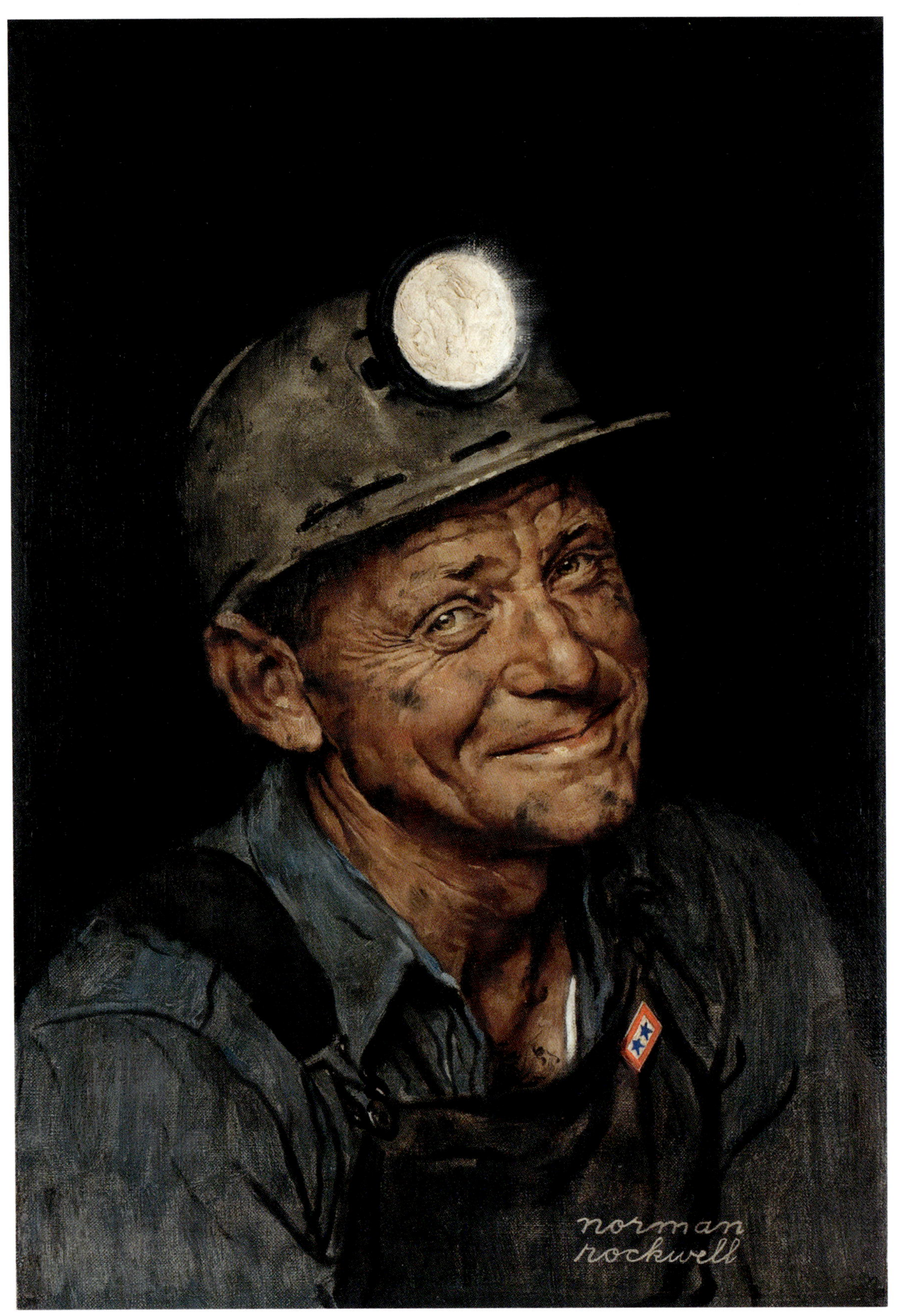

Pl. 21

Norman Rockwell, *Mine America's Coal (Portrait of a Coal Miner)*, 1943. Poster illustration for U.S. Office of War Information. Oil on canvas, 21 × 14 in. Norman Rockwell Museum Collection, Museum purchase. NRM.1978.12. Artwork Approved by the Norman Rockwell Family Agency.

Pl. 22

Norman Rockwell, *Rosie the Riveter*, 1943. Cover illustration for *The Saturday Evening Post*, May 29, 1943. Oil on canvas, 52 × 40 in. Crystal Bridges Museum of American Art, Bentonville, Arkansas. 2007.178. Artwork Approved by the Norman Rockwell Family Agency.

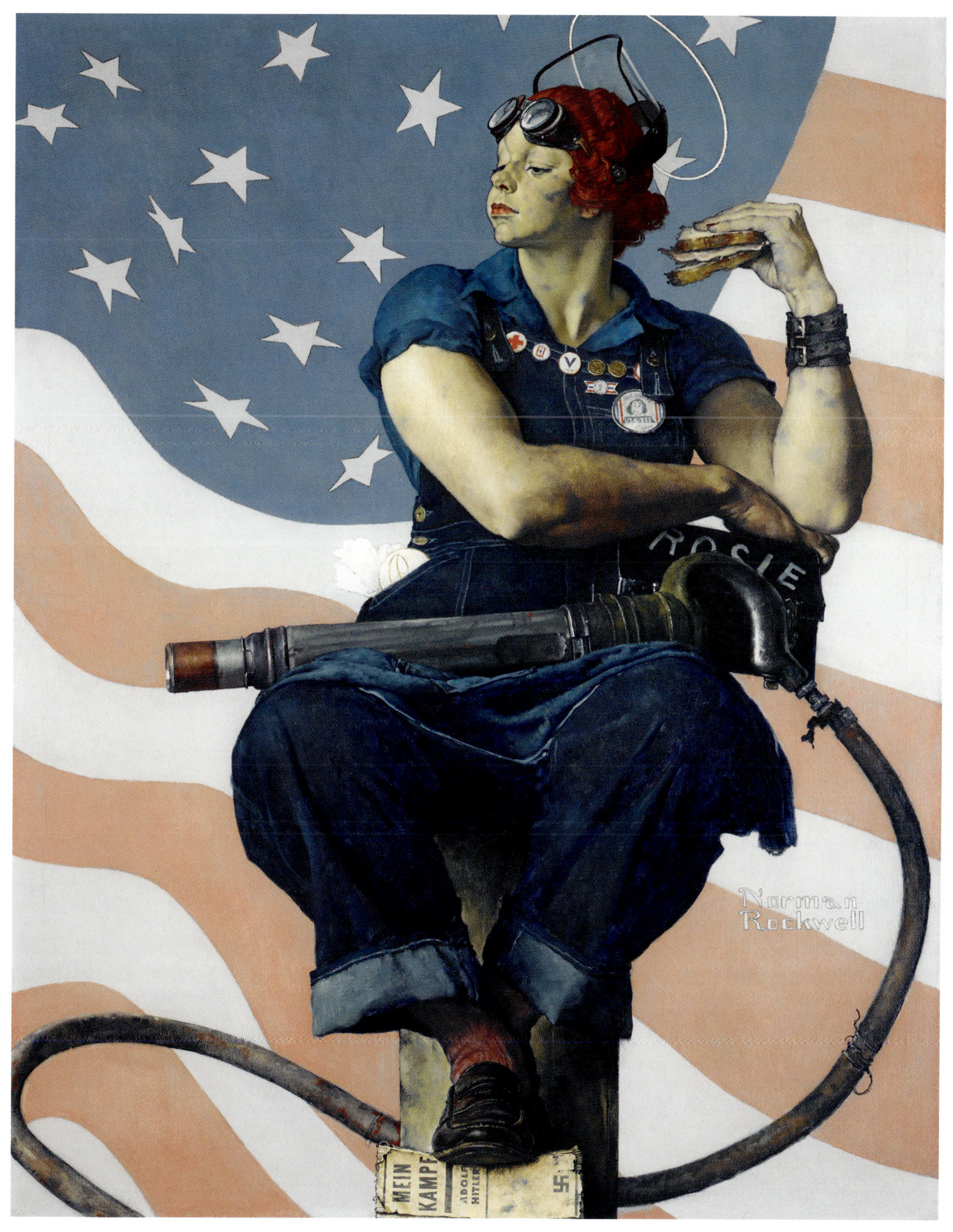
ROSIE
Norman
Rockwell
MEIN
KAMPF
ADOLF
HITLER

Pl. 23

Norman Rockwell, *The Tattoo Artist*, 1944. Cover illustration for *The Saturday Evening Post*, March 4, 1944. Oil on canvas, 43⅛ × 33⅛ in. Brooklyn Museum, Gift of the artist, 69.8. Artwork Approved by the Norman Rockwell Family Agency.

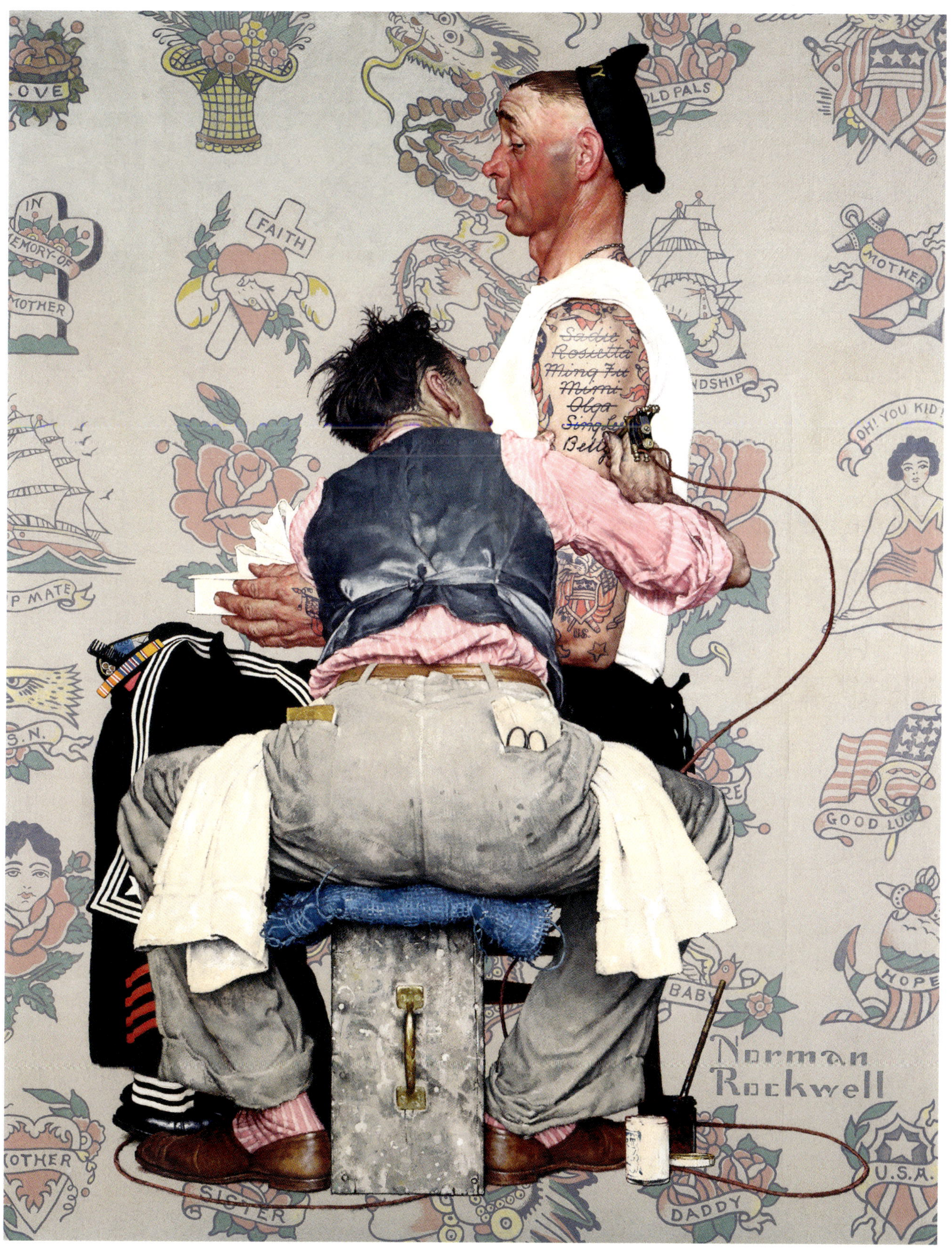
LOVE
OLD PALS
IN
EMORY-OF
MOTHER
FAITH
MOTHER
NDSHIP
OH! YOU KID!
P MATE
Rosietta
Mimi
Olga
S.N.
BABY
HOPE
SISTER
DADDY
U.S.A.
Norman
Rockwell

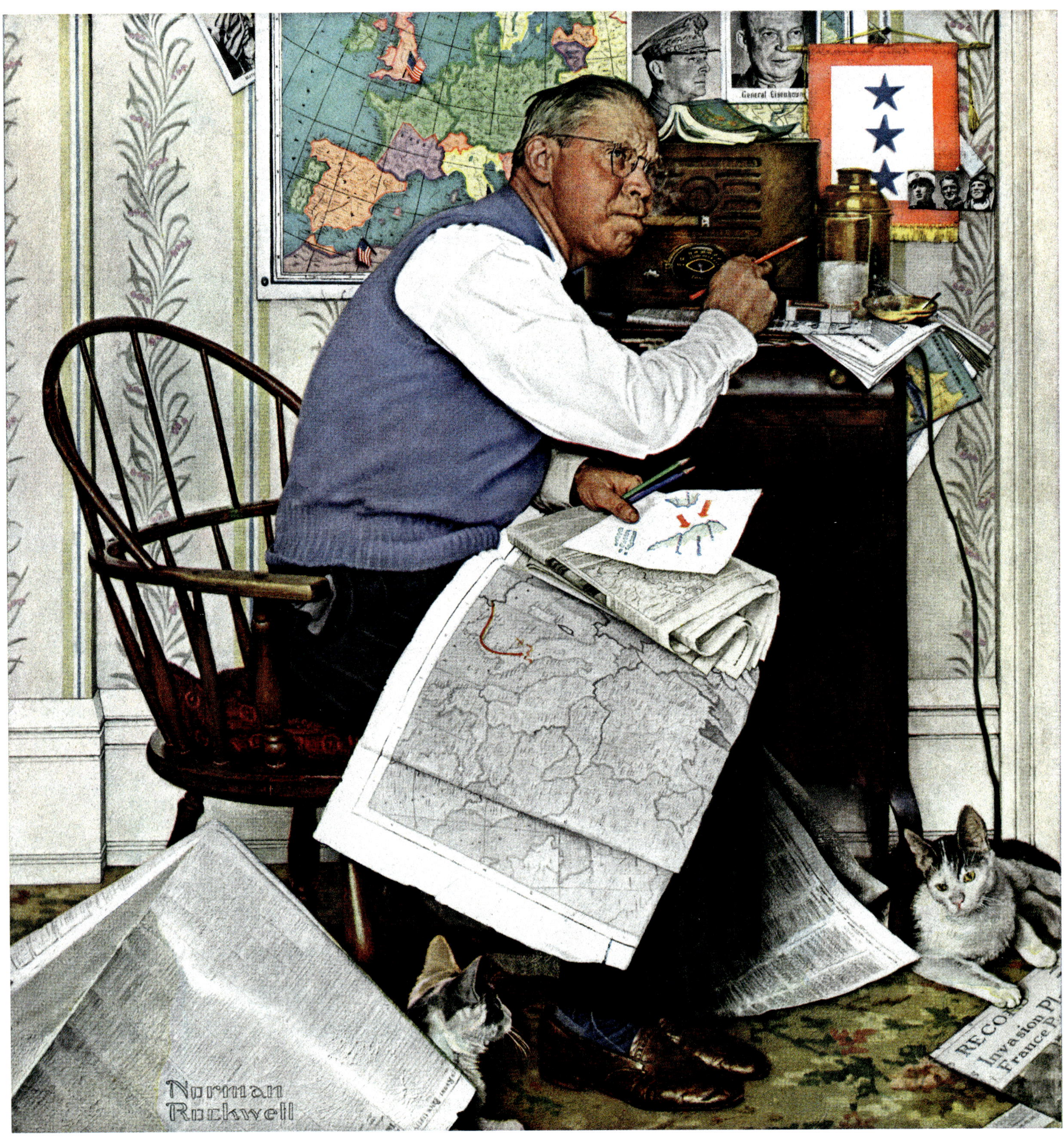
General Eisenhow
RECO
Invasion Pl
France P
Norman Rockwell

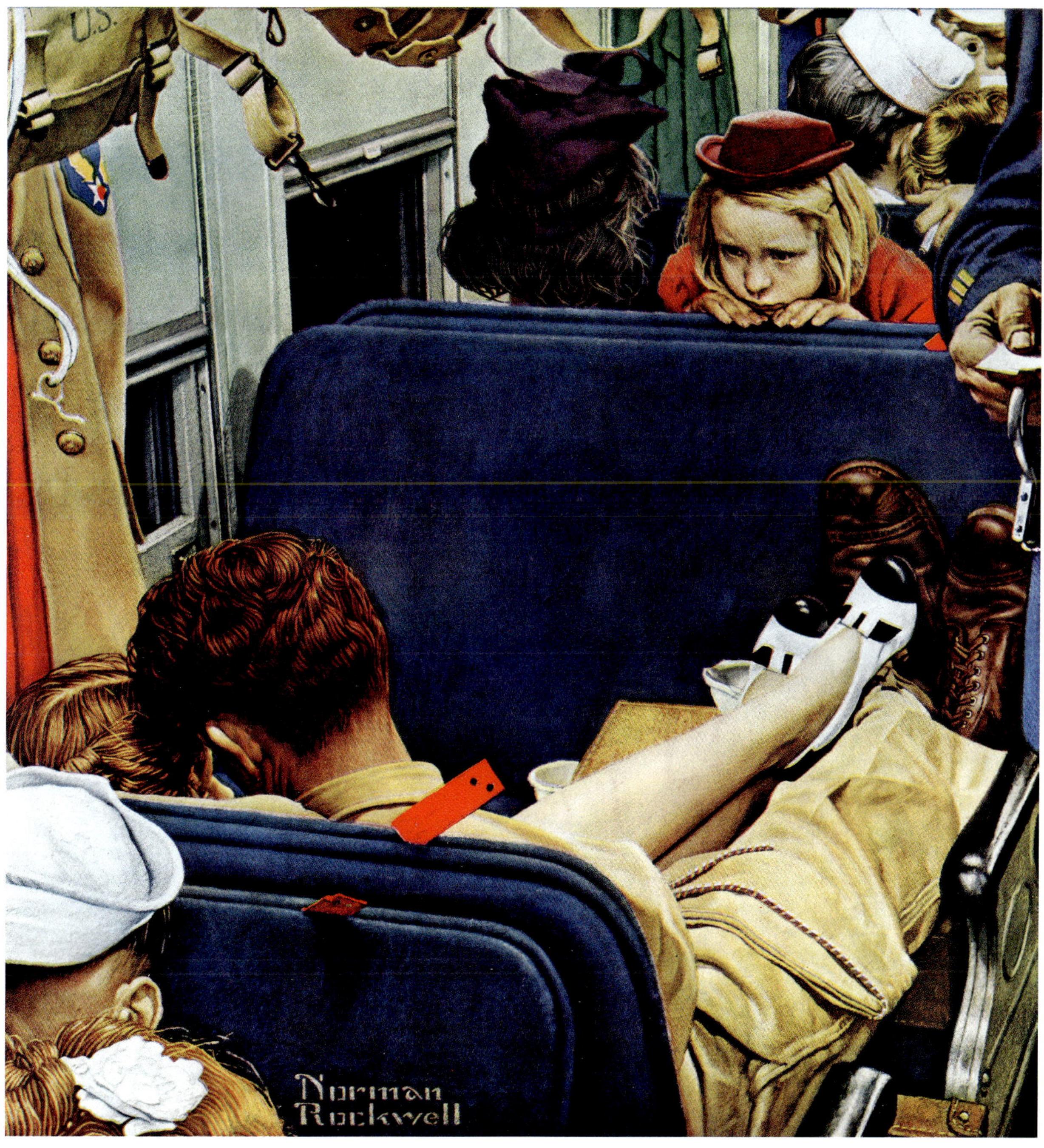

Pl. 24

Norman Rockwell, *Man Charting War Maneuvers*, 1944. Cover illustration for *The Saturday Evening Post*, April 29, 1944. Oil on canvas, 35 × 33 in. Collection of The Berkshire Eagle. Illustration provided by SEPS through Curtis Licensing. Artwork Approved by the Norman Rockwell Family Agency.

Pl. 25

Norman Rockwell, *Little Girl Observing Lovers on a Train*, 1944. Cover illustration for *The Saturday Evening Post*, August 12, 1944. Oil on canvas, 22 × 20 in. Private Collection. Illustration provided by SEPS through Curtis Licensing. Artwork Approved by the Norman Rockwell Family Agency.

Pl. 26
Norman Rockwell, *Willie Gillis: Gillis Heritage*, 1944. Cover illustration for *The Saturday Evening Post*, September 16, 1944. Oil on canvas, 13¼ × 10⅝ in. Private Collection. Illustration provided by SEPS through Curtis Licensing. Artwork Approved by the Norman Rockwell Family Agency.

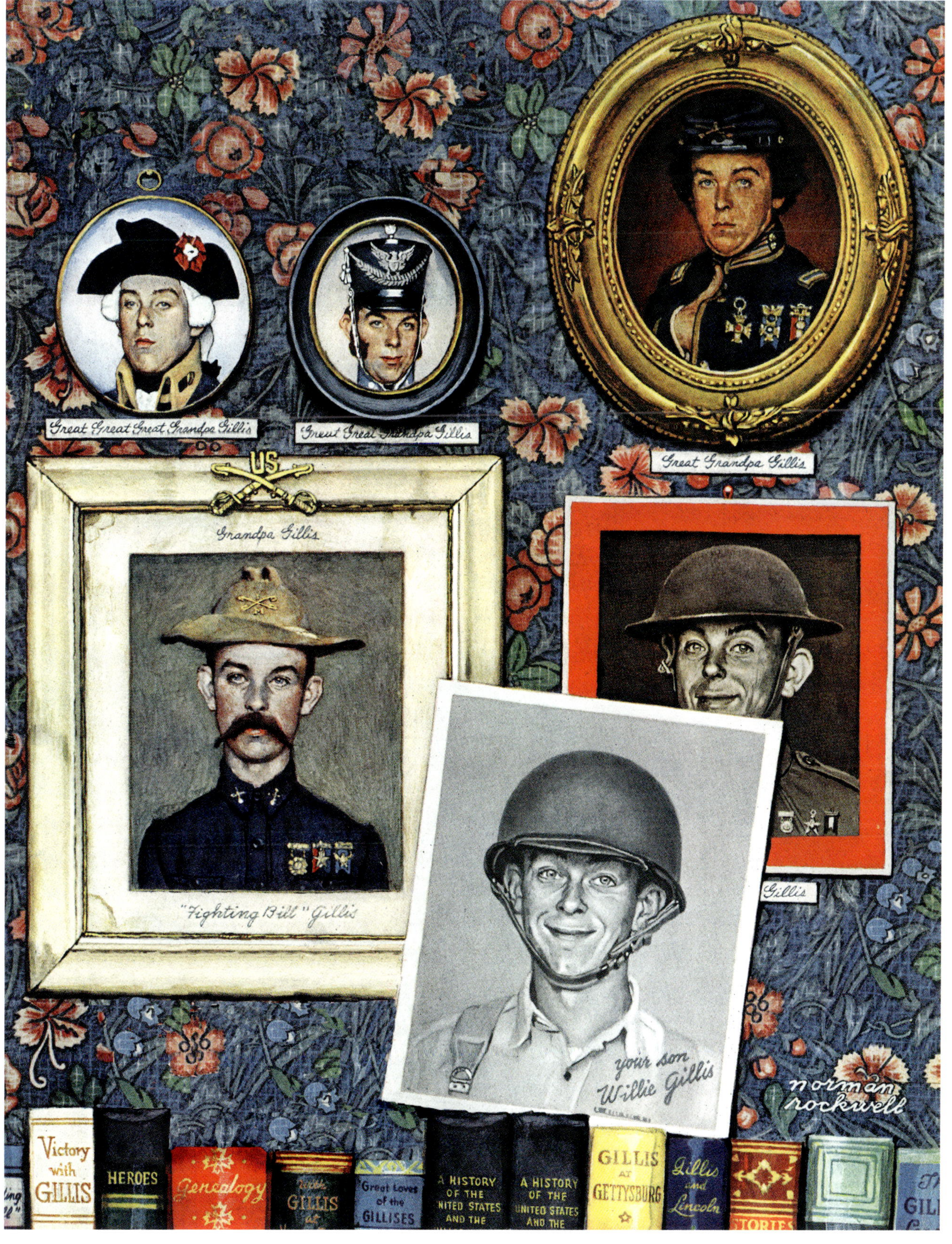

Great Great Great Grandpa Gillis
Great Great Grandpa Gillis
Great Grandpa Gillis
US
Grandpa Gillis
"Fighting Bill" Gillis
Gillis
your son
Willie Gillis
norman rockwell
Victory with GILLIS
HEROES
Genealogy
GILLIS
Great Loves of the GILLISES
A HISTORY OF THE
A HISTORY OF THE UNITED STATES AND THE
GILLIS AT GETTYSBURG
Gillis and Lincoln
STORIES

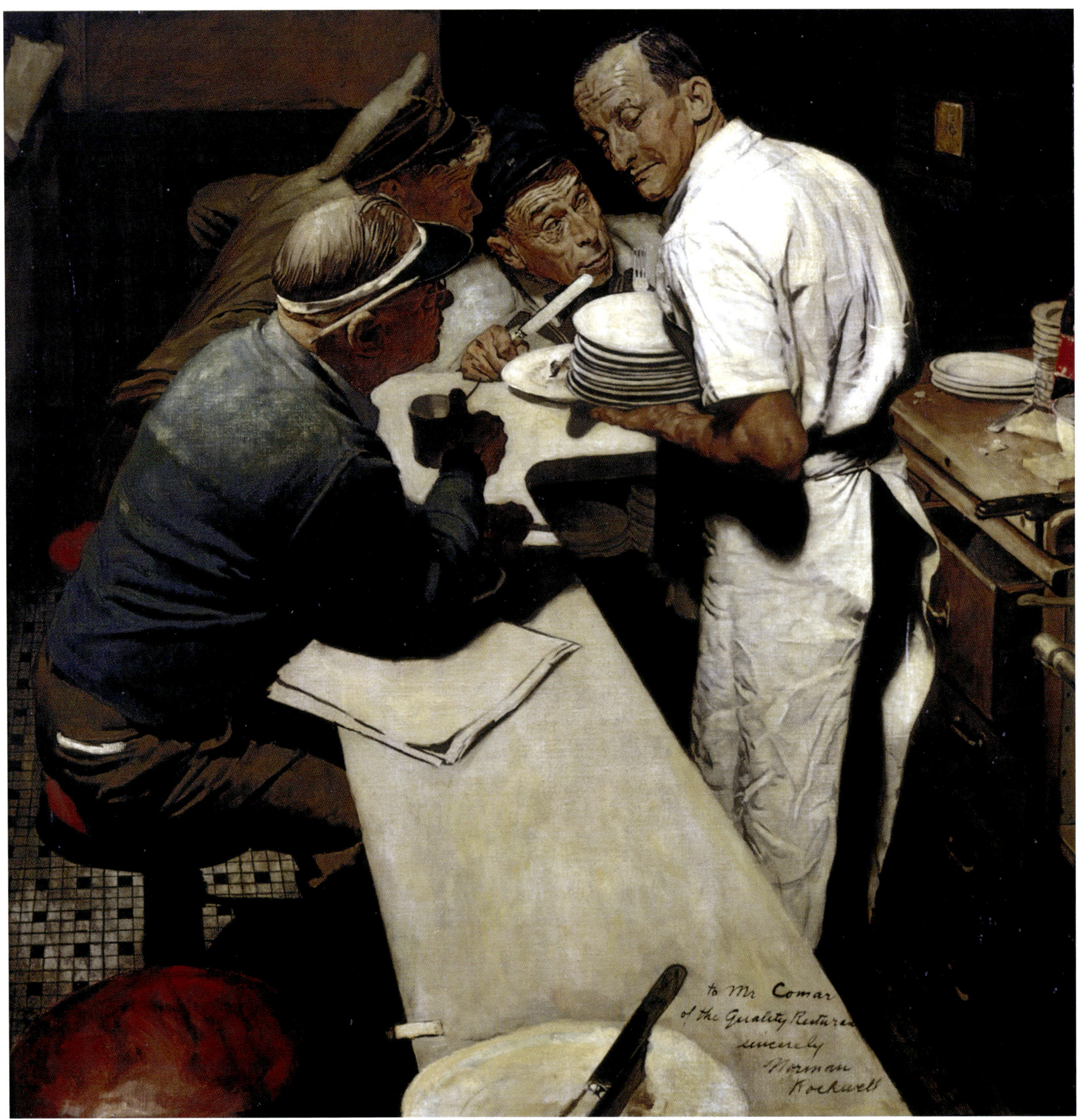
to Mr Comar
of the Quality Resturan
sincerely
Norman
Rockwell

Pl. 27

Norman Rockwell, *War News*, ca. 1945. Unpublished cover for *The Saturday Evening Post*. Oil on canvas, 41¼ × 40½ in. Norman Rockwell Museum Collection, Museum purchase. NRM.1976.02. Artwork Approved by the Norman Rockwell Family Agency.

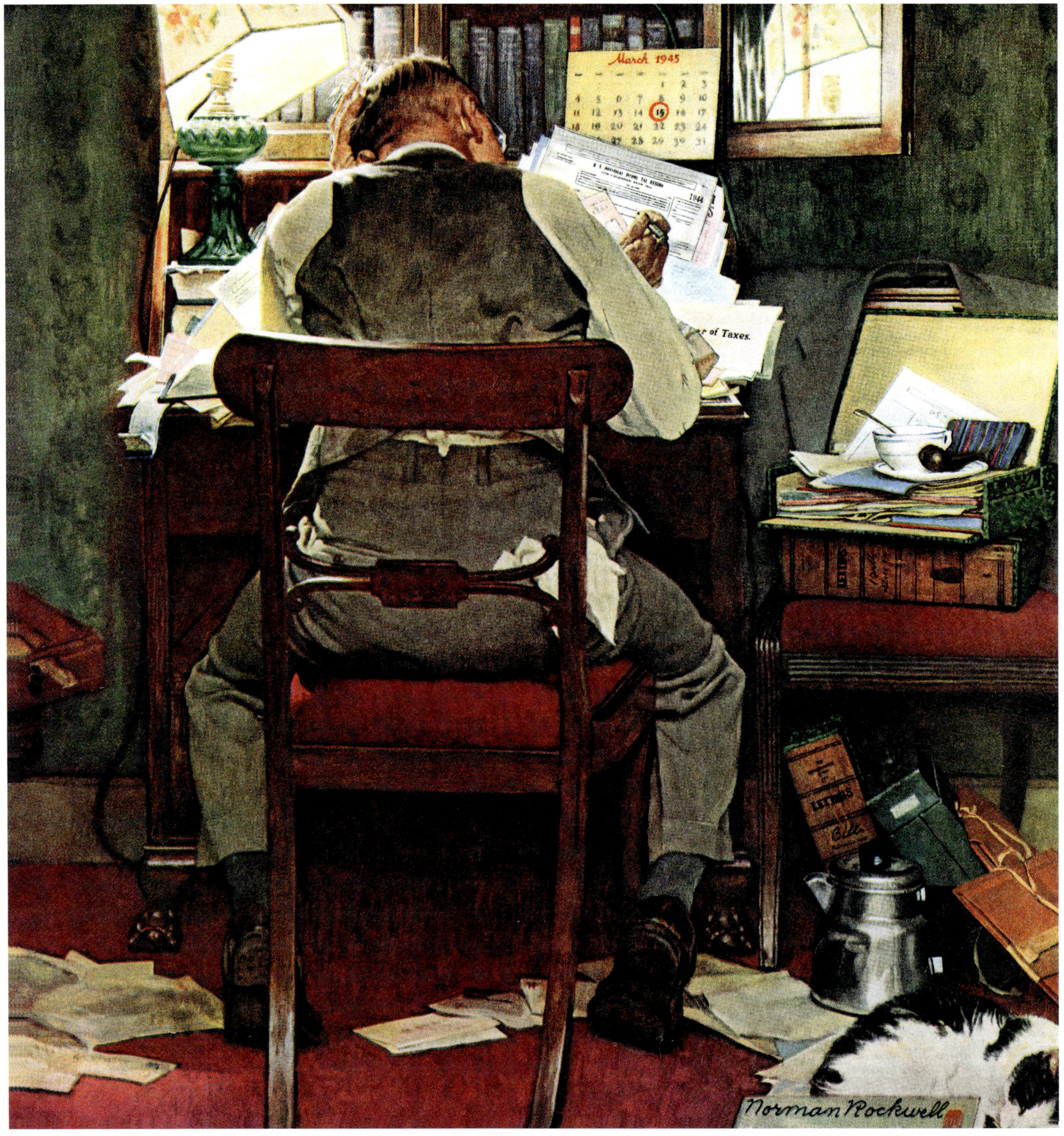
March 1945
of Taxes.
Norman Rockwell

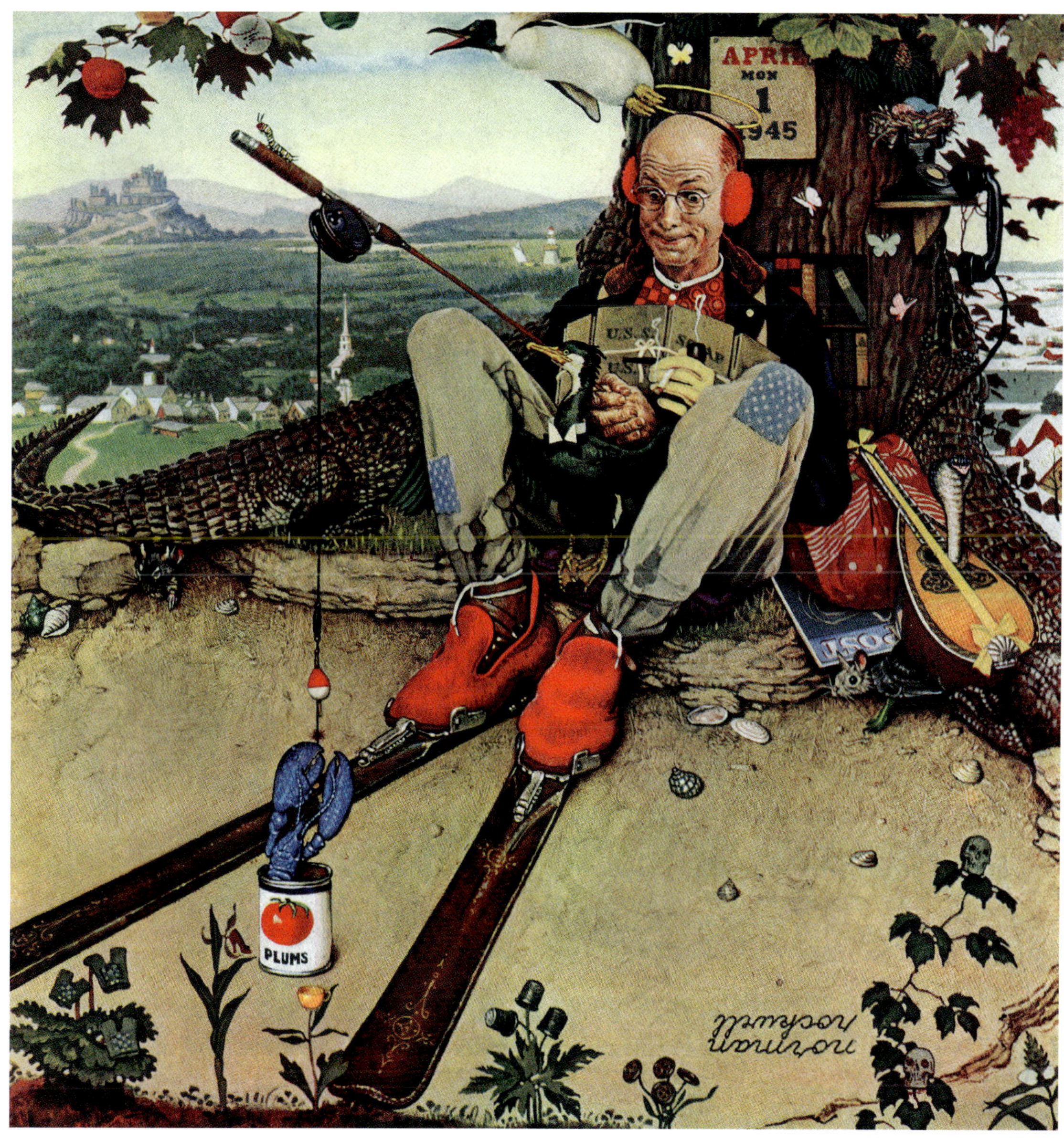

Pl. 28

Norman Rockwell, *Income Tax*, 1945. Cover illustration for *The Saturday Evening Post*, March 17, 1945. Oil on canvas, 22 × 20 in. Private Collection. Illustration provided by SEPS through Curtis Licensing. Artwork Approved by the Norman Rockwell Family Agency.

Pl. 29

Norman Rockwell, *April Fool: Fishing*, 1945. Cover illustration for *The Saturday Evening Post*, March 31, 1945. Oil on canvas, 22 × 20 in. Private Collection. Illustration provided by SEPS through Curtis Licensing. Artwork Approved by the Norman Rockwell Family Agency.

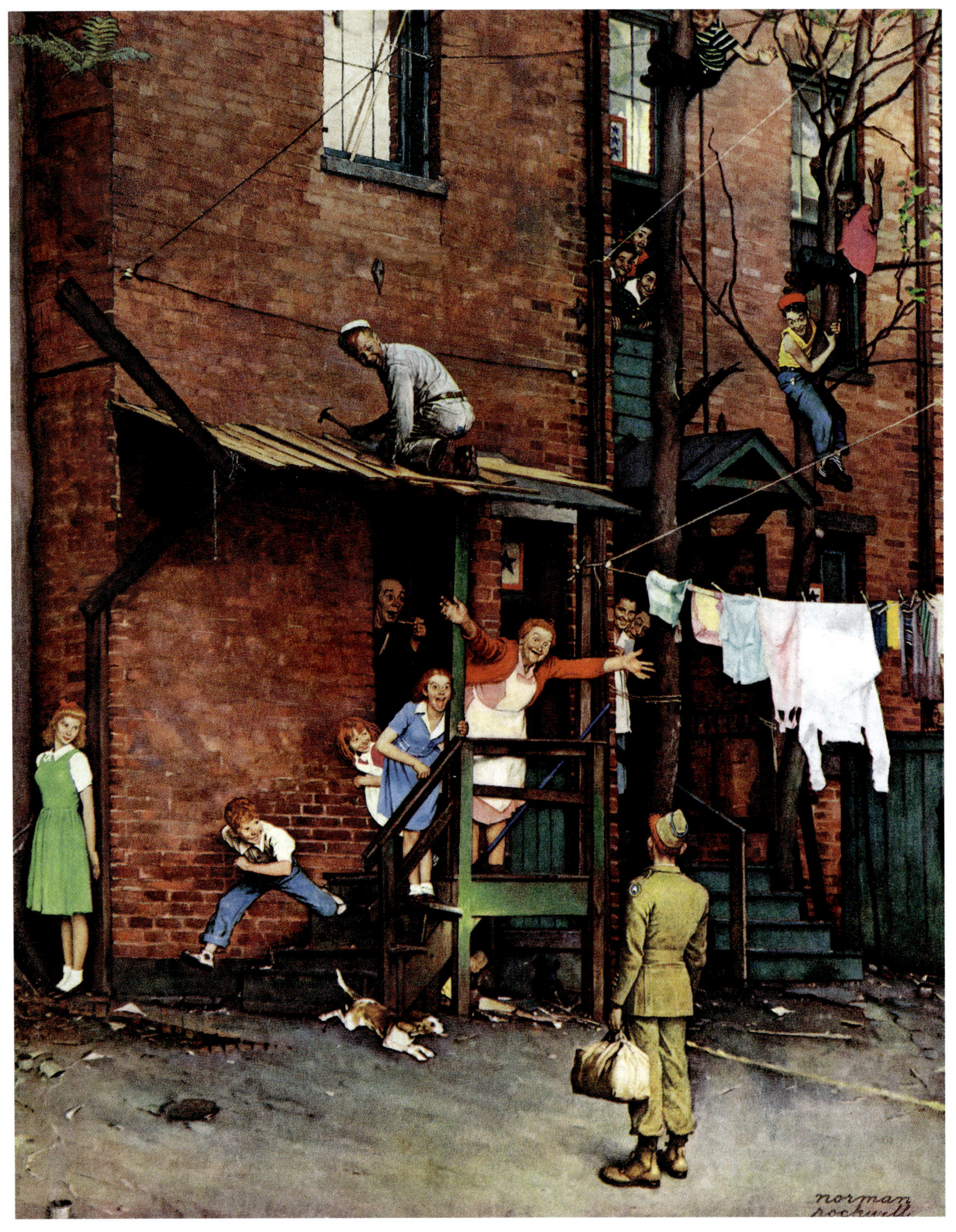
norman
rockwell

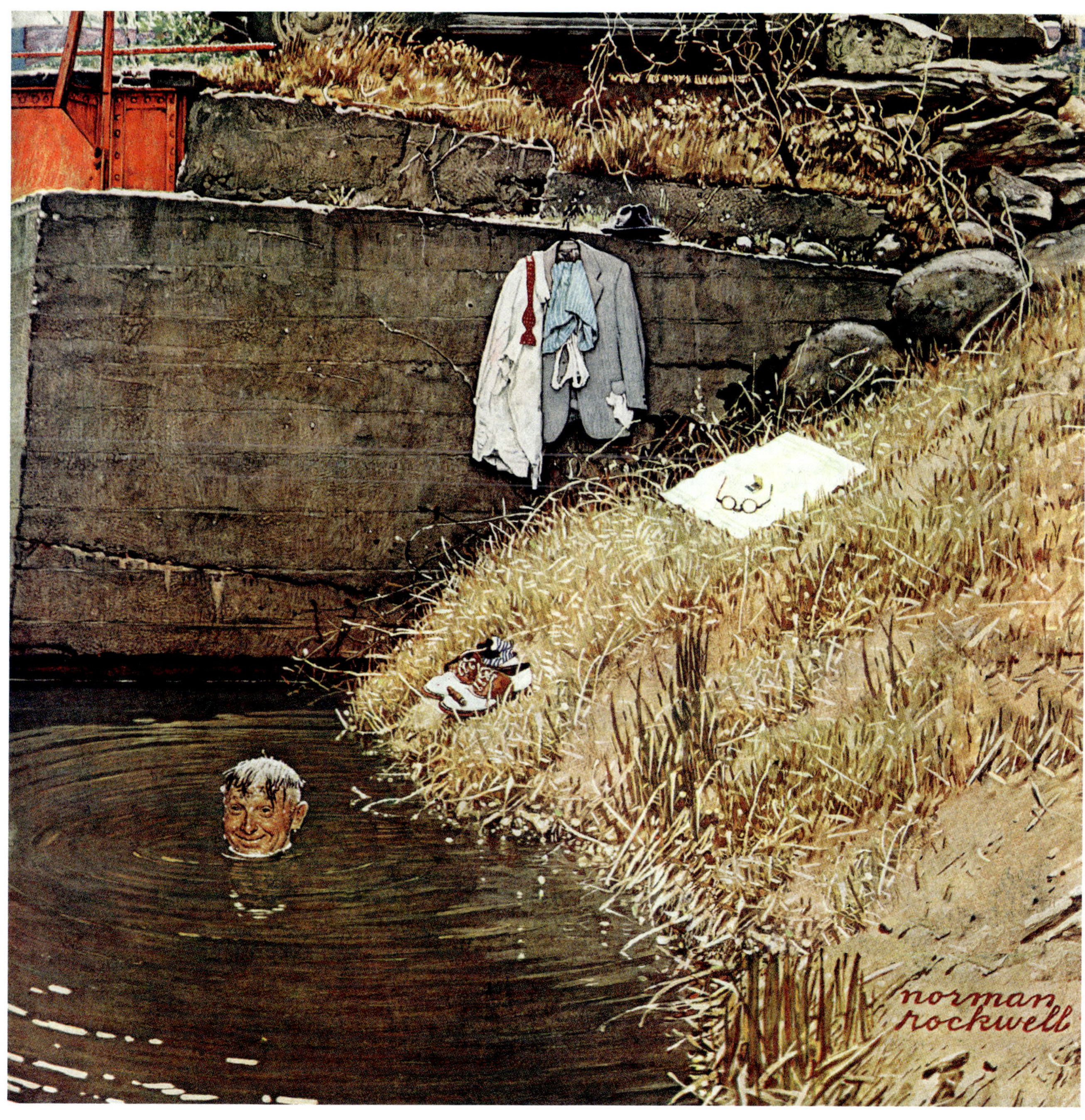

Pl. 30

Norman Rockwell, *The Homecoming*, 1945. Cover illustration for *The Saturday Evening Post*, May 26, 1945. Oil on canvas, 28 × 22 in. Private Collection. Illustration provided by SEPS through Curtis Licensing. Artwork Approved by the Norman Rockwell Family Agency.

Pl. 31

Norman Rockwell, *Salesman in Swimming Hole*, 1945. Cover illustration for *The Saturday Evening Post*, August 11, 1945. Oil on canvas. Private Collection. Illustration provided by SEPS through Curtis Licensing. Artwork Approved by the Norman Rockwell Family Agency.

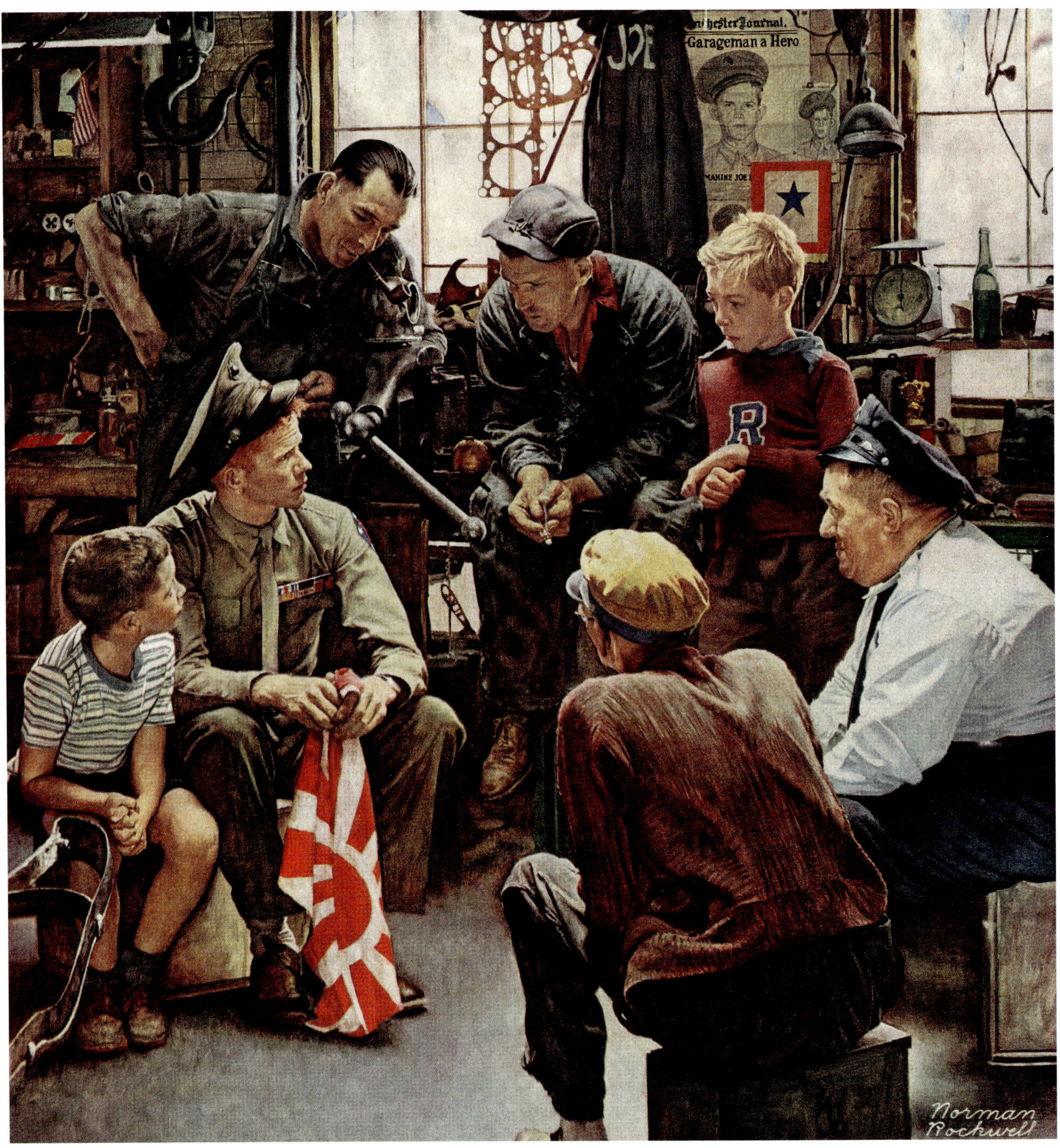
Garageman a Hero
JOE
Norman Rockwell

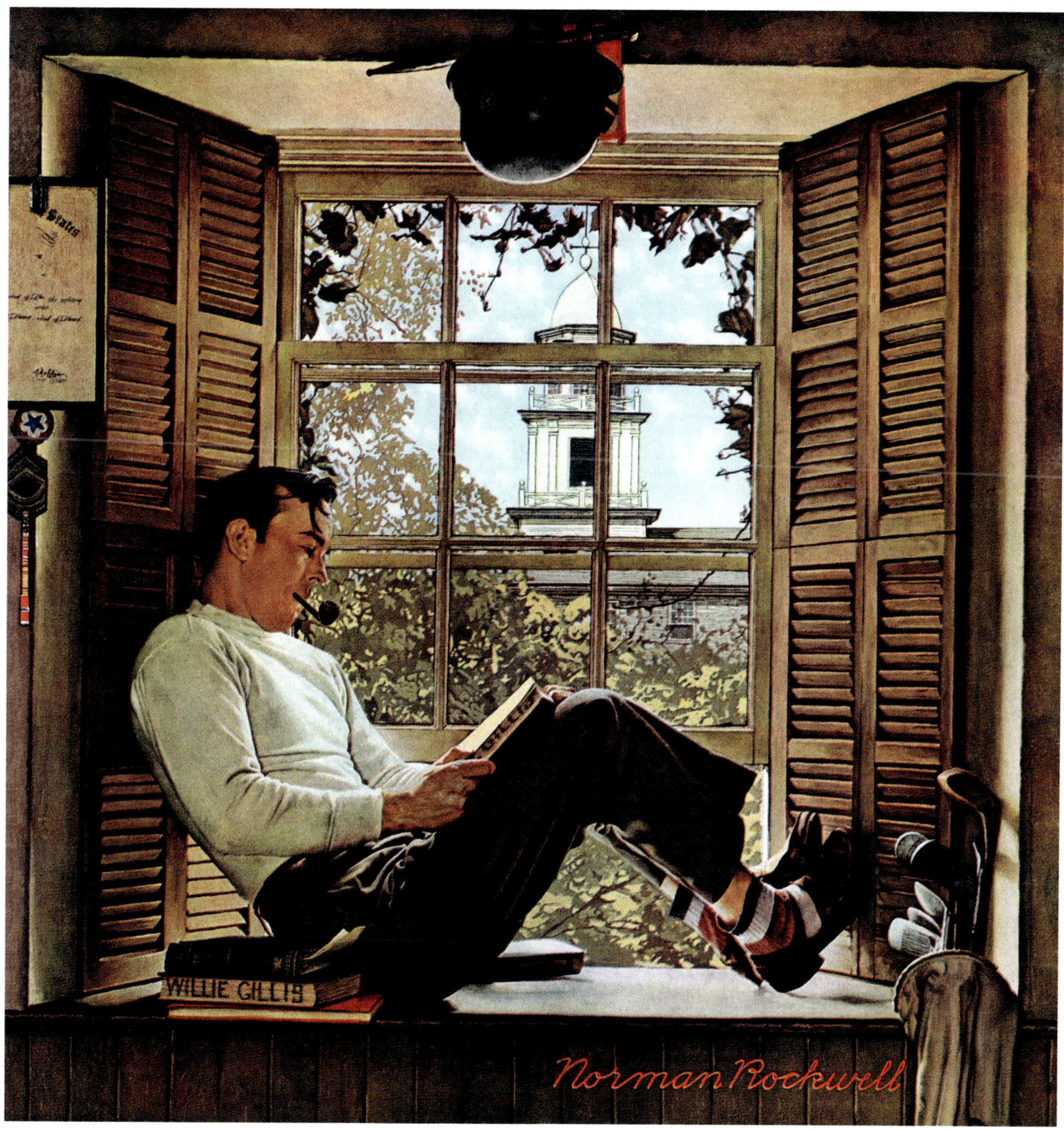

Pl. 32
Norman Rockwell, *Homecoming Marine*, 1945. Cover illustration for *The Saturday Evening Post*, October 13, 1945. Oil on canvas, 46 × 42 in. Private Collection. Illustration provided by SEPS through Curtis Licensing. Artwork Approved by the Norman Rockwell Family Agency.

Pl. 33
Norman Rockwell, *Willie Gillis in College*, 1946. Cover illustration for *The Saturday Evening Post*, October 5, 1946. Oil on canvas, 36 × 35 in. Private Collection. Illustration provided by SEPS through Curtis Licensing. Artwork Approved by the Norman Rockwell Family Agency.

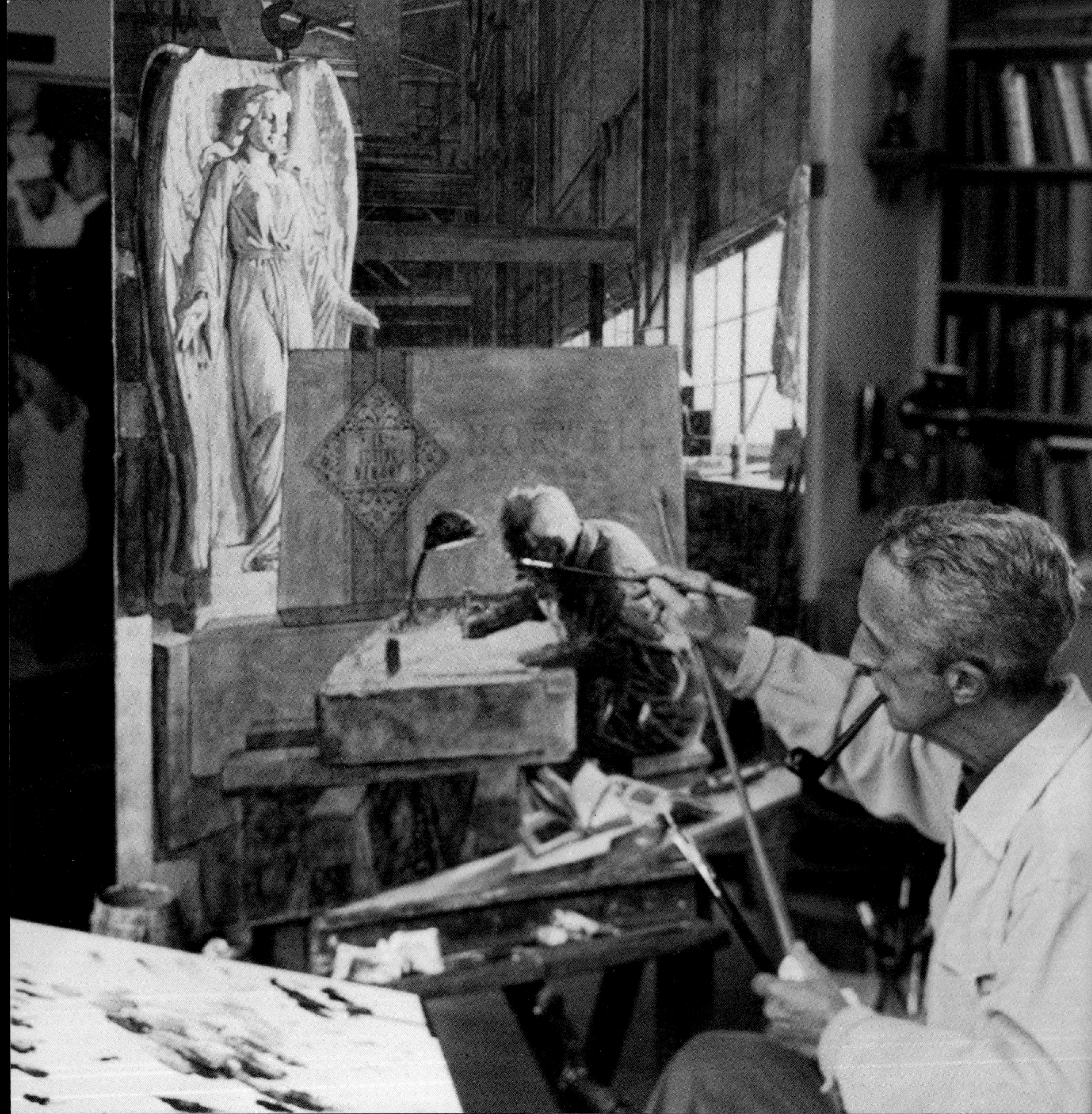

ROCK AND STONE

The Life-and-Death Art of Norman Rockwell

Alexander Nemerov

Norman Rockwell was the most earnest of artists. Is that a good thing or a bad thing? Herman Melville, in *The Confidence-Man*, wrote that the world "likes an earnest scene, and an earnest man, very well, but only in their place—the stage."[1] In actual life, not so much. Søren Kierkegaard, by contrast, praised earnestness as the deepest trait of a human being, the one thing that keeps the preacher steady every Sunday, or, to switch to Rockwell, every Saturday.[2] And so for years the master of *The Saturday Evening Post* was in earnest.

The three Rockwell paintings recently acquired by the Shelburne Museum—*Kneeling Girl* (Plate 34), *The Craftsman* (Plate 35), and a study for the latter work (Fig. 20)—are most decidedly in earnest. And what are they in earnest about? Death. The child in the first painting kneels before a fresh granite tombstone inscribed with the name "Newton." In blue jeans and pink blouse, her brown hair neatly braided, she folds her hands in prayer and stares at the fresh daisies she's laid on the grass. Three books at her side, neatly tied by a leather strap, tell us she's on her way home from school. The shadow of the stone says the sun is still high but starting to descend. We accept without thinking—such is Rockwell's skill—that the grave is that of a grandparent and not a parent or sibling or friend. Nothing is too tragic, everything is kempt and polite, part of the staid continuity of the seasons and the years, grandmothers and grandfathers and grandchildren like rows of stones, from colonial slate to new-chiseled granite, one big family in the school of life.

Is anything below? The girl kneels lightly, her knees rising a little from the grass. The soles of her feet do not touch the ground; no footprints flatten the green. The daisies, brought from elsewhere, do not mar the turf by growing from it. Resting on the grass, slightly above the blades, quite dead unto themselves, they forget their roots but retain the lift they had in life. Even the granite slab stays atop the earth, its heaviness distributed by the broad horizontal plinth that makes it float like a paper sailboat.

How different from the New England mourning of the *Stevenson Memorial*, Abbott Thayer's large homage of 1903 to the novelist and poet Robert Louis Stevenson, painted in Dublin, New Hampshire (Fig. 21).[3] There everything is weight: the rock inscribed with the name of the Samoan mountain on which Stevenson is buried; the lonely grief of the mourning angel, posed for by one of Thayer's housekeepers, also the heaviness of her gown, which Thayer had her wear soaked in plaster as she posed to create the right gravity. In memory not only of Stevenson but also Thayer's wife Kate, who died of depression and (like Stevenson) tuberculosis, the angel comes down to earth to mourn in elevation. But in Rockwell's painting everything is on the level, and his grave is not grave.

His cemetery is not creepy; the town is not creepy; death is not creepy. Nothing is like the New England gothic of H. P. Lovecraft, who makes the ten-year-old hero of his story "The Tomb" rattle the chains of an old granite vault

Pl. 34
Norman Rockwell, *Kneeling Girl*, 1955. Oil on canvas, 33⅜ × 31⅛ in. Collection of Shelburne Museum, gift of Polycor and Rock of Ages Corporation. 2024-12.3. © Rock of Ages Corporation.

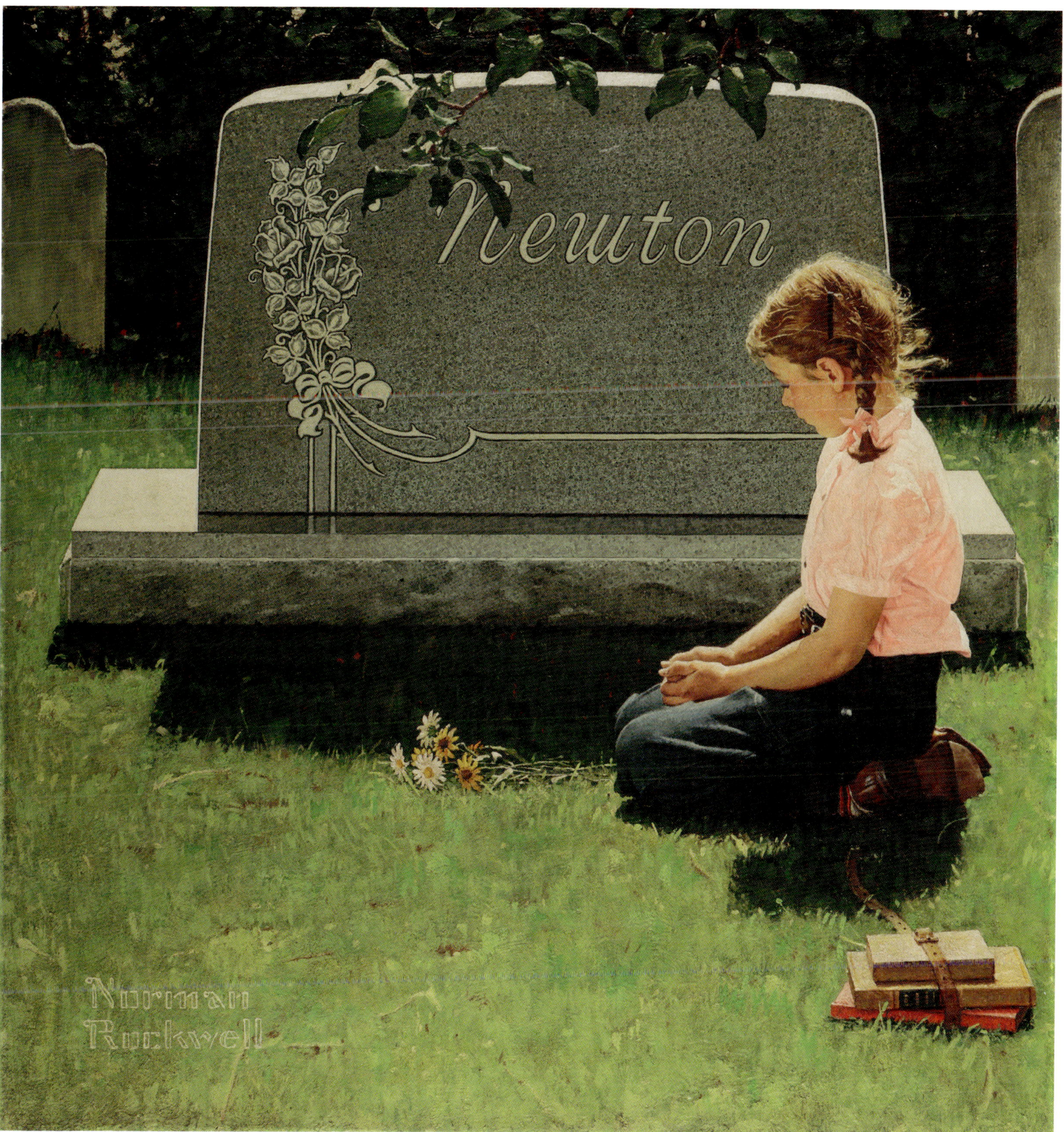
Newton
Norman
Rockwell

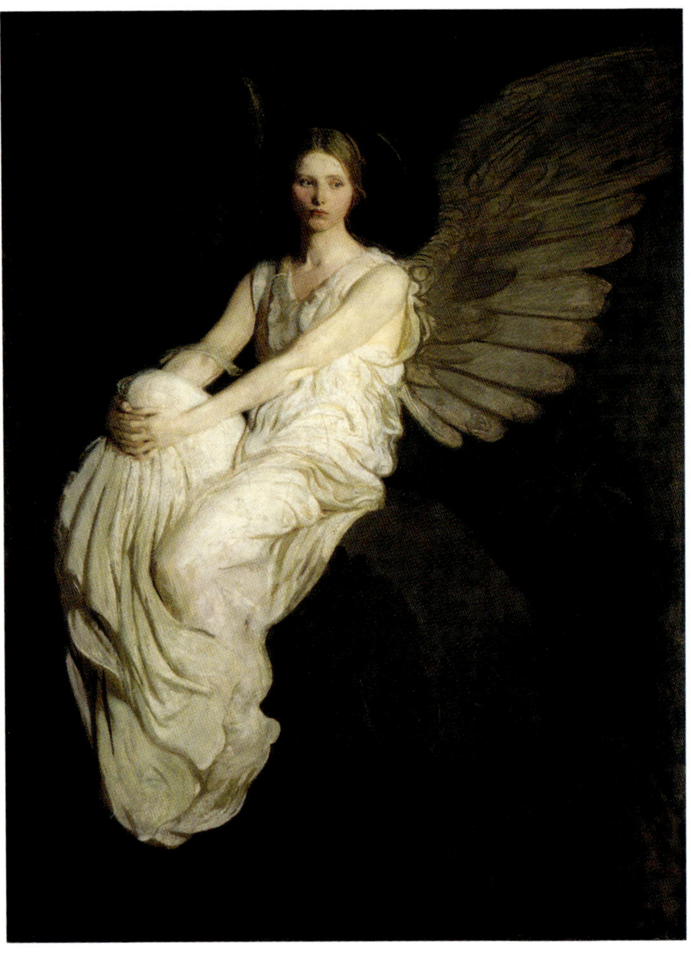

Fig. 21
Abbott Handerson Thayer, *Stevenson Memorial*, 1903. Oil on canvas, 81⅝ × 60⅛ in. Smithsonian American Art Museum, Gift of John Gellatly. 1929.6.127.

he finds in the forest, determined to break in, which eventually he does, sleeping there each night.[4] Rockwell, the anti-Lovecraft, keeps the girl safely on the surface. He rhymes the machine-tooled buds on Newton's stone with the braids of the girl's hair. Her downward gaze is as gentle as the green leaves bending over the grave. The strap tying the books is no snake of temptation, though it does rise to lick the girl's heel. It is not her first visit—or if it is, there will be more—but this is no mad, solitary quest. It is part of her education, as bound up with school as her books.

Imagine how beautiful and strange the painting would be if, in Lovecraftian fashion, Rockwell kept everything the same—the girl in her jeans and blouse and braids, with her books at her side—except *at night*? Then her vigil would be

Pl. 35
Norman Rockwell, *The Craftsman*, 1963. Oil on canvas, 47¼ × 38¼ in. Collection of Shelburne Museum, gift of Polycor and Rock of Ages Corporation. 2024-12.1. © Rock of Ages Corporation.

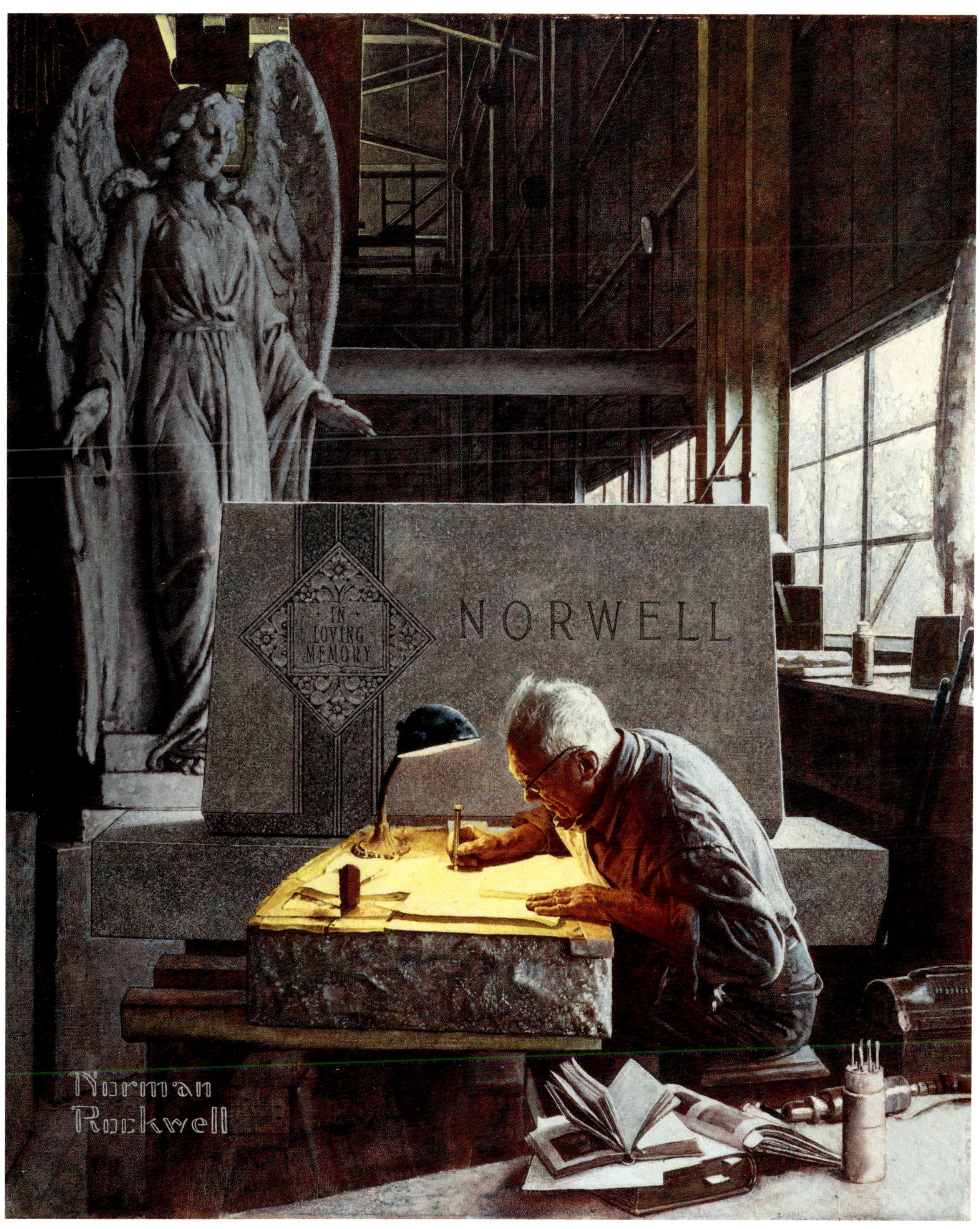
IN LOVING MEMORY
NORWELL
Norman Rockwell

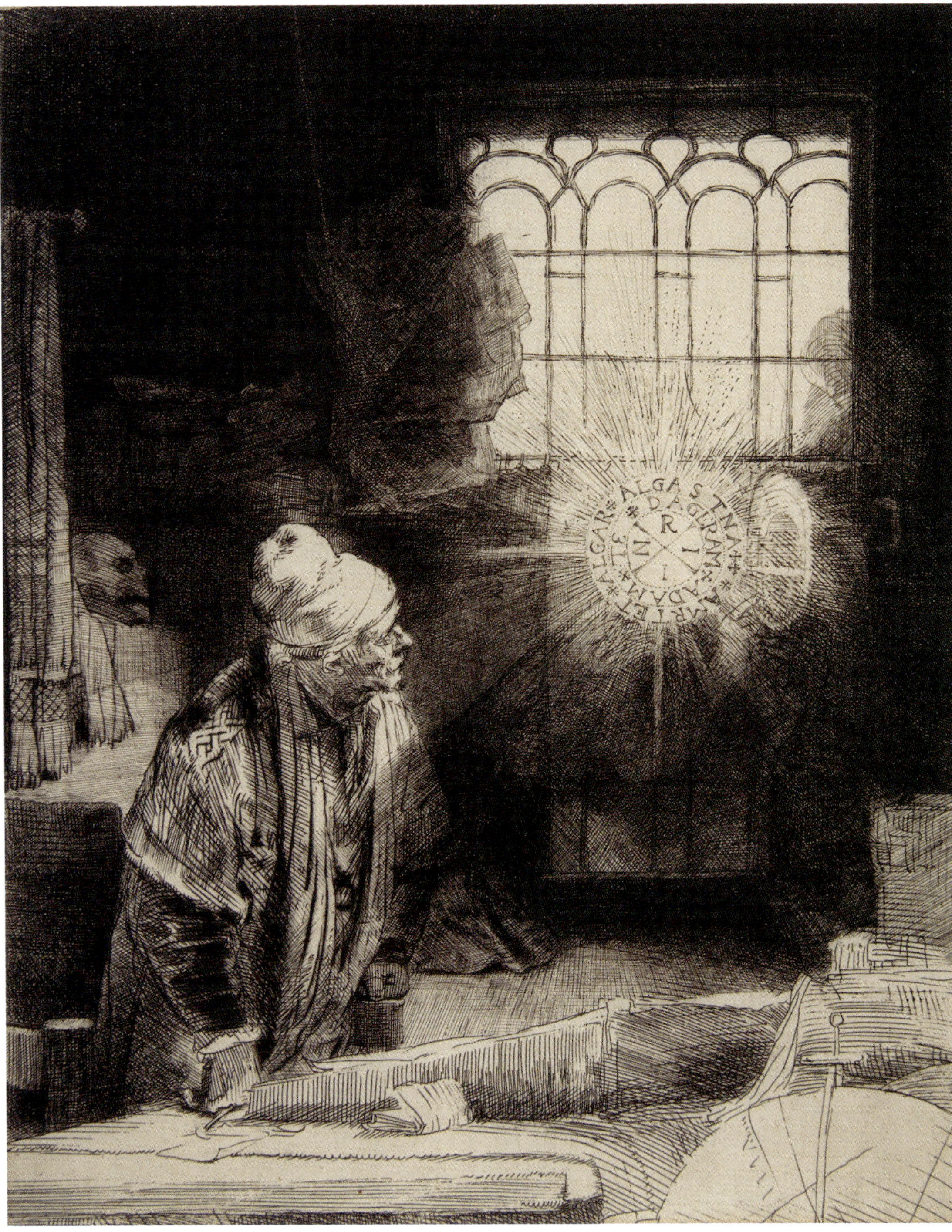

Fig. 22
Rembrandt, *Faust*, ca. 1652. Etching, $8\frac{1}{8} \times 9\frac{3}{8}$ in. The Metropolitan Museum of Art, Gift of Felix M. Warburg and his family, 1941. 41.1.19.

Fig. 23
Unidentified photographer, *Untitled* [Norman Rockwell painting *Kneeling Girl*], ca. 1955. Negative, 9⅞ × 7⅞ in. Vermont Granite Museum. 2021.74.526.

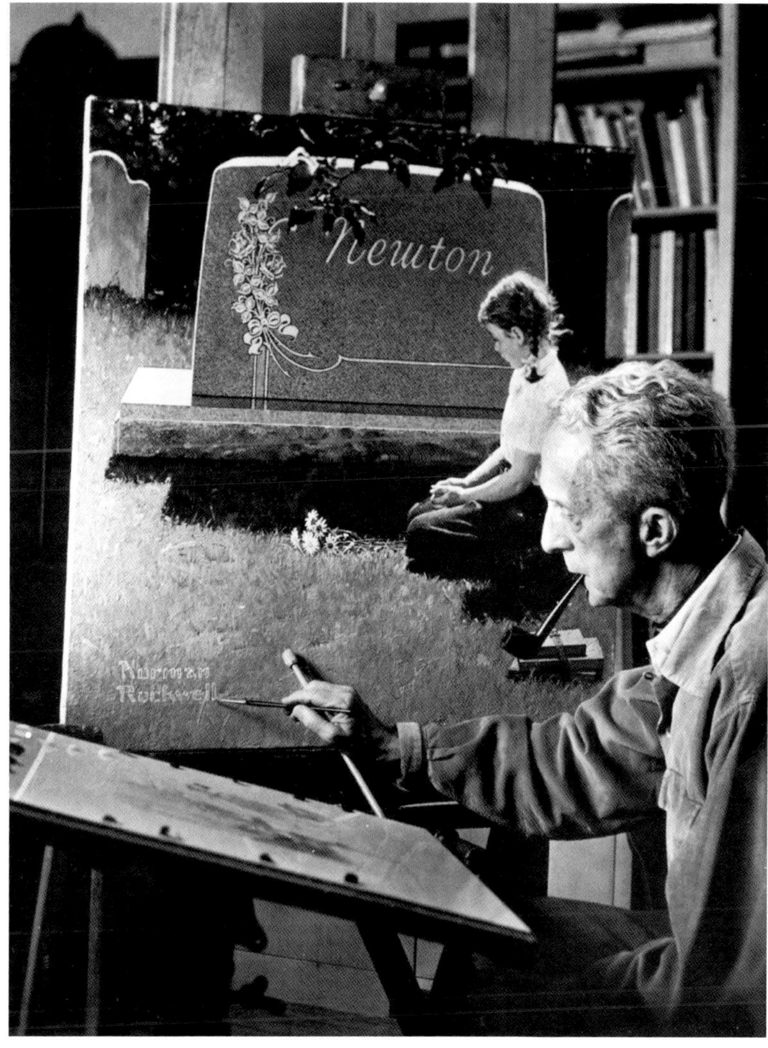

a true awakening, an insomniac devotion, a séance. But no such supernaturalism happens. Like the artist faithful in his task—a photograph shows Rockwell before his easel like the girl before the grave (Fig. 23)—the earnest one returns in the light of day.

It is good that they are earnest because Death awaits—he is the Craftsman in the other painting. In his darkened warehouse, the grim reaper works patiently at his task, incising a new name in his rolls. One of his angels looks on, held upright by a hook hanging from the ceiling, making sure the master enters the name correctly. Uncannily, the angel's halo drops down to become the desk lamp guiding the man's hand. Like Rembrandt's Faust, the humble Vermont artisan becomes a type of mystic, if for no other reason than his habitual proximity to the underworld (Fig. 22). The phrase "In Loving Memory" seems like a version of the kabbalistic diagram radiating before Rembrandt's philosopher.

None too subtly, the name "Norwell" suggests Rockwell's own name—fittingly in the year of the last of his *Saturday Evening Post* illustrations, bringing to a conclusion a forty-six-year span of work. Always doubtful and sad about his talent, the most modest of artists, Rockwell was earnest enough to know when his time was up. The photograph of him painting the picture shows again a fateful alignment: this time between the painter and the artisan (Fig. 24). So does Rockwell write his own name—ne'er well, nor well, not well, fare thee well—on the rock.

Is a poet's earnestness about death different from Rockwell's? In 2011 the artist Eric Aho, who lives in Putney, Vermont, made nine drawings of the Vermont poet Ruth Stone at her house in Goshen, in the mountains above Middlebury. Stone was then ninety-six years old; she died three months later. One of the drawings shows her seated inside her screen porch, turned away from the artist (Fig. 25). The darkened panels of the porch, like the shaded window of the gabled second story above her, imply that a poetry of death is a darkened frame: a non-illumination, a patient presence. The porch becomes an antechamber, a holding cell adjoined to the house proper, a hermitage of reflection. It makes her more accessible to the outside, more visible than if she were in the house, but emphasizes her apartness. Her back to us, she communes with herself. Into the mind of a child the mystery goes, welling down and emerging in the divinations of darkened windows. Poetry is not green grass or a rock of ages but an ancient woman turned little girl in a commemoration of herself that is no recollection, no regret, but a continual becoming of youth and age in a new growth of solitude.

Poetry, famously, is not famous. It is not a matter of spreading the word. Poetry is found by chance—found as a message in a bottle, as the poet Osip Mandelstam wrote a few years before Ruth Stone was born.[5] The person who happens to find a poem, Mandelstam said, is the person for whom it was intended. It is mystically personal, a fateful and sacred encounter, written by a stranger for another stranger who, in discovering it, becomes the poet's kin. Mourning and love happen in a space as small as the bottle, without an inch to share, yet whole worlds open in the privacy of the encounter. "You can talk to yourself all you want to," Stone wrote in "Being a Woman," one of her poems. "After all, you were the only one who ever heard / What you were saying."[6] Beautiful how that "you" is both the poet and the solitary reader.

By contrast, a communal culture of death means spreading the word to as many as possible—it requires advertising.

Fig. 24
Unidentified photographer, *Untitled* [Norman Rockwell painting *The Craftsman*], ca. 1963. Photograph, 10 × 8⅛ in. Vermont Granite Museum. 2021.74.512.

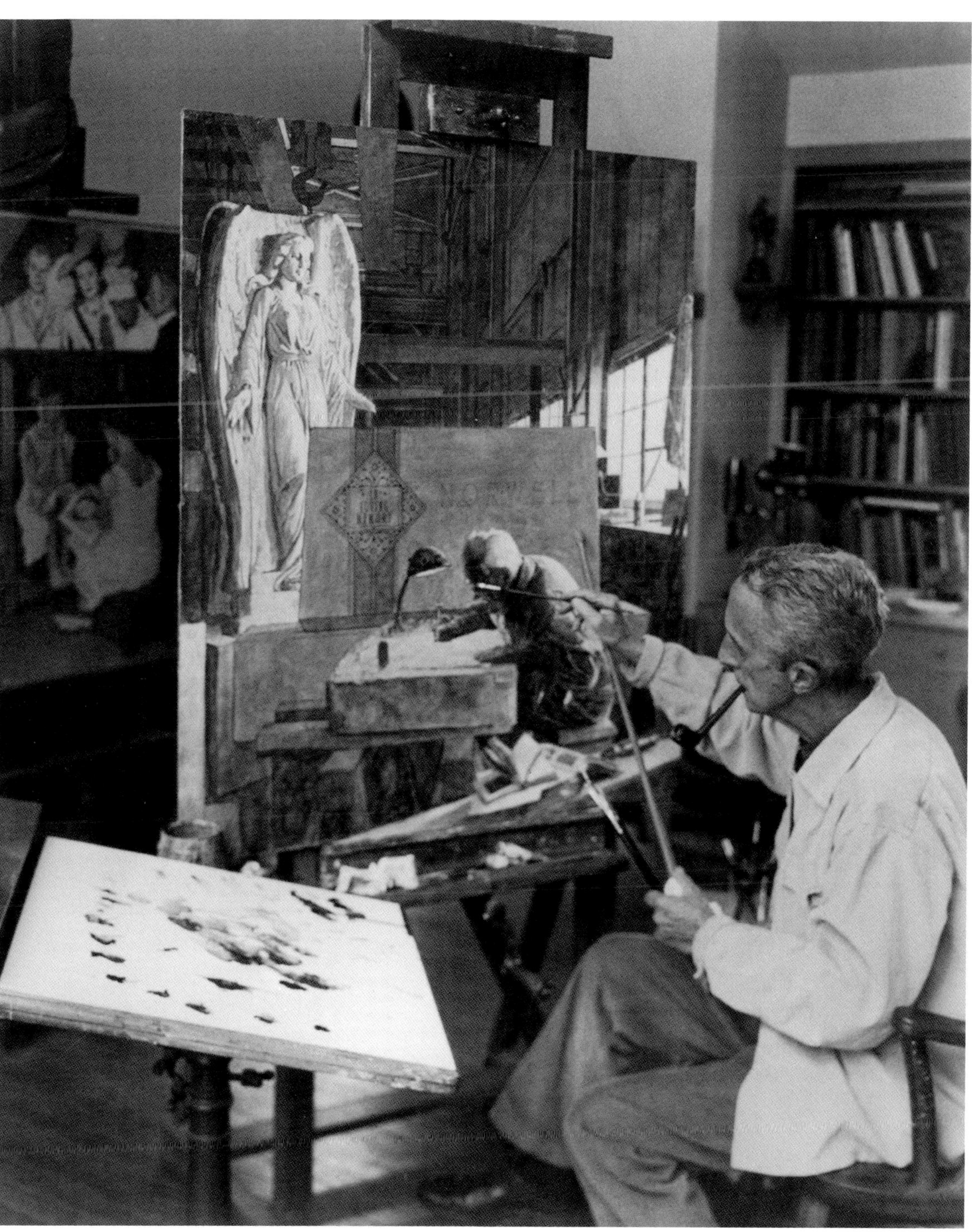

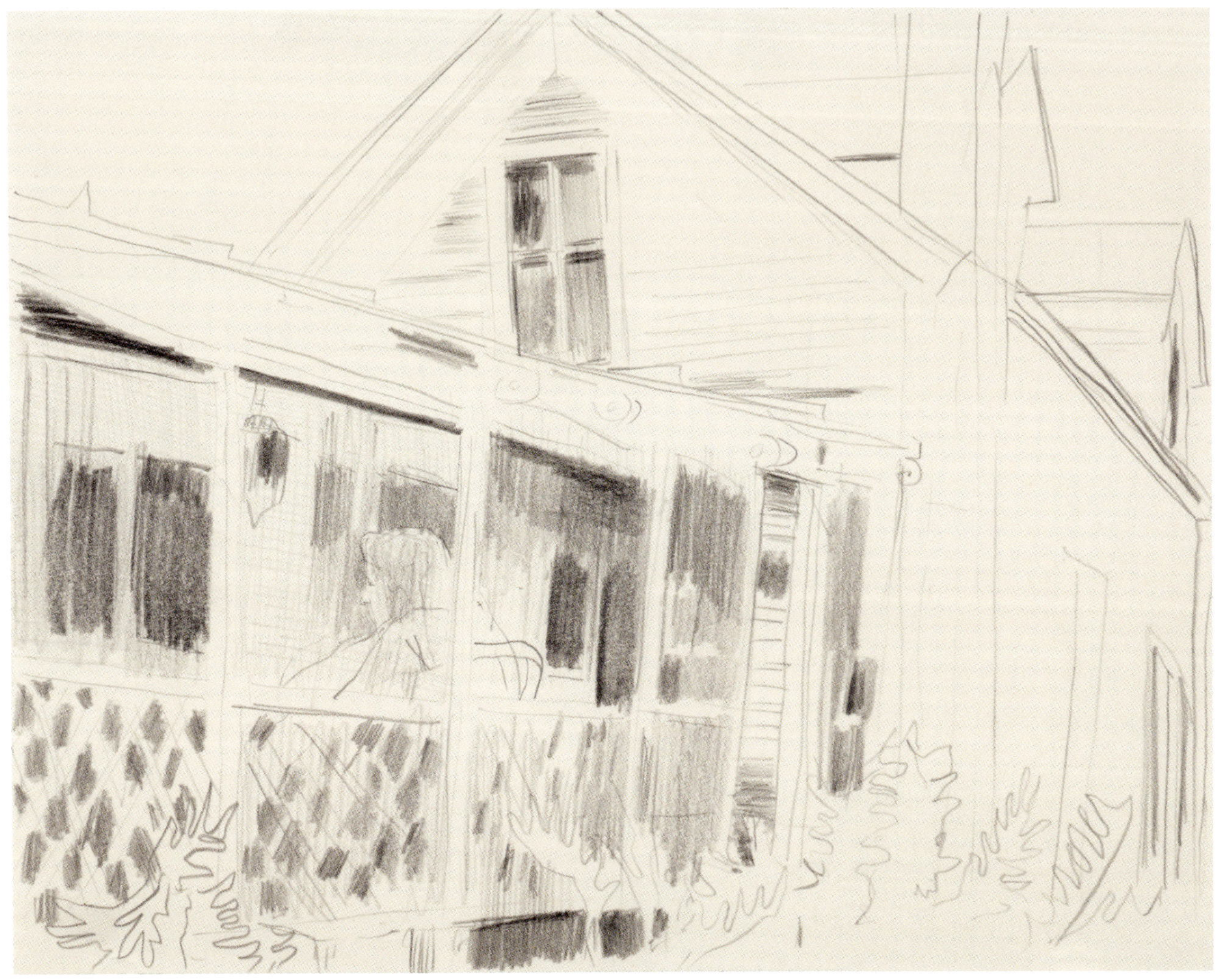

Fig. 25
Eric Aho, *Ruth Stone on her Porch (Goshen, Vermont)*, 2009. Graphite on paper, 11 × 14 in. Courtesy of the artist and DC Moore Gallery, New York.

In a multi-page ad, Rock of Ages dealers work the phones—listening, occasionally speaking, cordial, helpful (Fig. 26). They are not the Four Horsemen of the Apocalypse but the one hundred and thirty-four Middlemen of the Inevitable. As emissaries from heaven—ranked in rows and grids like the angels and saints in a medieval altarpiece—they sell their clients on the idea of their deaths. If we think of it all a little more grimly, they do not speak with their clients at all. They all speak simultaneously with their boss, the Grim Reaper himself, a being so omnipresent that he is not above speaking with more than a hundred of his minions at once—the most unholy of Zoom meetings. But the poet on the

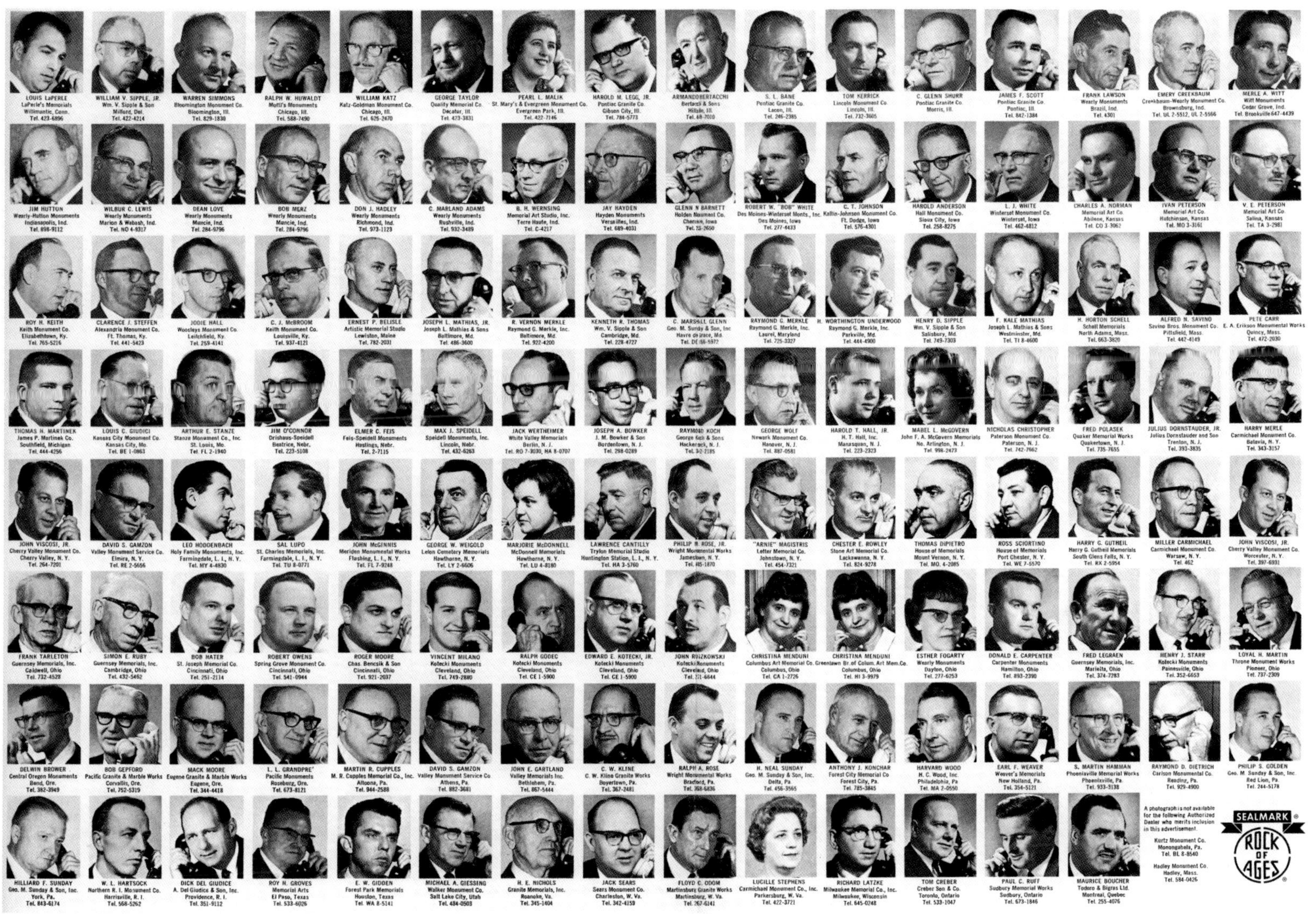

Fig. 26
Rock of Ages, *Top Rock of Ages Authorized Dealers, Life Magazine Insert*, 1966. Ink on paper, 11¾ × 8½ in. Vermont Granite Museum. 2021.76.571.

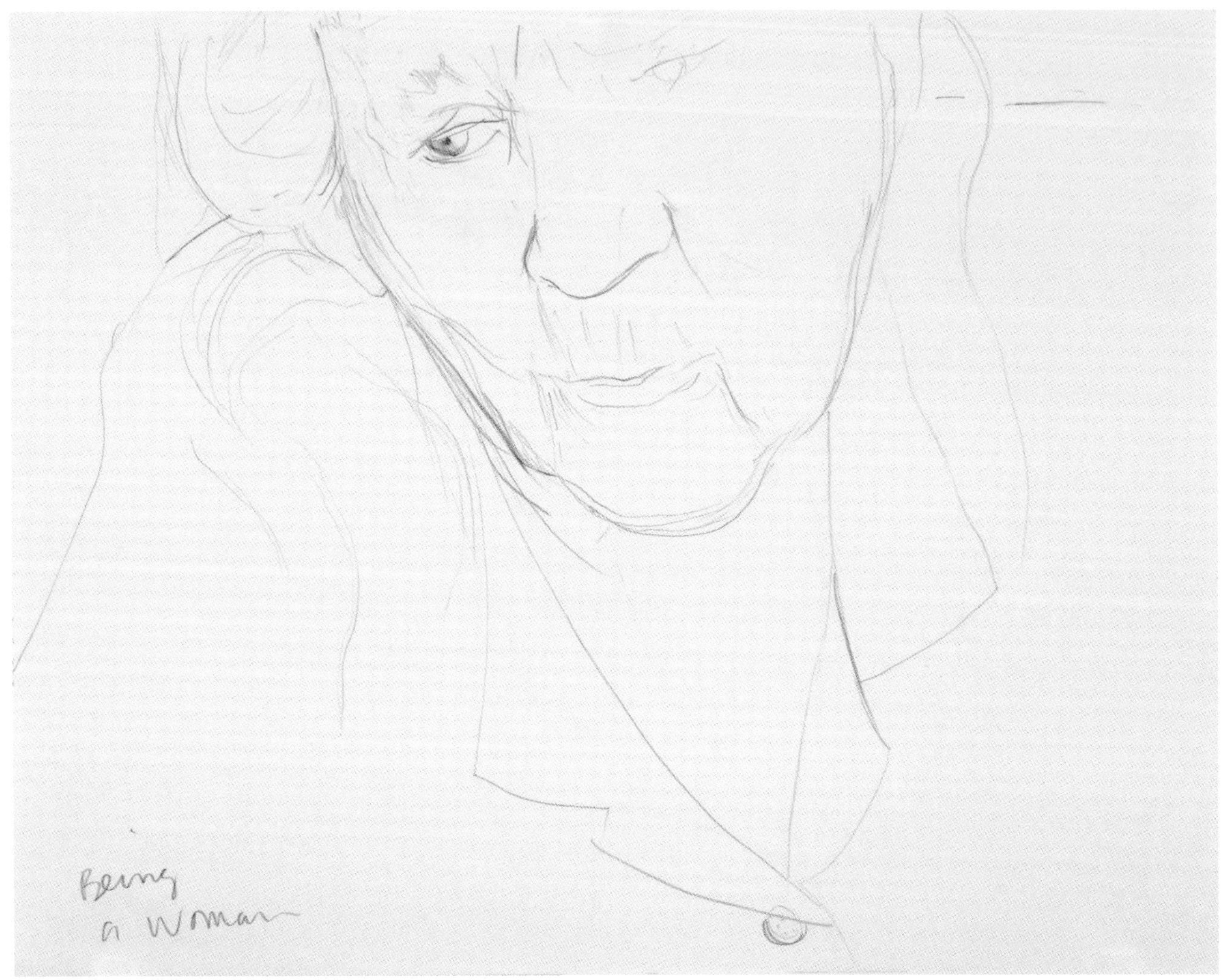

Fig. 27
Eric Aho, *Ruth Stone Reciting her Poem "Being a Woman,"* 2009. Graphite on paper, 11 × 14 in. Courtesy of the artist and DC Moore Gallery, New York.

porch speaks to no one but herself and, for that reason, to another one out there somewhere. The words stay within the porch but waft through the screen, seeking to save the life of a stranger. Rockwell, by contrast, treats the canvas like a slab.

Was his earnestness too accepting of death? The answer hinges on how he responds to the phrase *going away*. In Aho's eight close-up drawings of Ruth Stone, the poet is not all there (Fig. 27). The artist does not bother to fill in all the lines. He lets the warm air interfuse her being. She grows "translucent," in his word, becoming one with the atmosphere. As he sketched her, Stone recited her poetry, which Aho recalls she summoned from nowhere, drawing it down out of thin air.[7] So the poet gave the cue to the artist for how to picture her—to attend to the invisible from which she gathers her words, an invisible into which she disappears even as he looks. Her muses are the Sylphs that Alexander Pope wrote of, the gliding lights that "sport and flutter in the fields of air."[8] As they alight upon her, she too grows Sylph-like, ready for her posthumous role as invisible guide to others. By contrast, Rockwell's craftsman and kneeling girl worry so much about granite that they forget the air they breathe.

Yet maybe Rockwell was closer to Stone than we might think. Admittedly, the opposite seems to be the case. For decades his art had required the studied approval of his editors at *The Saturday Evening Post* and of advertising agencies such as Harold Cabot & Company, which managed the Rock of Ages account. There is nothing translucent in Rockwell's art. Everything is given, hard, delineated, set forth so that there can be no mistake, no place for the mind to wander and, in wandering, be lost to an element beyond itself. Death for the kneeling girl becomes a polite affair, as boxed and businesslike as the advertising agency and granite company had a right to expect. The solitude of the artist becomes too readily the same as that of the little girl and the craftsman—as if the name Norman Rockwell had been chiseled in the annals of time long before he was born and all this melancholic man had to do, in living life, was to execute the grave marker that awaited him the day he was born.

But, yes, Rockwell talked to himself in these works. Even though everyone "got" his art, in another sense he was the only one who heard what he was saying. This muttering, this chanting, this incanting, was perhaps his own witch's hex, his own way of "being a woman," of being unheard in a man's world, of combating the directions of death in the pursuit of something that, for once, could not be set in stone. The little girl at the grave is a figure for him, posed into piety, scripted into the honor roll, yet alone with her thoughts. One of the study photographs Rockwell made of her happens to show three books by her side—just stand-ins grabbed from the artist's bookshelves for the books in the painting—but telling all the same (Fig. 28). Of the two whose spines face us, one is on Diego Velázquez (1599–1660), perhaps the greatest painter ever, whose tomb, along with the church in which it was housed, was destroyed without a trace in the early nineteenth century. The other is Samuel Chamberlain's *New England Doorways* (Fig. 29). For the little girl, death is a threshold, a New England doorway, a non-existence in futurity that she dwells on because, like the artist, she does not understand it.

In this respect the girl has a brother—the little boy cowering at the end of a diving board in a painting of eight years earlier (Plate 36). All alone, imploring the lord, he is like Isaac laying down his head prior to God's ordained sacrifice, a person of "fear and trembling."[9] His sister over at the cemetery is a mite more mature than him. She is trained in the decorum of adult behavior, acculturated

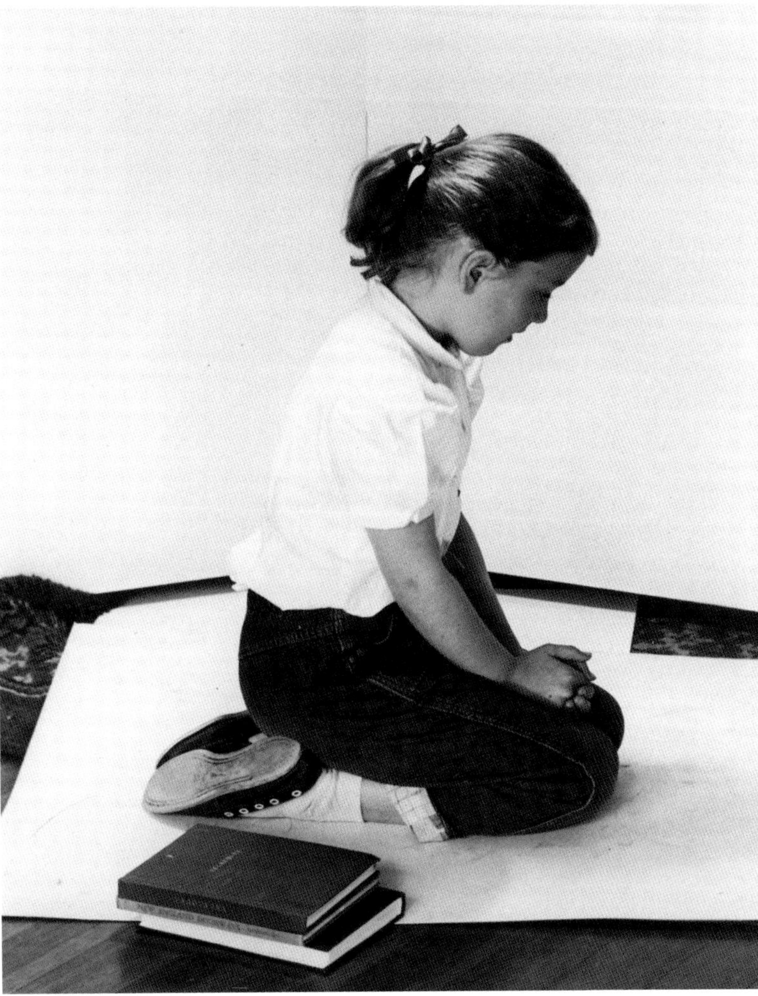

Fig. 28
Unidentified photographer, *Reference Photo for Kneeling Girl*, 1954. Photograph, 10⅜ × 8¼ in. Vermont Granite Museum. 2021.74.515.

to know when adults will look on her and how to win their approval—which in this case is an appearance of "accepting" death that mirrors their own fear-easing postures. But the little boy on the diving board has no scruples about being just a kid, a laughingstock, terrified of mortality. Like an aristocrat sticking his neck out on the guillotine, he wonders what it is to die. His sister, too, in her quiet way, is willing to come right up to the edge—to let the question of the Beyond frazzle her hair into light-struck strands.

And if the plunge for both should be into a freezing river, if it should be like one of Aho's *Ice Cut* paintings—for instance, the one subtitled *Violet Kennebec*

Fig. 29
Written and photographed by Samuel Chamberlain, published by Hastings House Publishers, *New England Doorways*, 1939, p. 42. Hardcover book, 8 3/8 × 6 1/4 × 7/16 in. Collection of Shelburne Museum Archives.

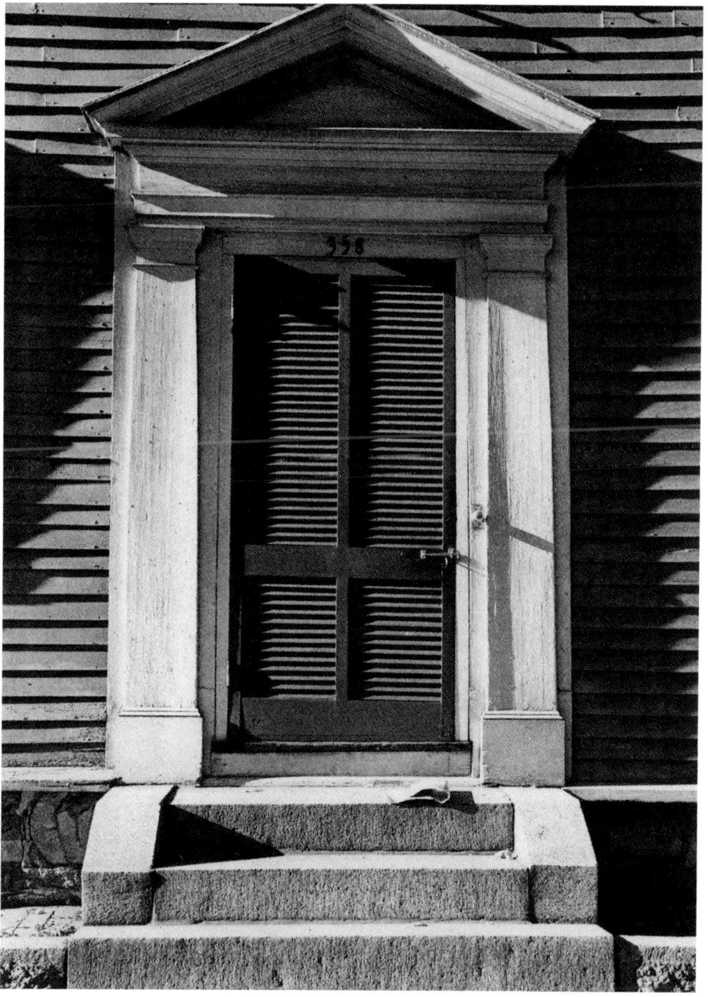

(Fig. 30)—what should we make of that? If the day could go magically from summer to winter in those twenty feet between the diving board and the destination, the spray of time is what releases the diver to another depth. Aho, who began making his *Ice Cut* paintings after the death of his father in 1996, finds his own Rock of Ages, a cemetery without names. The tomb of ice awaits the body or has been found as empty as the one the Three Marys visited, a mystery. And Rockwell, no less than Aho, returns to it like a preacher on Sunday.

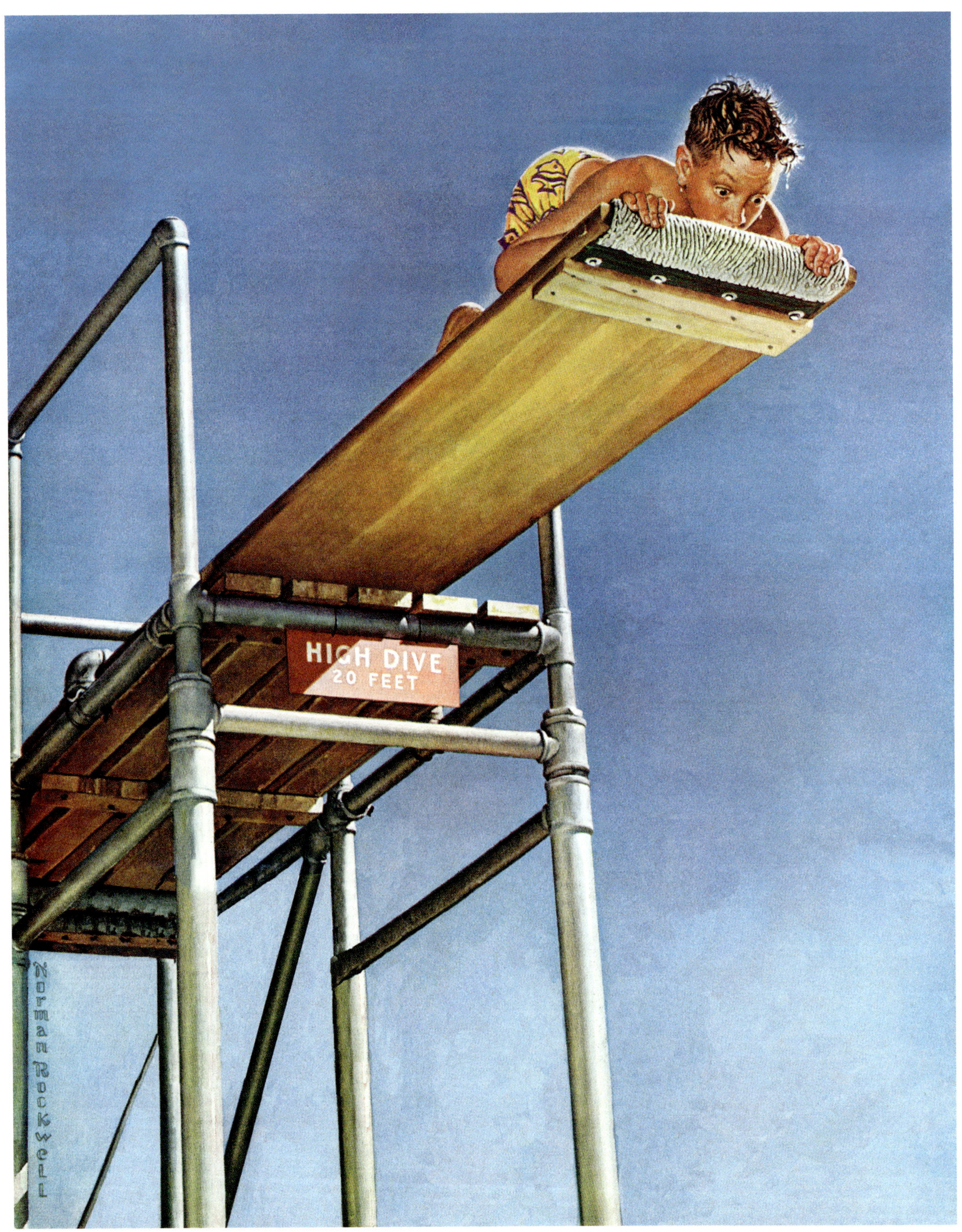
HIGH DIVE
20 FEET
Norman Rockwell

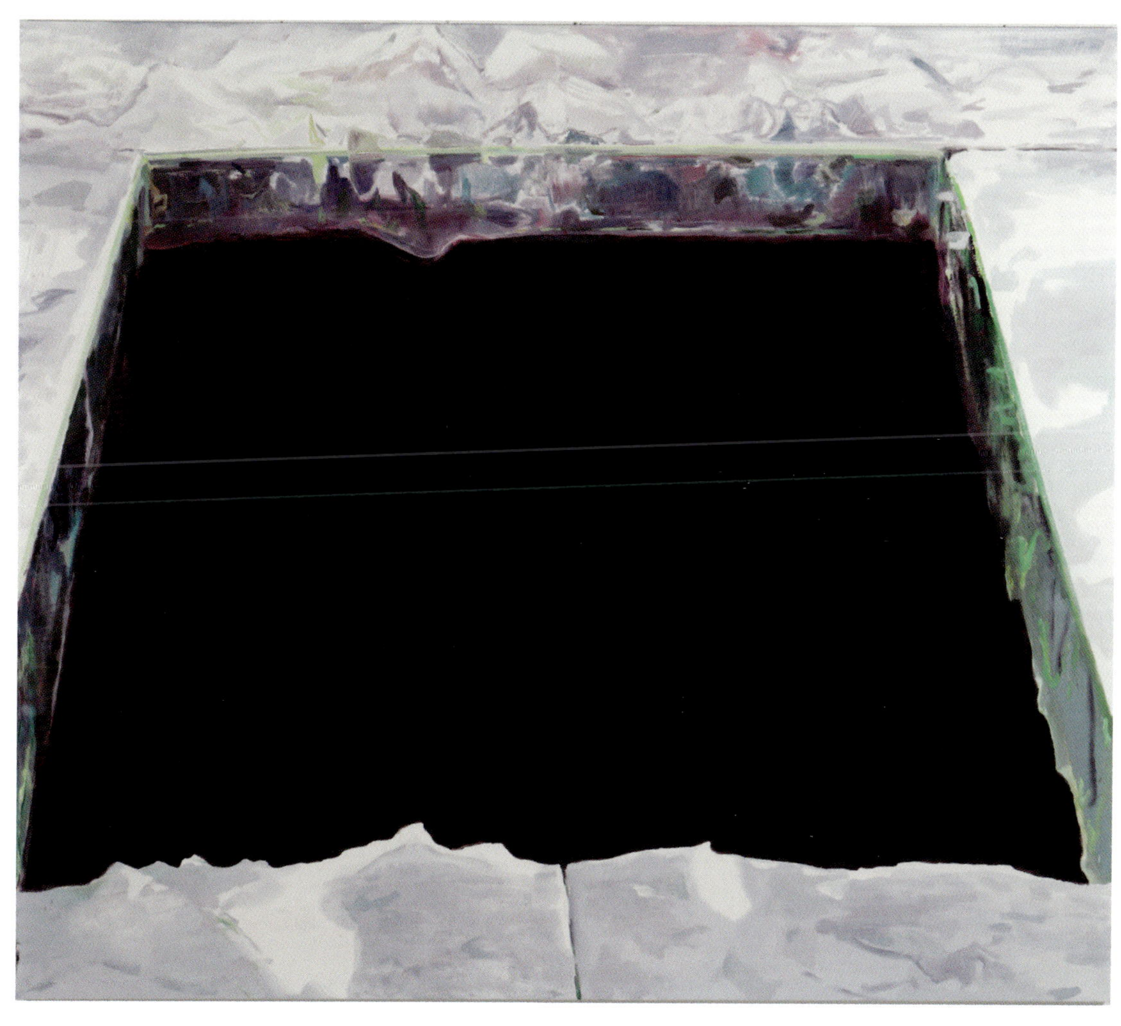

Pl. 36
Norman Rockwell, *High Dive*, 1947. Cover illustration for *The Saturday Evening Post*, August 16, 1947. Oil on canvas, 35 × 27 in. Private Collection. Illustration provided by SEPS through Curtis Licensing. Artwork Approved by the Norman Rockwell Family Agency.

Fig. 30
Eric Aho, *Ice Cut (Violet Kennebec)*, 2022. Oil on linen, 80 × 90 in. Farnsworth Art Museum, Rockland, Maine, Museum Purchase, Lynne Drexler Acquisition Fund, 2022.28. Courtesy of the artist and DC Moore Gallery, New York.

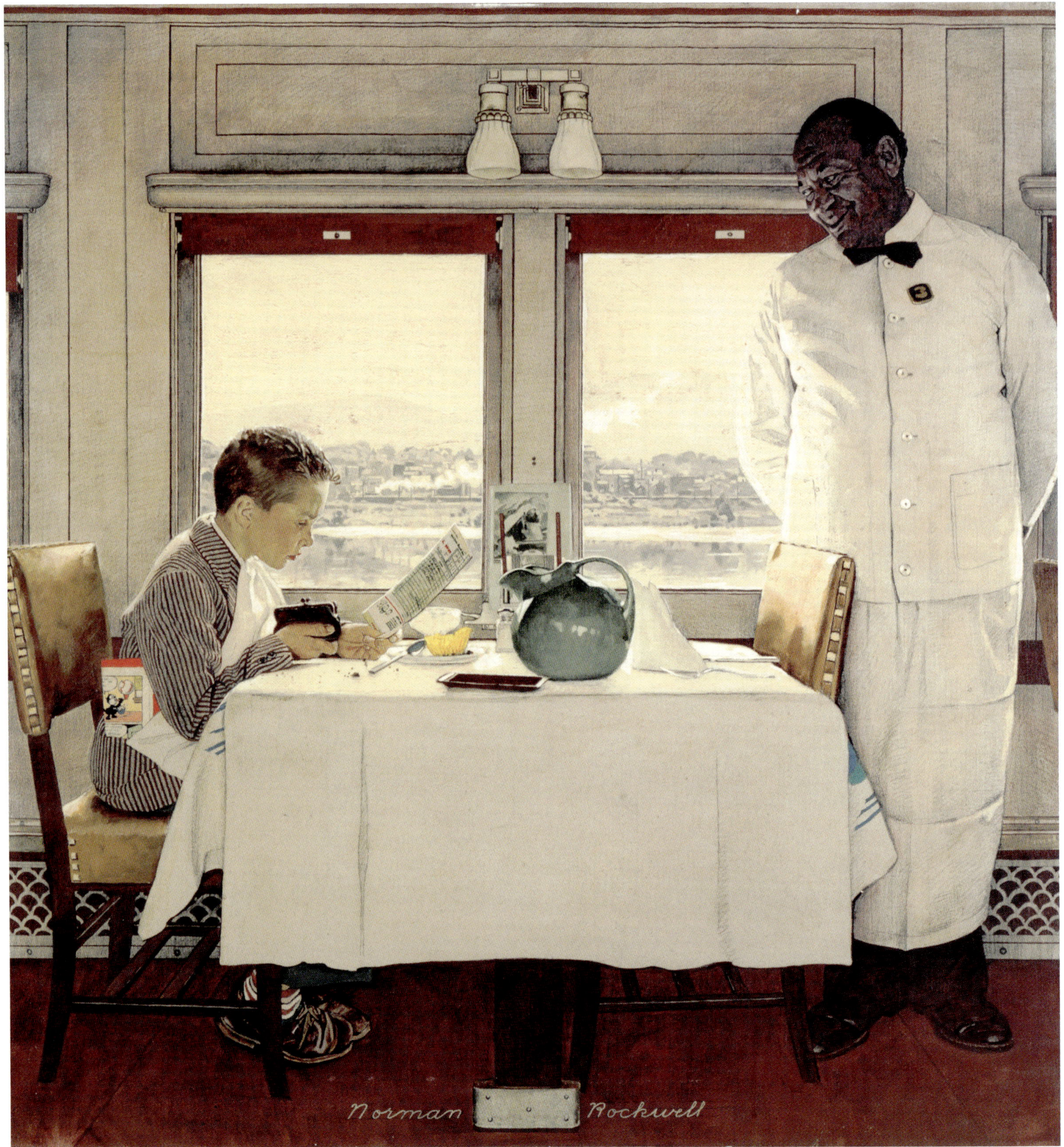
Norman Rockwell

Pl. 37

Norman Rockwell, *Boy in a Dining Car*, 1946. Cover illustration for *The Saturday Evening Post*, December 7, 1946. Oil on canvas, 38 × 36 in. Norman Rockwell Museum Collection, Museum purchase. NRM.1988.02.

Pl. 38

Norman Rockwell, *Going and Coming*, 1947. Cover illustration for *The Saturday Evening Post*, August 30, 1947. Oil on canvas, 38 × 36 in. Norman Rockwell Museum Collection, Norman Rockwell Art Collection Trust. NRACT.1973.009. Artwork Approved by the Norman Rockwell Family Agency.

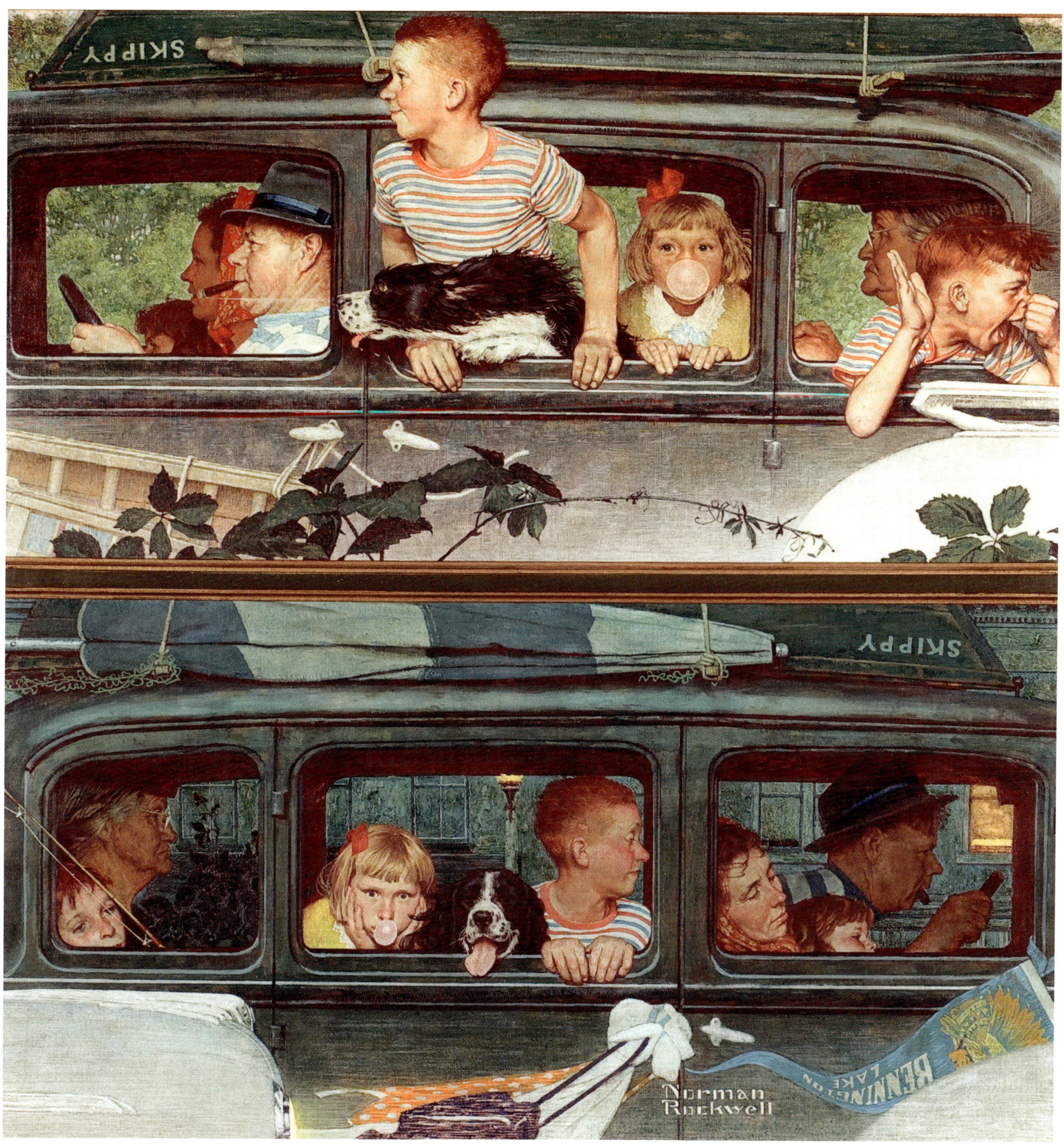
SKIPPY
SKIPPY
LAKE
BENNINGTON
Norman
Rockwell

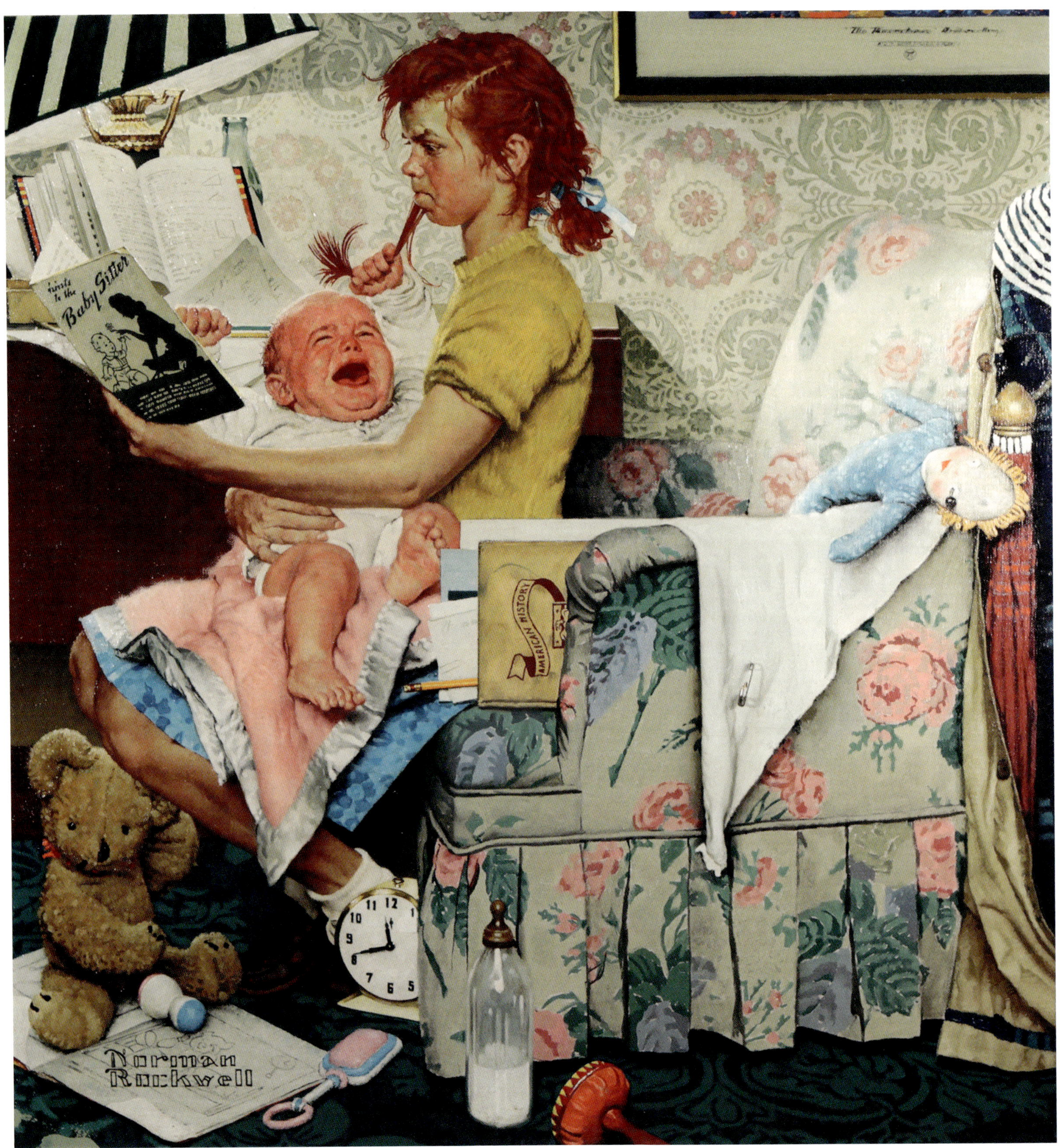
Baby Sitter
AMERICAN HISTORY
Norman Rockwell

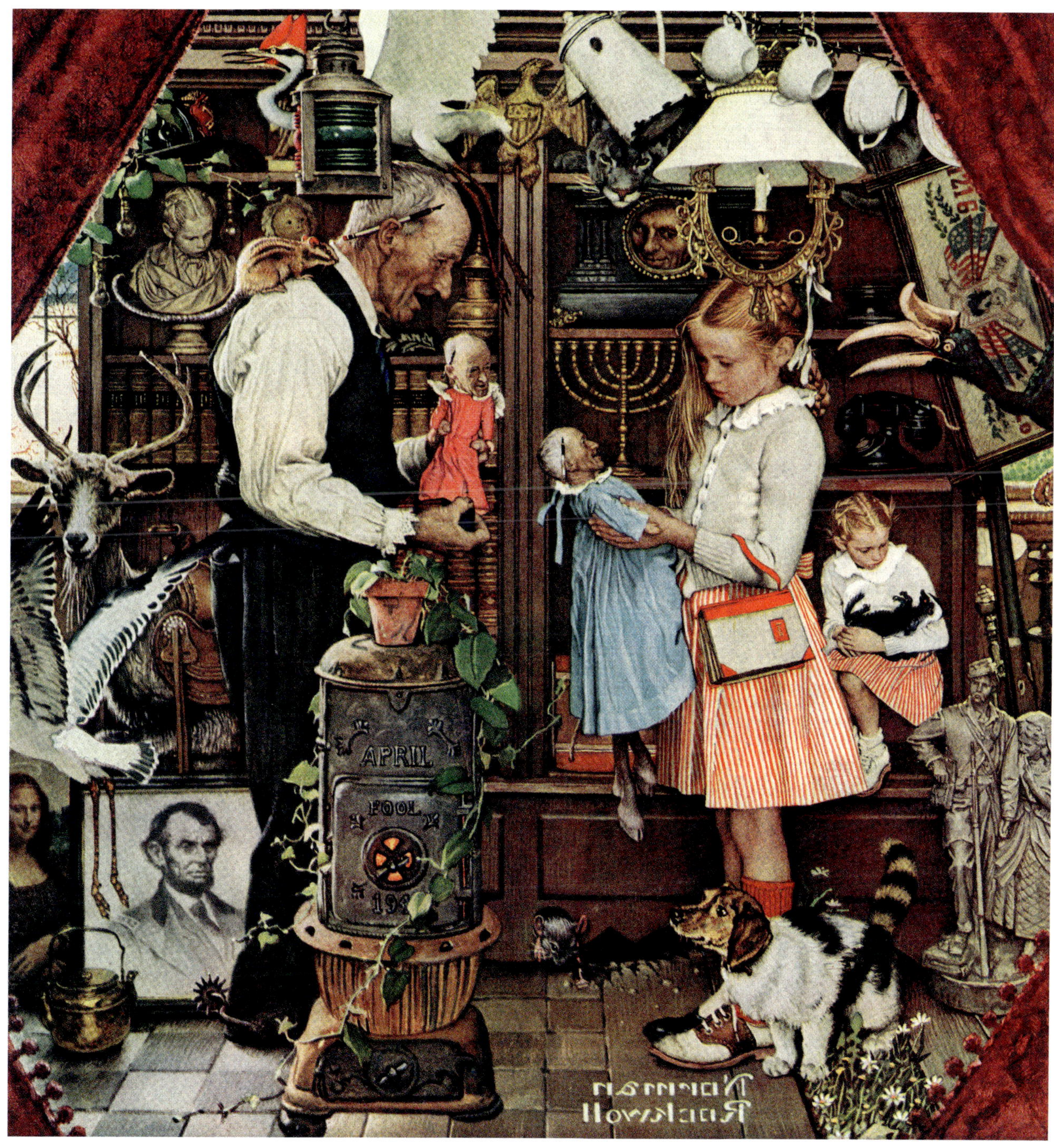

Pl. 39
Norman Rockwell, *The Babysitter*, 1947. Cover illustration for *The Saturday Evening Post*, November 8, 1947. Oil on canvas, 28 × 26 in. Fleming Museum of Art, University of Vermont. Artwork Approved by the Norman Rockwell Family Agency.

Pl. 40
Norman Rockwell, *April Fool: Girl with Shopkeeper*, 1948. Cover illustration for *The Saturday Evening Post*, April 3, 1948. Oil on canvas. Private Collection. Illustration provided by SEPS through Curtis Licensing. Artwork Approved by the Norman Rockwell Family Agency.

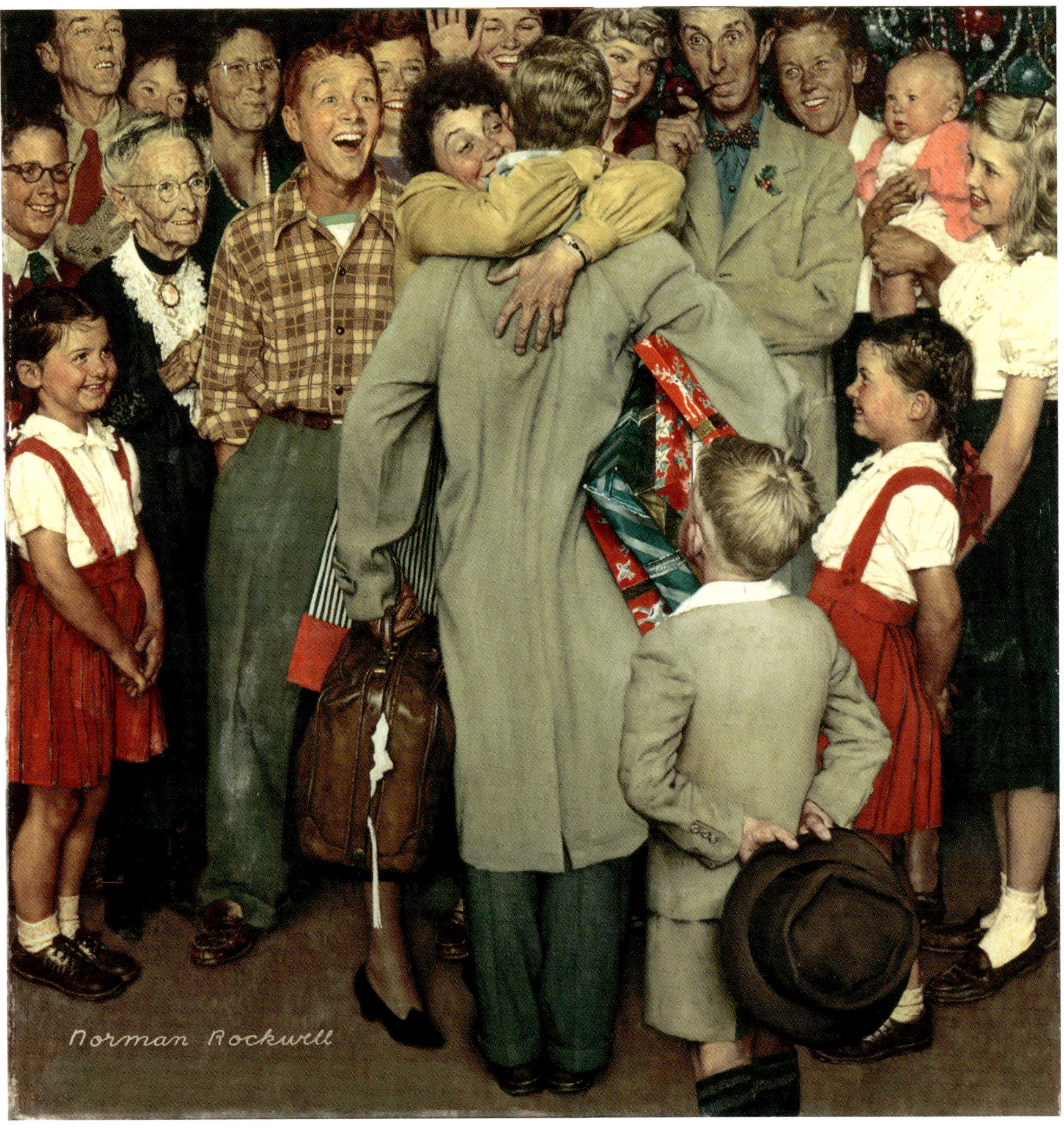

Pl. 41
Norman Rockwell, *Christmas Homecoming*, 1948. Cover illustration for *The Saturday Evening Post*, December 25, 1948. Oil on canvas, 35½ × 33½ in. Norman Rockwell Museum Collection, Museum purchase, NRM.1978.10.

Pl. 42
Norman Rockwell, *Prom Dress*, 1949. Cover illustration for *The Saturday Evening Post*, March 19, 1949. Oil on canvas. Private Collection. Illustration provided by SEPS through Curtis Licensing. Artwork Approved by the Norman Rockwell Family Agency.

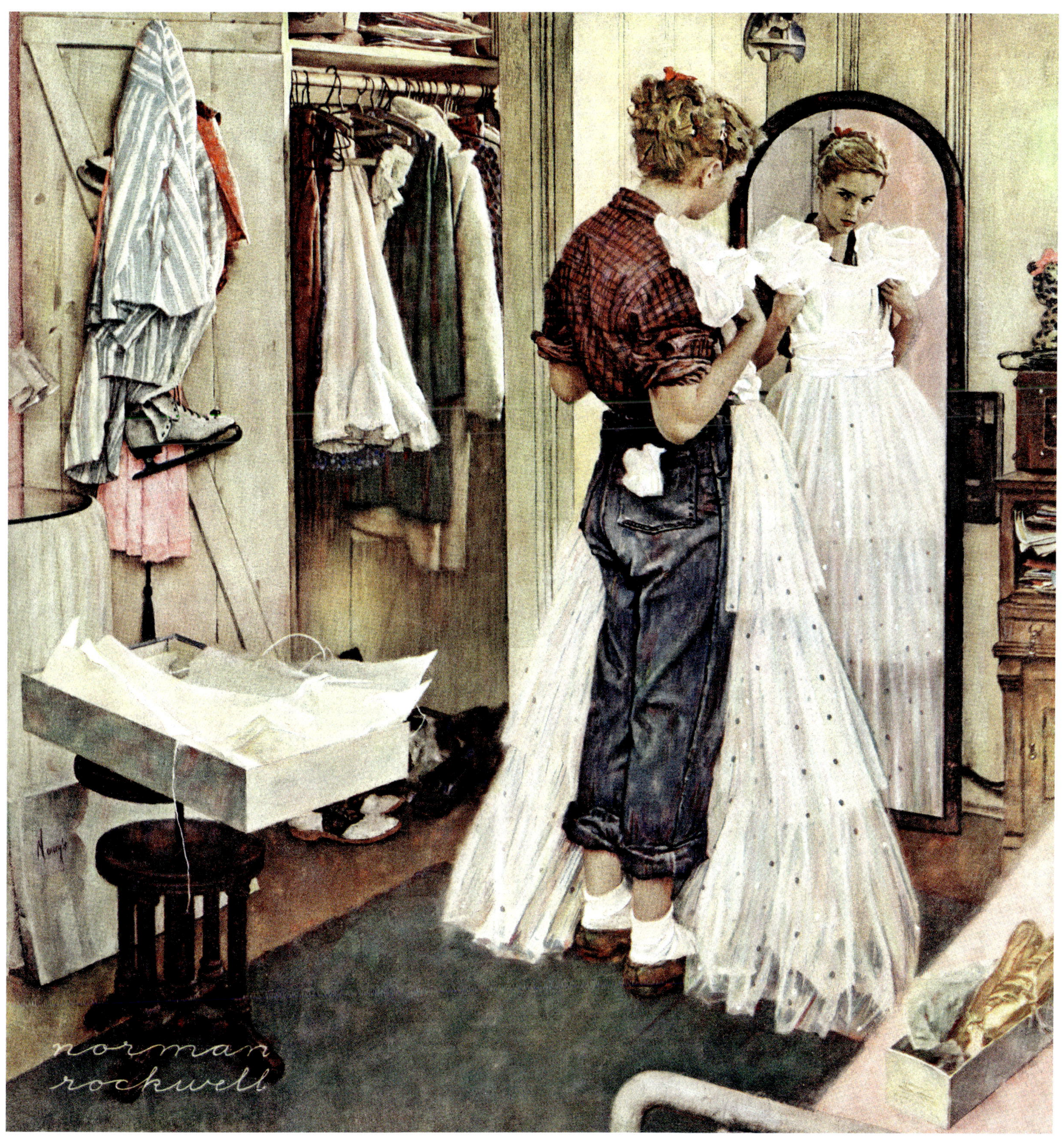
norman
rockwell

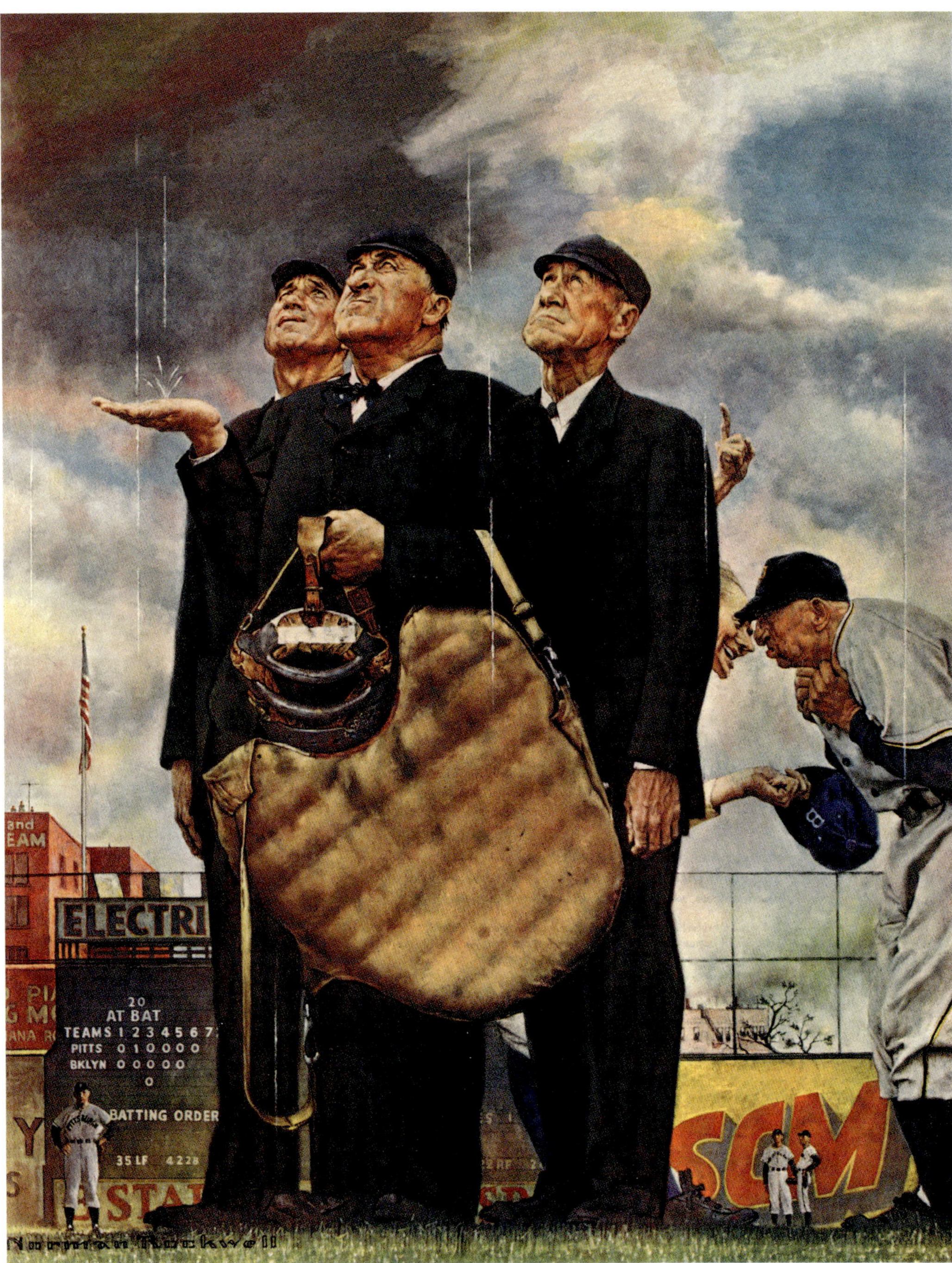

Pl. 43

Norman Rockwell, *Game Called Because of Rain (Tough Call)*, 1949. Cover illustration for *The Saturday Evening Post*, April 23, 1949. Oil on canvas, 42¾ × 40½ in. National Baseball Hall of Fame and Museum, Cooperstown, New York. Illustration provided by SEPS through Curtis Licensing. Artwork Approved by the Norman Rockwell Family Agency.

Pl. 44

Norman Rockwell, *Before the Date*, 1949. Cover illustration for *The Saturday Evening Post*, September 24, 1949. Oil on canvas. Private Collection. Illustration provided by SEPS through Curtis Licensing. Artwork Approved by the Norman Rockwell Family Agency.

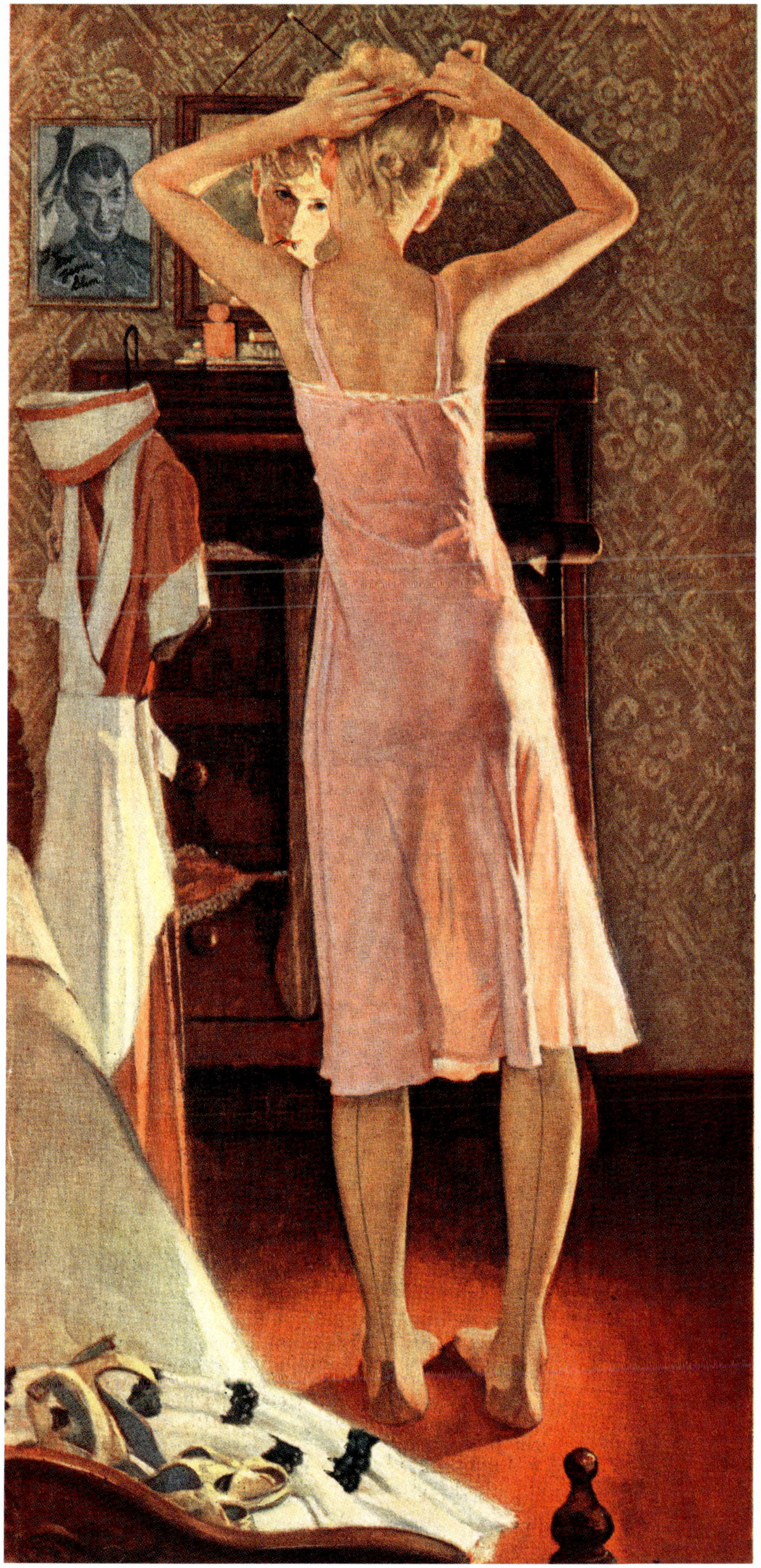

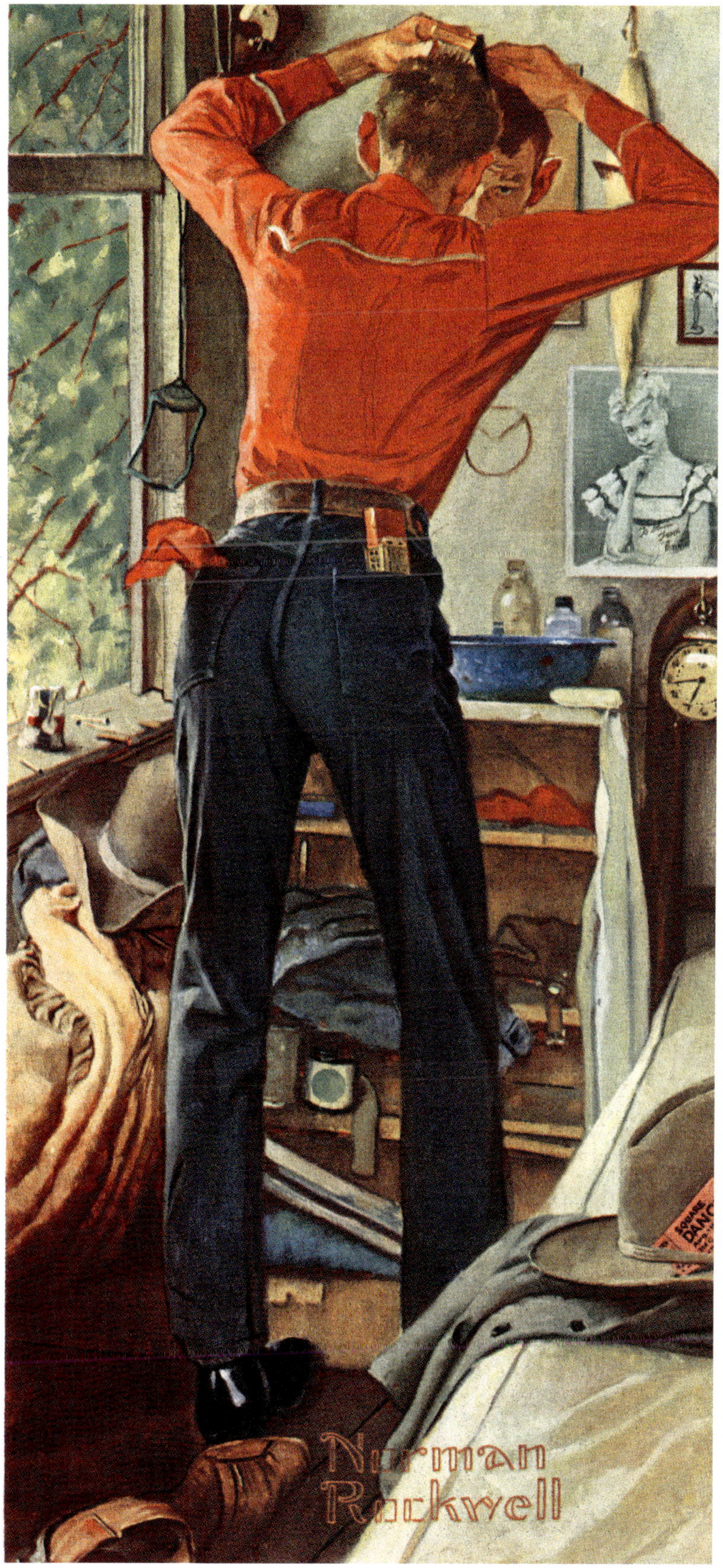

Norman
Rockwell

Pl. 45

Norman Rockwell, *The New Television Set*, 1949. Cover illustration for *The Saturday Evening Post*, November 5, 1949. Oil on canvas, 46 1/16 × 43 3/8 in. Los Angeles County Museum of Art, Gift of Mrs. Ned Crowell. 55.42. Illustration provided by SEPS through Curtis Licensing. Artwork Approved by the Norman Rockwell Family Agency.

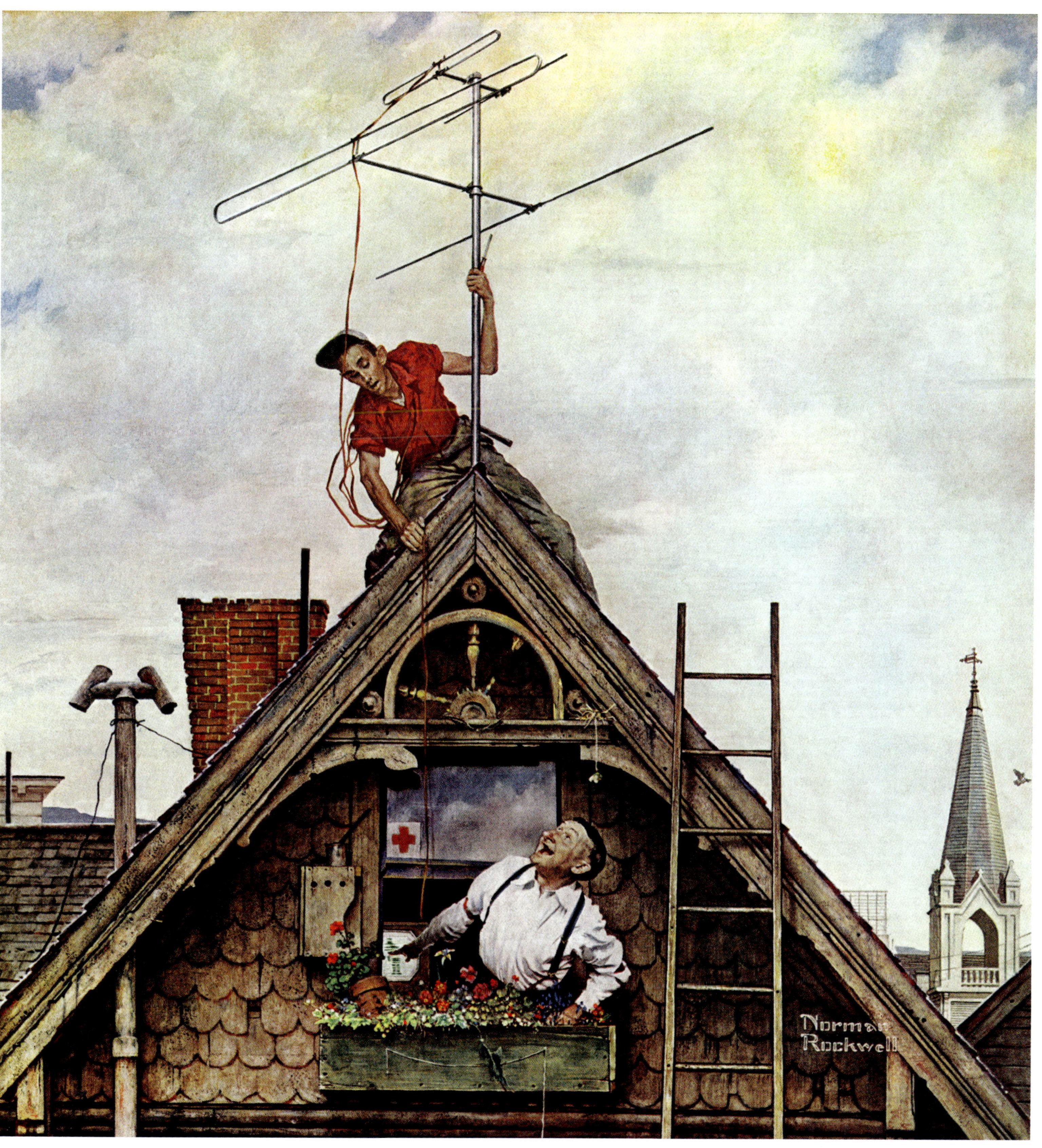
Norman
Rockwell

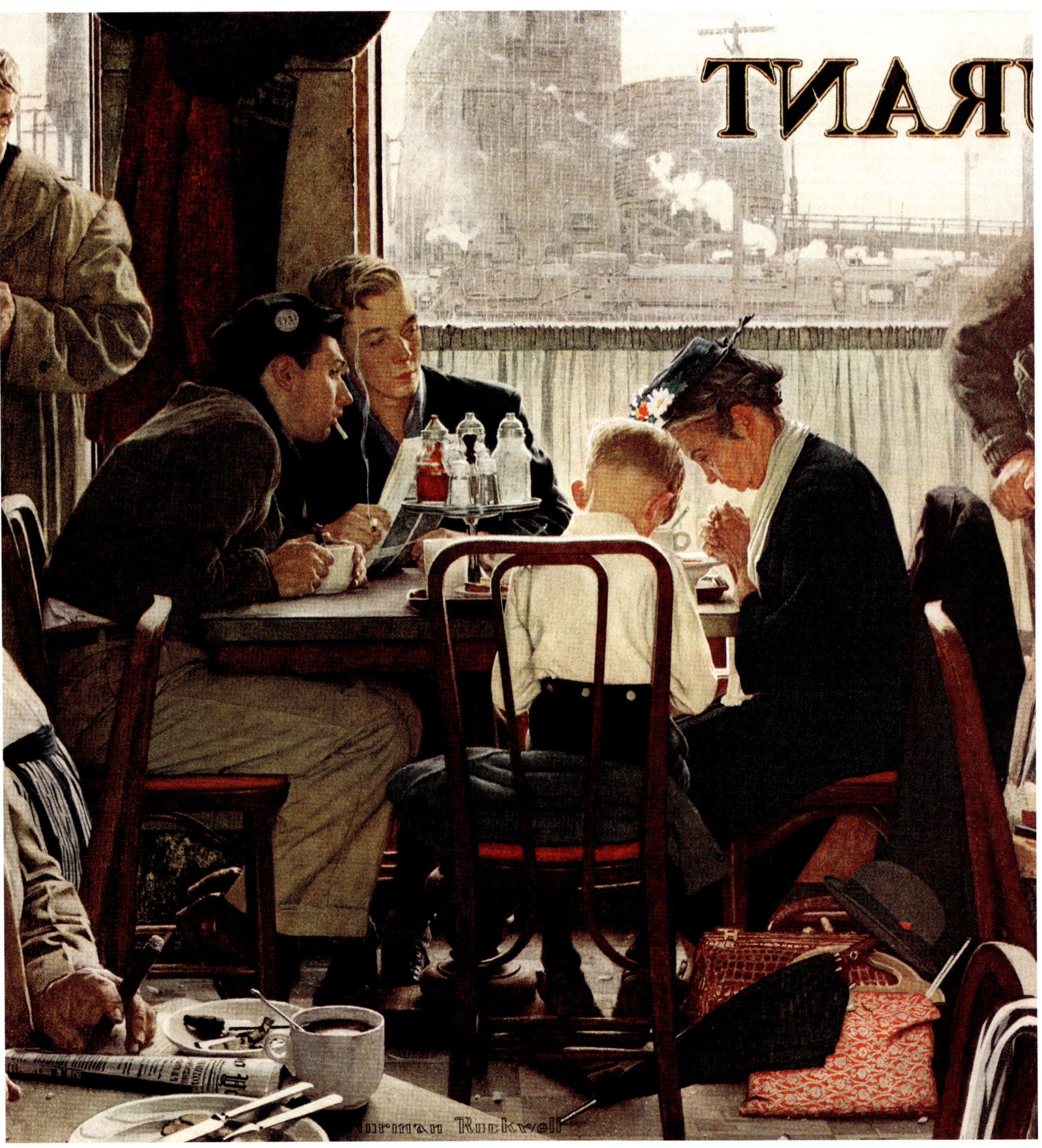

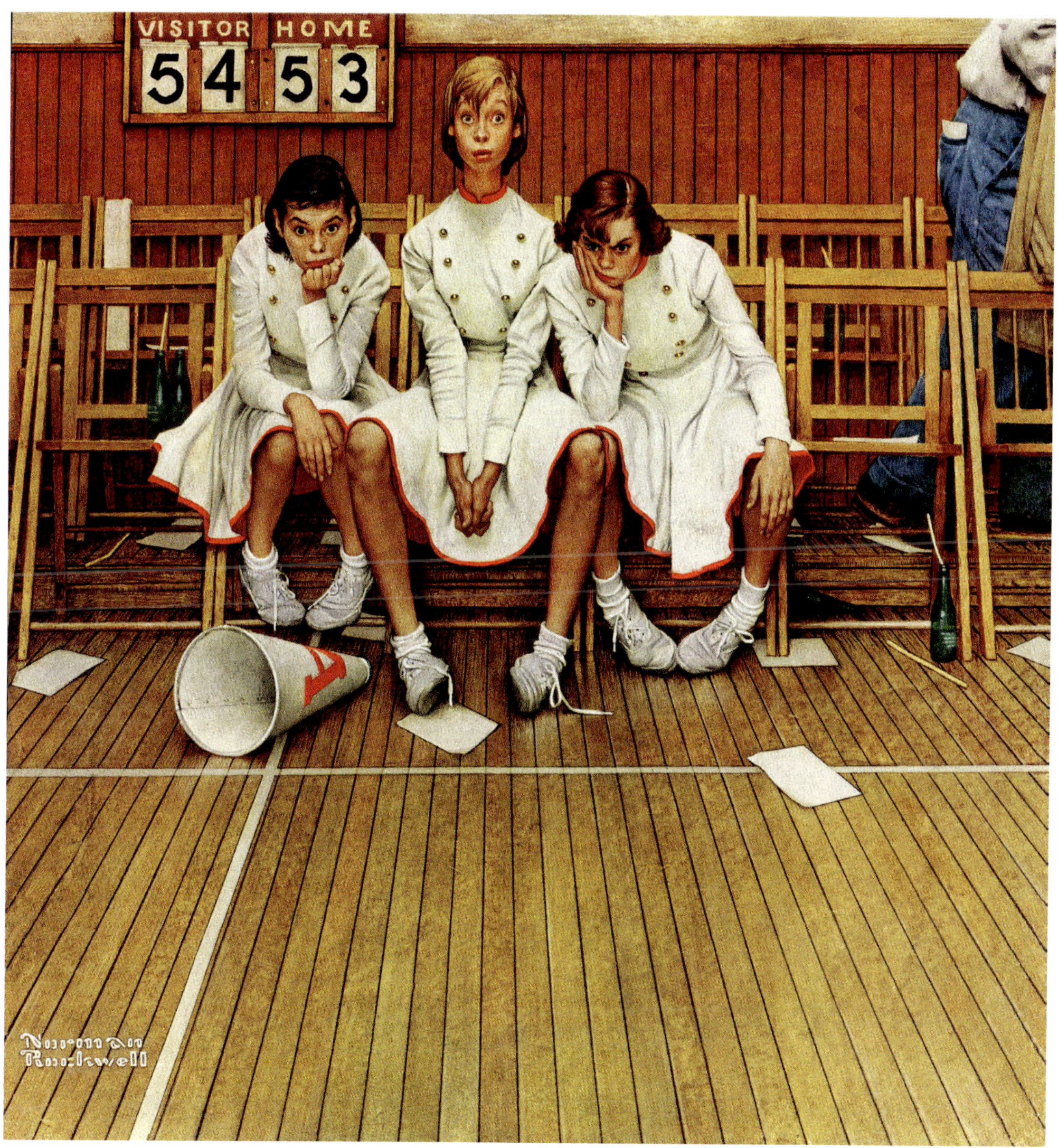

Pl. 46
Norman Rockwell, *Saying Grace*, 1951. Cover illustration for *The Saturday Evening Post*, November 24, 1951. Oil on canvas, 42 × 40 in. Private Collection. Illustration provided by SEPS through Curtis Licensing. Artwork Approved by the Norman Rockwell Family Agency.

Pl. 47
Norman Rockwell, *Cheerleaders (Losing the Game)*, 1952. Cover illustration for *The Saturday Evening Post*, February 16, 1952. Oil on Masonite, 17¼ × 16⅜ in. Private Collection. Illustration provided by SEPS through Curtis Licensing. Artwork Approved by the Norman Rockwell Family Agency.

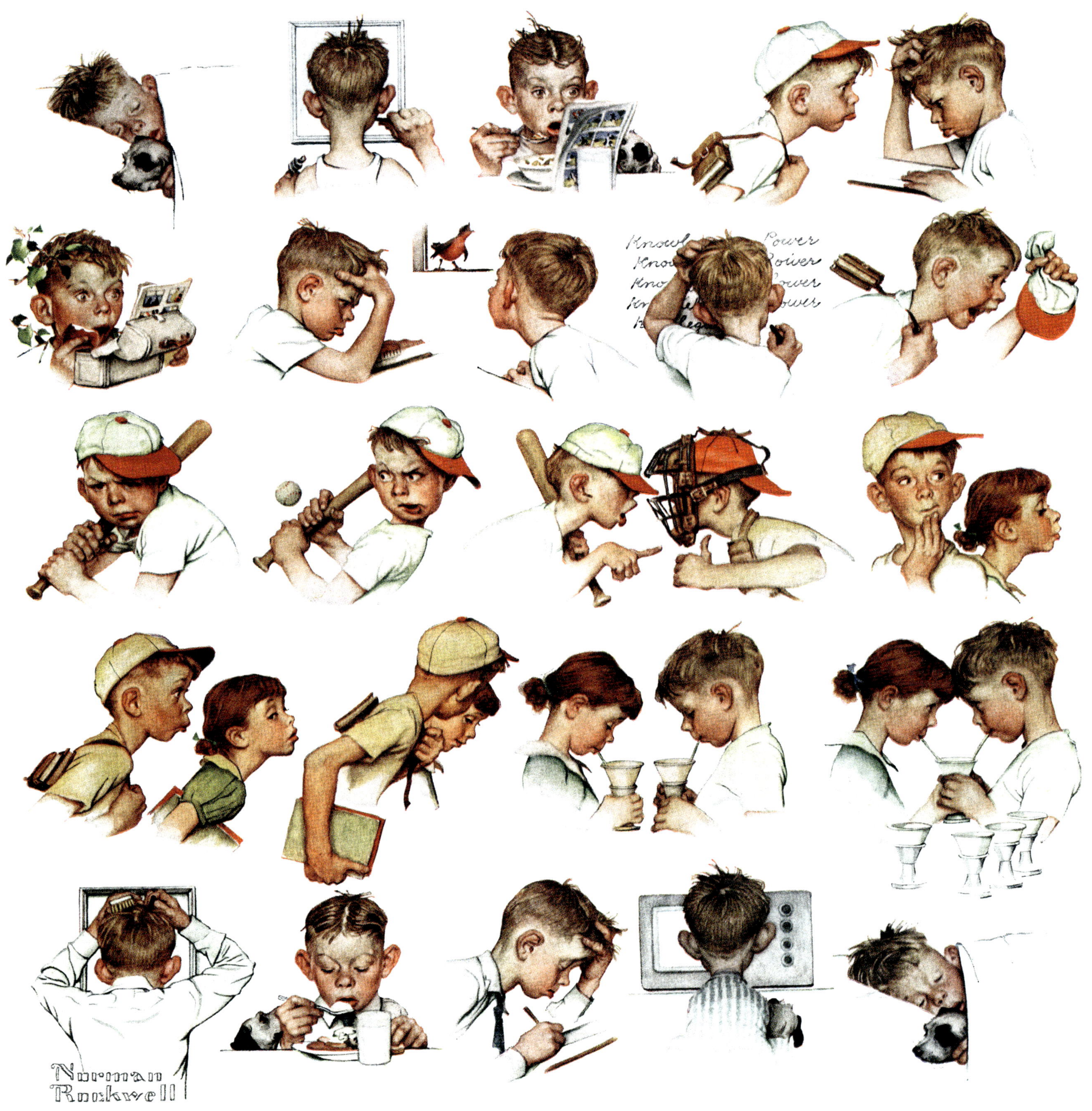
Norman
Rockwell

Pl. 48

Norman Rockwell, *Day in the Life of a Boy*, 1952. Cover illustration for *The Saturday Evening Post*, May 24, 1952. Oil on canvas. Private Collection. Illustration provided by SEPS through Curtis Licensing. Artwork Approved by the Norman Rockwell Family Agency.

Pl. 49

Norman Rockwell, *Day in the Life of a Girl*, 1952. Cover illustration for *The Saturday Evening Post*, August 30, 1952. Oil on canvas, 40 × 37¼ in. Norman Rockwell Museum Collection, Museum purchase. NRM.1980.02.

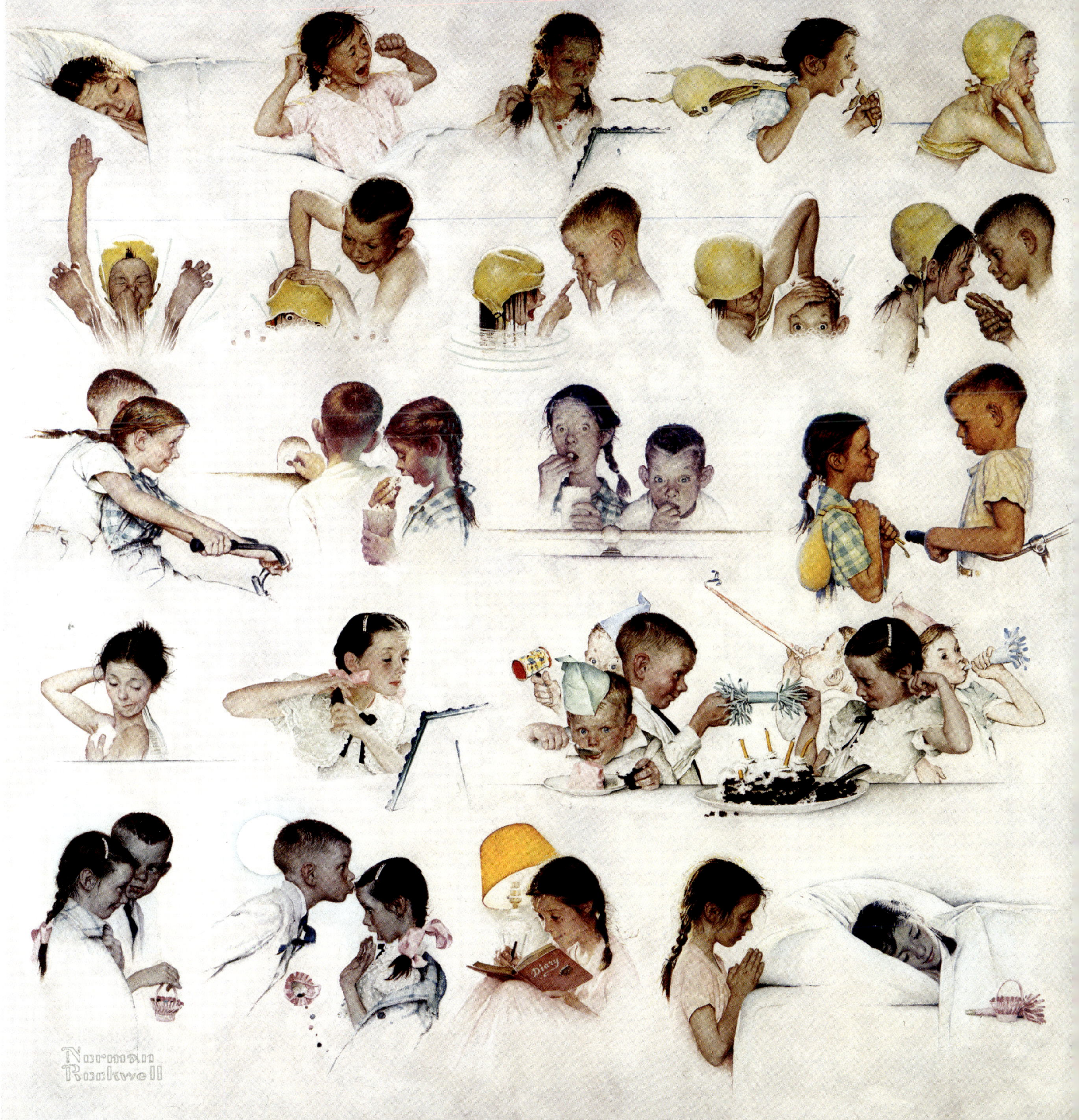
Diary
Norman
Rockwell

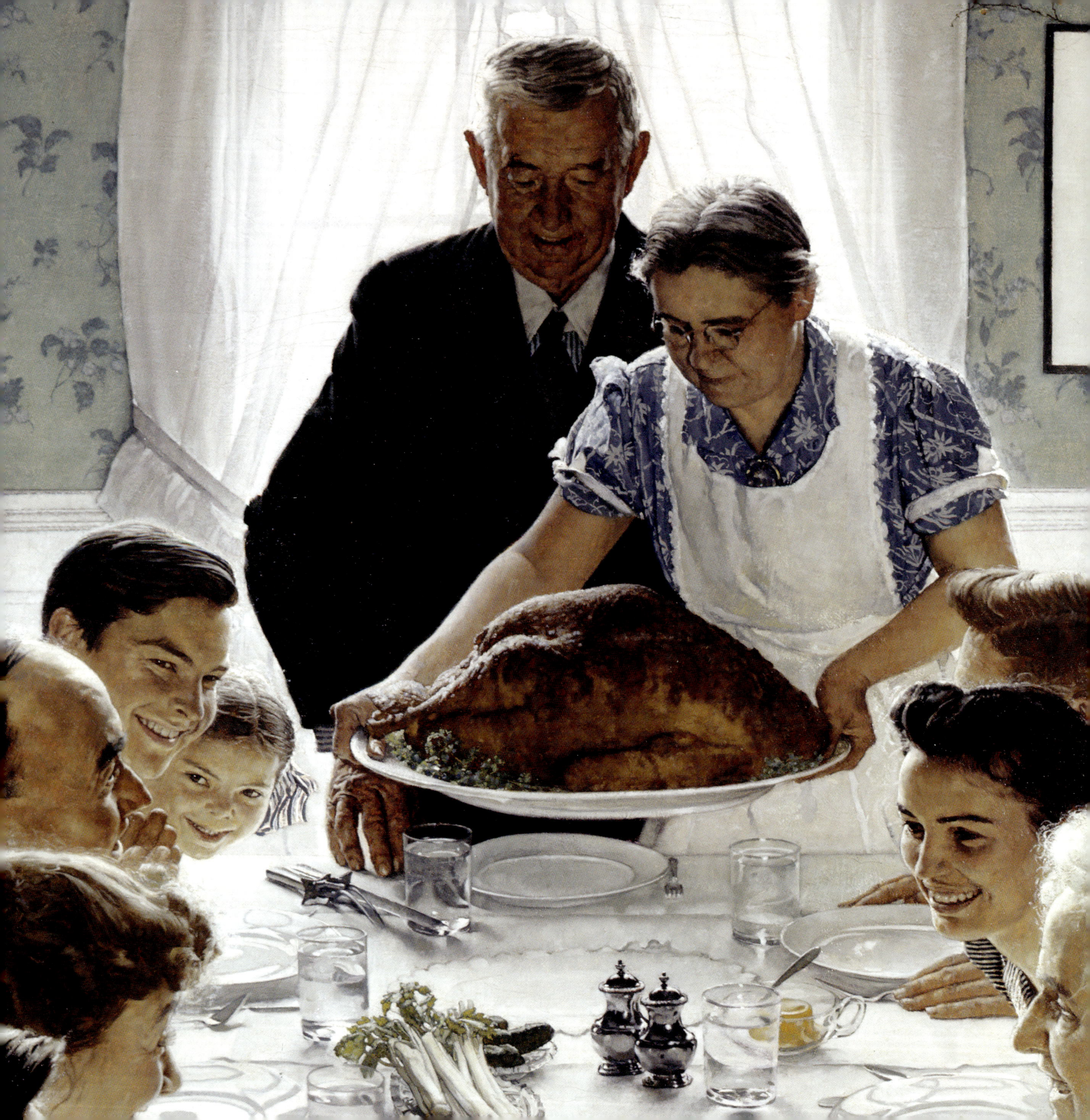

NORMAN ROCKWELL'S ARLINGTON YEARS

1938–55

1938

- Seeking reprieve from their busy lives in New Rochelle, New York, Norman and Mary Rockwell traveled north in the fall of 1938 to visit Arlington, Vermont—and fell instantly in love with the village and its surrounding countryside. The trip, made after time spent in rural England, stirred Rockwell's own nostalgic memories of childhood excursions to the country. The couple resolved to find a farmstead where they could raise their three young sons—Jarvis, Thomas, and Peter—and where Rockwell could work in peace. By chance, the Rockwells discovered Arlington during an overnight stay at the Colonial Inn, situated near the town hall and the home of writer Dorothy Canfield Fisher. Enchanted by the town's charm and its sense of community, they decide then and there to purchase an old farmhouse nearby (Fig. 31). Over the winter, while temporarily back in New York, they arrange for renovations to the property, including converting a barn into Rockwell's new studio.

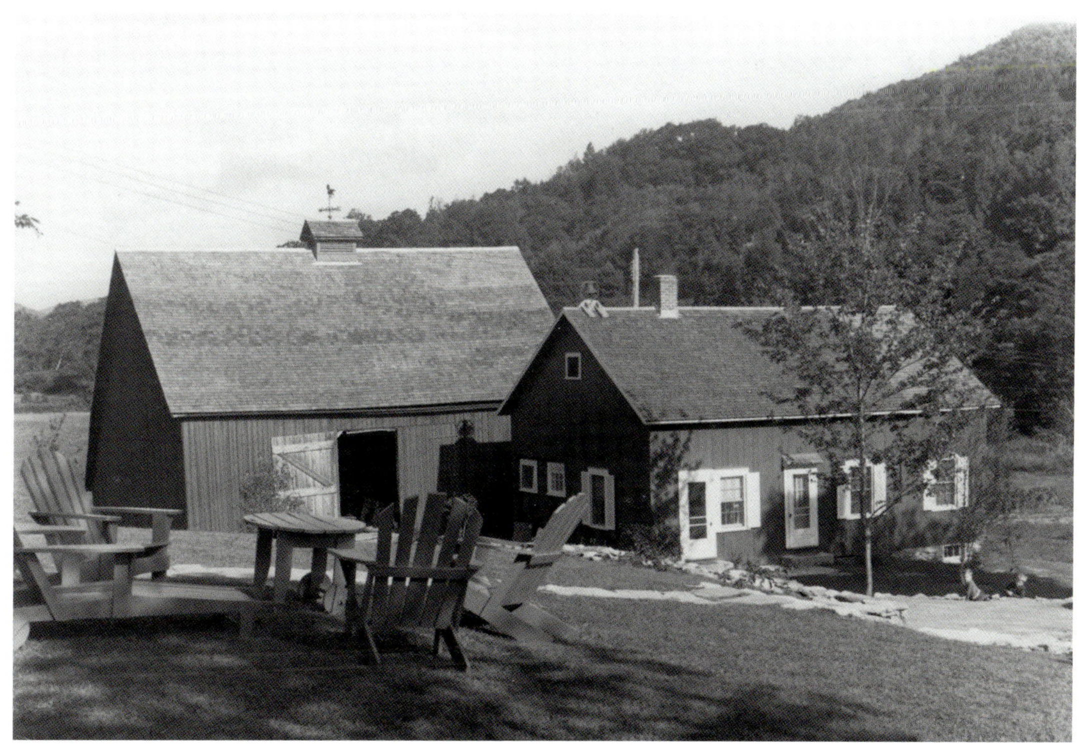

Fig. 31
Unidentified photographer, *Arlington (Jarvis and Tommy in foreground)*, pre-1943. Silver gelatin print, 4⅝ × 6⅞ in. Norman Rockwell Museum Collection, Norman Rockwell Art Collection Trust, Studio Collection. ST.1976.20032.172.34. Artwork Approved by the Norman Rockwell Family Agency.

- Unbeknownst to the Rockwells, another illustrator from New Rochelle, Gene Pelham, had also recently moved with his wife to start a family in Arlington. About a year later, the two artists encountered each other by chance in town, rekindling a professional connection from their earlier days in New York. Pelham soon began assisting Rockwell in his studio—photographing models, sourcing costumes and props, and helping stage scenes that would serve as the basis for Rockwell's paintings.

1939

- By early 1939, the Rockwell family had fully settled into their new home in Arlington—marking the beginning of one of the most productive and defining chapters of Rockwell's career. Over the course of their fourteen-year sojourn in the Green Mountain State, Rockwell would find in the town's people and ethos a deep well of inspiration that grounded his art in genuine community life.
- That same year, Rockwell completed his first *Saturday Evening Post* cover from his Arlington studio, *Marble Champion (Girl Playing Marbles)*, published on September 2, 1939 (Fig. 32; see also Plate 5). The painting captures a young boy—modeled by Rockwell's eldest son, Jarvis, in his debut appearance—locked in concentration over a game of marbles, his red cap providing a bright focal point. During Rockwell's Vermont years, he would go on to paint more than 175 covers for *The Saturday Evening Post*, often enlisting friends and neighbors from Arlington as models, infusing his illustrations with the warmth and authenticity of small-town life.
- In Arlington, Rockwell also reconnected with fellow *Saturday Evening Post* illustrators and close friends John "Jack" Atherton and Mead Schaeffer (Fig. 33). The trio, all living nearby, became an informal artistic circle—meeting often to exchange ideas, offer critiques, and lend one another moral support. Their families occasionally modeled for each other's paintings, further blending their professional and personal worlds. Though their artistic temperaments differed—Atherton's work more of an outlier with modernist restraint and dystopias—they shared a deep mutual respect and a steadfast commitment to the craft of illustration. Together, they helped transform Arlington into an unexpected center of American visual culture in the 1940s.

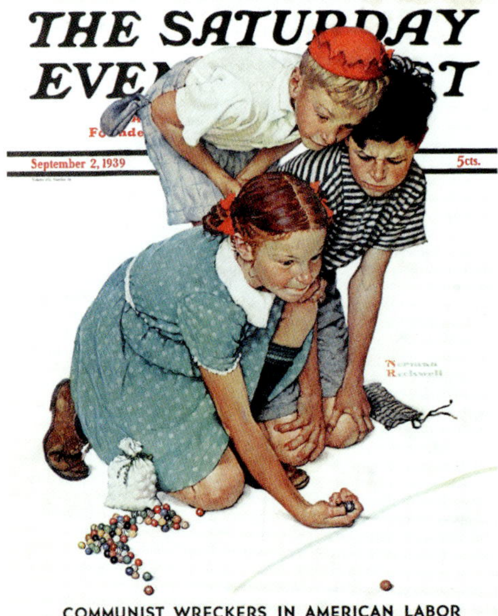

Fig. 32
Designed by Norman Rockwell, *Marble Champion (Girl Playing Marbles)*, *The Saturday Evening Post*, September 2, 1939. Cover illustration tear sheet, 14¼ × 11¼ in. Norman Rockwell Museum Collection, Gift of John A. & Laura C. Savio. RC.2007.1.186.

1940

- By 1940, Rockwell had become deeply woven into the fabric of Arlington life. The town's residents—shopkeepers, farmers, teachers, and children—had become his trusted collaborators, posing for his sketches and photographs and inspiring the scenes that appeared on *The Saturday Evening Post* covers seen by millions across the country. Rockwell was now drawing almost exclusively from his immediate community, capturing the gestures, humor, and New England stoicism of everyday Vermonters. Now Arlington was no longer merely a picturesque setting, but a living studio filled with willing participants in Rockwell's vision of American life.

- Rockwell's reputation as Vermont's most celebrated artist grew with his growing community involvement in and out of Arlington. For instance, in February, he was invited to serve as a judge for Dartmouth College's Winter Carnival Queen Contest, alongside fellow Vermont painter Paul Sample, then the college's artist-in-residence. The event reflects Rockwell's growing stature as both a cultural figure and a beloved member of his adopted greater community.

- Rockwell undertook a major literary commission, illustrating the Heritage Press edition of *The Adventures of Huckleberry Finn*. His twelve illustrations for Mark Twain's classic novel reveal Rockwell's exceptional ability to translate narrative into image—combining his love of storytelling with his gift for character observation. The project offered him an opportunity to explore more dramatic and emotionally varied subjects than his magazine covers, reaffirming his versatility and mastery as an illustrator.

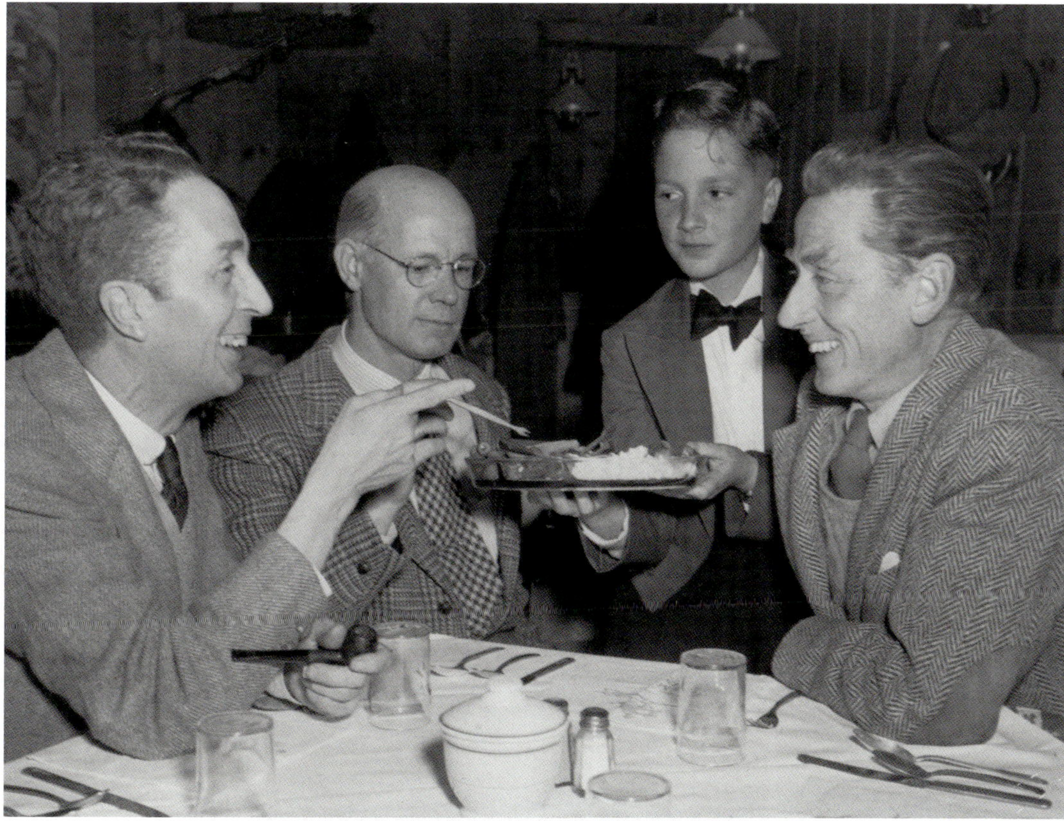

Fig. 33
Aldo Merusi, *Norman Rockwell with Mead Schaeffer, John Atherton, and Peter Rockwell*, date unknown. Silver gelatin print, 7½ × 9½ in. Norman Rockwell Museum Collection, Norman Rockwell Art Collection Trust, Studio Collection. ST.1976.20032.178.241. Artwork Approved by the Norman Rockwell Family Agency.

1941

- In January 1941, President Franklin D. Roosevelt delivered his landmark *State of the Union* address to Congress, articulating four fundamental human rights that should be safeguarded everywhere in the world: Freedom of Speech, Freedom of Worship, Freedom from Want, and Freedom from Fear. These ideals struck a profound chord with Rockwell. Already deeply attuned to the rhythms of American life, he was moved to interpret Roosevelt's vision in the language he knew best, illustration. Though it would take him two years to bring the concept fully to life, Roosevelt's words planted the seed for what would become Rockwell's most ambitious and enduring wartime project, "The Four Freedoms."

- That same year, with the world at war, Rockwell's work for *The Saturday Evening Post* began to reflect the growing national tension and spirit of service. He introduced a new recurring character, the fictional young soldier Willie Gillis, whose lighthearted adventures offered reassurance and humanity amid uncertainty. "The Willie Gillis" series, which ultimately appeared on eleven *Saturday Evening Post* covers between 1941 and 1946, chronicled the life of an everyman private, who at times is presented as naive, earnest, and endearing, as he navigates the realities of wartime America. Modeled by Arlington teenager Robert Otis Buck, Willie Gillis embodied the experiences of countless young men and their families, blending humor and heart at a time when both were in short supply.

1942

- As the United States entered World War II, Rockwell, like many American artists, turned his attention to the war effort. That year, he completed his first wartime illustration—a vivid depiction of a machine gunner (Fig. 34)—marking a shift in subject and tone from the gentle humor of his prewar *Saturday Evening Post* covers. Rockwell's new focus expanded to themes of duty, sacrifice, and national unity. Over the next several years, he would contribute numerous wartime paintings and posters in support of the country's mobilization, using his art to bolster morale and promote the ideals of service and freedom.
- Later that year, Rockwell and Schaeffer traveled from Arlington to Washington, D.C., to meet with officials at the Ordnance Department. Both artists hoped to find meaningful ways to lend their talents to the war effort. During this visit, Rockwell presented a bold idea, to illustrate President Roosevelt's recently declared Four Freedoms, translating the lofty ideals of democracy into relatable scenes of everyday American life. To Rockwell's disappointment, the government officials declined his proposal. Undeterred, Rockwell returned to Arlington determined to bring the project to life on his own terms. When he shared the concept with editors at *The Saturday Evening Post*, they immediately recognized its potential and agreed to publish the series. This decision set in motion what would become one of Rockwell's greatest artistic and civic achievements in the visual embodiment of Roosevelt's Four Freedoms in four paintings that would soon inspire its viewers and help raise substantial funds in war bonds.

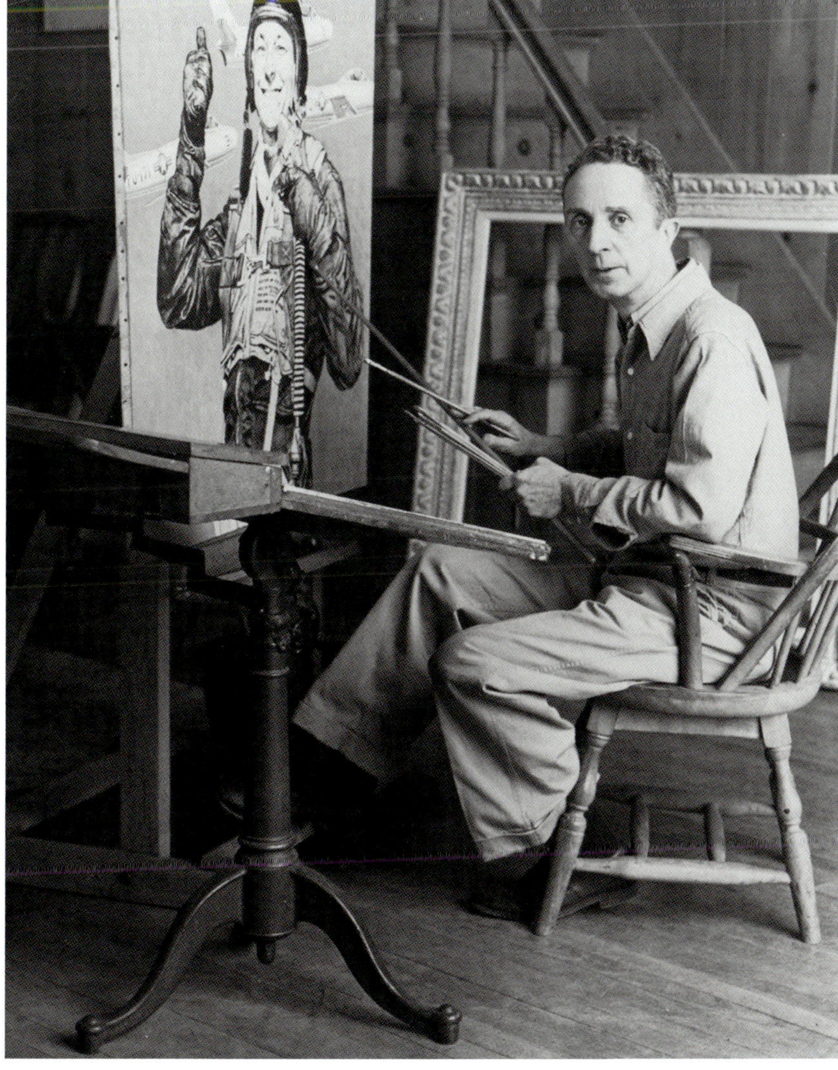

Fig. 34
Unidentified photographer, *Norman Rockwell painting Global U.S. Air Force (Pilot)*, ca. 1952. Photographic print, 10 × 8 in. Norman Rockwell Museum Collection, Norman Rockwell Art Collection Trust, Studio Collection. ST.1976.20032.97.14. Artwork Approved by the Norman Rockwell Family Agency.

1943

- By early 1943, Norman Rockwell had completed "The Four Freedoms" series—*Freedom of Speech*, *Freedom of Worship*, *Freedom from Want*, and *Freedom from Fear* (see Plates 15–18). Drawing inspiration from President Roosevelt's 1941 address, Rockwell translated these abstract ideals into intimate, human scenes drawn from the lives of his Arlington neighbors. Before sending the paintings to *The Saturday Evening Post* in Philadelphia, Rockwell first unveiled them locally at the West Arlington Grange Hall, offering townspeople—many of whom had modeled for the works—the chance to see themselves and their community reflected in this stirring visual expression of American values.
- When *The Saturday Evening Post* published "The Four Freedoms" in four consecutive issues between February and March 1943, each painting was accompanied by essays and short stories expanding on its theme. The series was met with overwhelming acclaim, striking a deep emotional chord with readers across the nation. The original canvases soon embarked on a sixteen-city U.S. War Bond tour, organized by the Treasury Department, where they were viewed by thousands and helped raise over $130 million in war bonds, ultimately transforming Rockwell's paintings into enduring symbols of patriotism.
- That same year, Rockwell completed another wartime masterpiece, *Rosie the Riveter* (see Plate 22), his tribute to the women who had entered the workforce to support the war effort. Depicted in workwear and with muscular confidence, Rockwell's Rosie embodied both strength and femininity, becoming an icon of American resilience and industrial might.

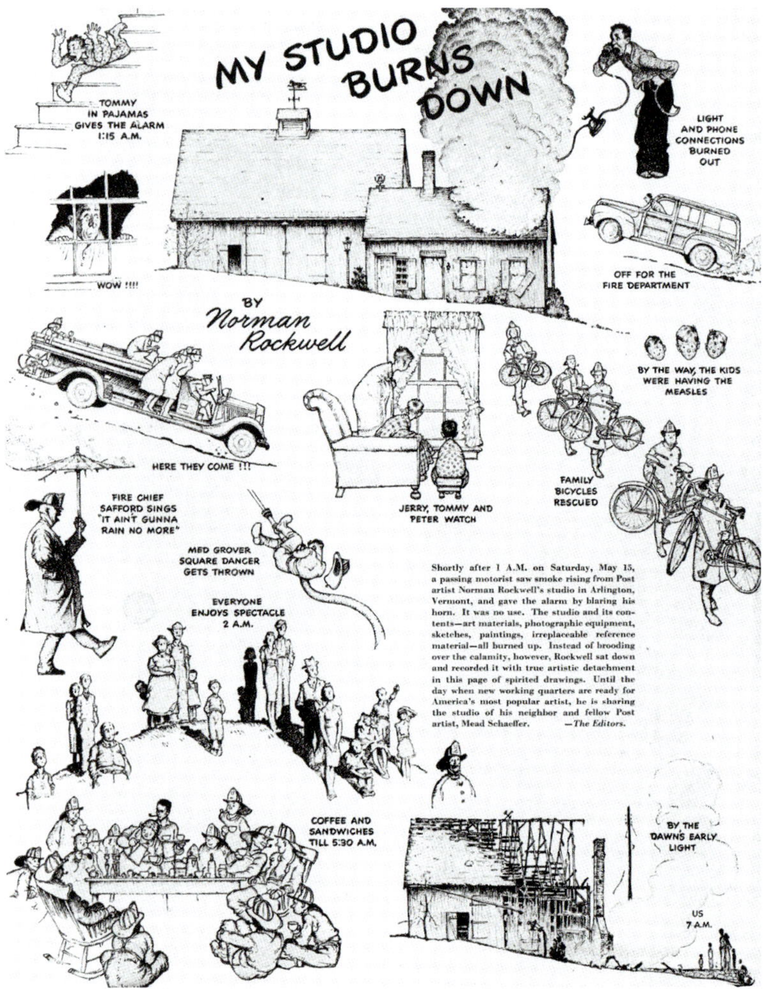

MY STUDIO BURNS DOWN

BY Norman Rockwell

TOMMY IN PAJAMAS GIVES THE ALARM 1:15 A.M.

LIGHT AND PHONE CONNECTIONS BURNED OUT

WOW !!!!

OFF FOR THE FIRE DEPARTMENT

BY THE WAY, THE KIDS WERE HAVING THE MEASLES

HERE THEY COME !!!

FAMILY BICYCLES RESCUED

FIRE CHIEF SAFFORD SINGS "IT AINT GUNNA RAIN NO MORE"

JERRY, TOMMY AND PETER WATCH

MED GROVER SQUARE DANCER GETS THROWN

EVERYONE ENJOYS SPECTACLE 2 A.M.

Shortly after 1 A.M. on Saturday, May 15, a passing motorist saw smoke rising from Post artist Norman Rockwell's studio in Arlington, Vermont, and gave the alarm by blaring his horn. It was no use. The studio and its contents—art materials, photographic equipment, sketches, paintings, irreplaceable reference material—all burned up. Instead of brooding over the calamity, however, Rockwell sat down and recorded it with true artistic detachment in this page of spirited drawings. Until the day when new working quarters are ready for America's most popular artist, he is sharing the studio of his neighbor and fellow Post artist, Mead Schaeffer. —*The Editors.*

COFFEE AND SANDWICHES TILL 5:30 A.M.

BY THE DAWN'S EARLY LIGHT

US 7 A.M.

Fig. 35
Norman Rockwell, *My Studio Burns*, 1943. Illustration for *The Saturday Evening Post*, July 17, 1943. Tear sheet, 14¼ × 11¼ in. Norman Rockwell Museum Collection, Norman Rockwell Illustrated Ephemera. RC.2011.3.17.9. Artwork Approved by the Norman Rockwell Family Agency.

- Tragedy struck Rockwell in May 1943, when his Arlington studio caught fire, destroying virtually everything inside, including paintings, sketches, costumes, props, and his invaluable library of reference materials. The loss was devastating, but Rockwell's characteristic humor and perseverance soon resurfaced; he even alluded to the incident in a playful drawing (Fig. 35).

- Refusing to let the fire setback his momentum, the Rockwells purchased the McKee house located down the road on the West Arlington Green shortly thereafter and swiftly constructed a new studio (Fig. 36). The new studio became both a creative refuge and a community hub, allowing Rockwell to continue his remarkable output as well as become more engaged with the community through their new location on West Arlington's main green.

1944

- Among the many paintings completed that year was *The Tattoo Artist* (see Plate 23). In this humorous depiction, a sailor is adding yet another name to a growing list of former sweethearts tattooed on his arm. The tattooist is portrayed by Schaeffer, who anecdotally told Rockwell he was taken aback by the size and appearance of his back end.

1945

- As World War II ended, Rockwell's work turned toward the theme of reunions. His painting *The Homecoming* (also known as *Homecoming G.I.*) stands among his most heartfelt tributes to America's returning soldiers. Painted with characteristic empathy, the scene shows a uniformed young man embraced by family and neighbors on a sunlit stoop, an image that distilled the nation's collective joy and gratitude at the war's end (see Plate 30).

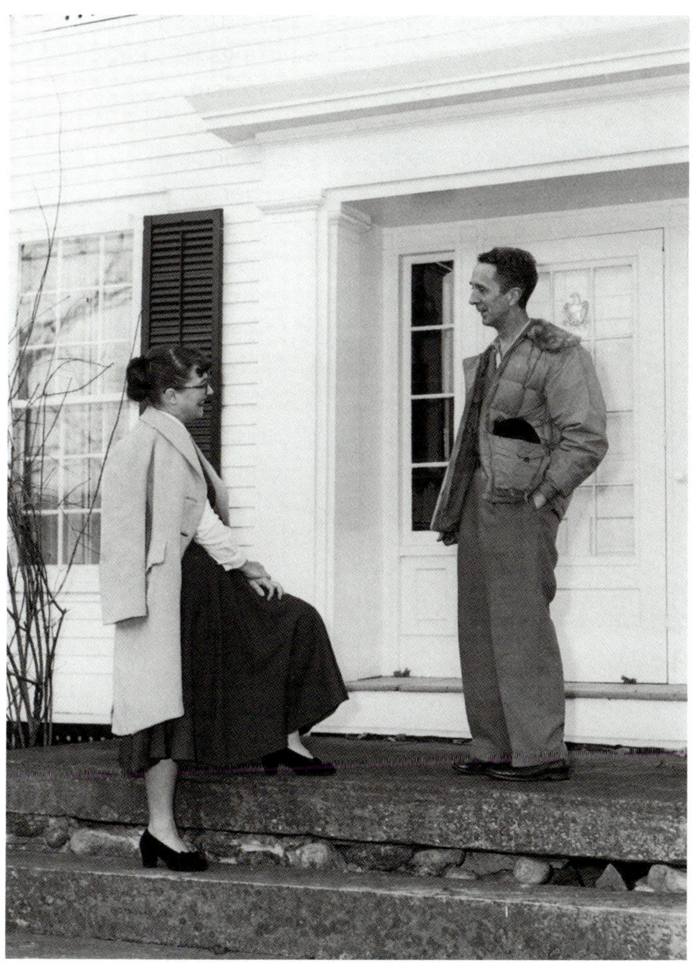

Fig. 36
Arthur Johnson, *Norman and Mary Rockwell in Arlington, Vermont*, ca. 1939–53. Silver gelatin print, 6½ × 6¼ in. Norman Rockwell Museum Collection, Norman Rockwell Art Collection Trust, Studio Collection. ST.1976.20032.178.227. Artwork Approved by the Norman Rockwell Family Agency.

- That same year, Rockwell's stature as one of America's foremost illustrators was affirmed when he was honored at the Palace of the Legion of Honor in San Francisco, alongside artists such as Thomas Hart Benton, John Sloan, and Charles Sheeler. The recognition placed Rockwell firmly within the broader narrative of American art beyond his popular notoriety.

1946

- In 1946, the artistic community in Arlington continued to flourish with the arrival of another *Saturday Evening Post* illustrator, George Hughes. Hughes's lively depictions of postwar domestic life complemented Rockwell's narrative and sentimental approach. With Rockwell, Schaeffer, Atherton, Pelham, and now Hughes all living and working within a few miles of one another, Arlington had become an extraordinary enclave of American illustration.

1947

- Rockwell's engagement with Vermont's artistic life deepened in 1947, when he participated in the annual Southern Vermont Artists exhibitions in Manchester, an important regional showcase that connected professional and emerging artists alike. His presence lent prestige to the event and reinforced his commitment to supporting local creative communities.

- During this year, Rockwell's work received high accolades when the Metropolitan Museum of Art in New York included his paintings created for the motion pictures *The Song of Bernadette* and *The Razor's Edge* in an exhibition celebrating motion picture art. The presentation of his illustrations in such an esteemed institution signaled a growing acknowledgment of Rockwell's artistry beyond popular culture and magazine illustration.

- Closer to home, a new Arlington landmark opened its doors, the Green Mountain Restaurant and Diner, a rustic family eatery that quickly became a favorite gathering place for the town's artists. Rockwell, Schaeffer, Hughes, and others were frequent patrons, their presence turning the diner into an informal salon of sorts. Its walls soon filled with prints and reproductions of their work, transforming it into a local shrine to the community's artistic spirit.

1948

- In 1948, Rockwell completed one of his most beloved *Saturday Evening Post* covers, *The Gossips*, a humorously choreographed depiction of a rumor passed from one person to the next (see Plate 1). The composition features more than a dozen faces, nearly all of them Arlington residents, including his wife, Mary, and himself, appearing at the end of the chain. Drawing upon the quirks and humor of small-town life, the painting encapsulates Rockwell's deep affection for his small Vermont community.

- That same year, Rockwell extended his influence beyond Vermont by joining the founding faculty of the Famous Artists School, a pioneering correspondence-based art program designed to bring professional instruction to aspiring illustrators nationwide. Among its founding members were several of Rockwell's peers, including his Arlington colleague Atherton. The initiative reflected Rockwell's belief in mentorship and craftsmanship (Fig. 37).

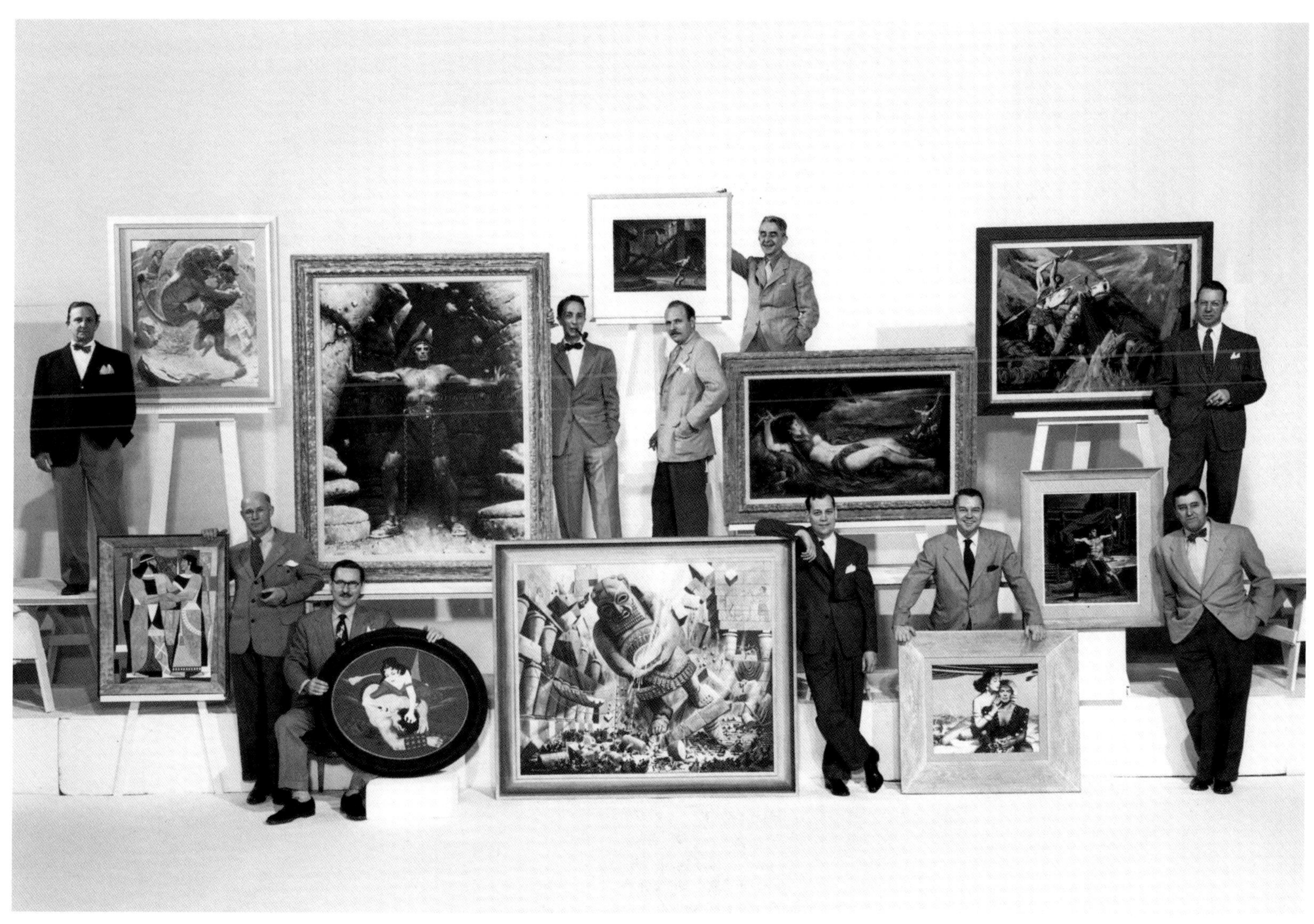

Fig. 37
Pagano Studios, *Famous Artists School faculty posing with their "Samson" paintings*, date unknown. Photographic print, 9¾ × 13¾ in. Norman Rockwell Museum Collection, Famous Artists School Collection, Gift of Magdalen & Robert Livesey, RC.2013.11.31.4. Artwork Approved by the Norman Rockwell Family Agency.

• Rockwell is paired with Anna Mary Robertson ("Grandma") Moses, who lived nearby, just over the Vermont border in New York, in a charming publicity event orchestrated by Joyce C. Hall, president of Hallmark Cards. To celebrate Moses's eighty-eighth birthday, Rockwell decorated an enormous cake with buttercream scenes inspired by her 1946 painting *Out for Christmas Trees* (Fig. 38). The playful gesture delighted the public and drew national attention to the pair, whose works, albeit stylistically distinct, shared a celebration of rural American life and community. Rockwell reprised his role as cake decorator the following year, cementing an enduring friendship with the self-taught painter.

Fig. 38
Unidentified photographer, *Grandma Moses' 80th Birthday Party (Grandma Moses, her son Hugh Moses, Hugh's wife, and Norman Rockwell)*, 1948. Silver gelatin print, 10 × 8 in. Norman Rockwell Museum Collection, Norman Rockwell Art Collection Trust, Studio Collection. ST.1976.20032.178.241. Artwork Approved by the Norman Rockwell Family Agency.

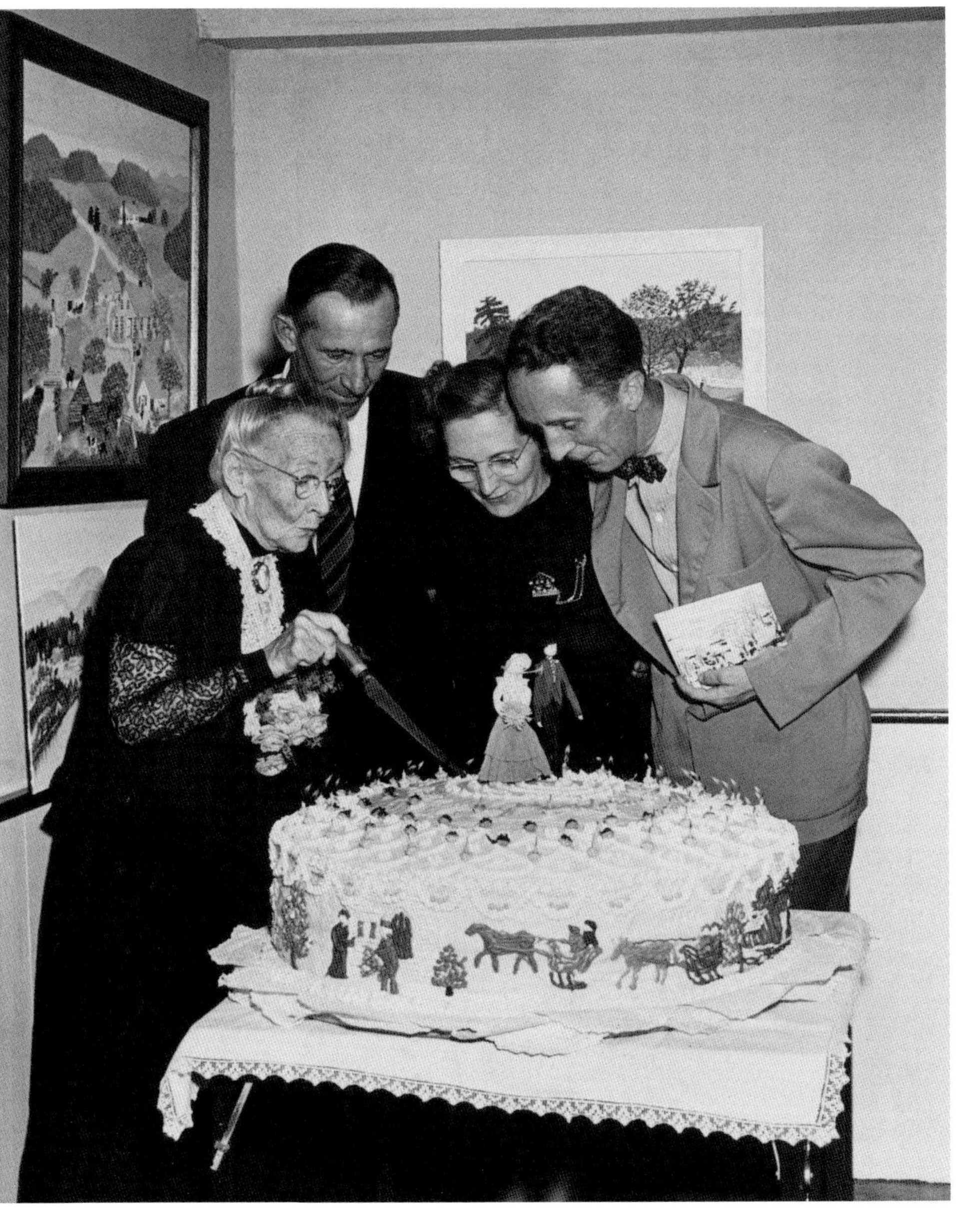

1949

- In 1949, Rockwell is formally recognized by his adopted state, receiving an honorary Doctor of Fine Arts degree from the University of Vermont, honoring his contributions to American art.

- That same year, he created *Christmas Homecoming*, which graced *The Saturday Evening Post*'s Christmas issue (see Plate 41). The painting, a warm and emotionally resonant portrayal of reunion and joy, depicts a returning serviceman embraced by his family at the holidays. The models include Rockwell's wife Mary, his three sons, and many of their close friends and neighbors, among them, "Grandma" Moses, as well as Rockwell himself.

1950

- In 1950, Rockwell completed one of his acknowledged masterpieces, *Shuffleton's Barbershop*, based on the real-life barbershop of his neighbor Frank Shuffleton in nearby East Arlington (see Plate 4). Bathed in the soft glow of evening light, the scene depicts three musicians gathered in the back room after hours, their quiet camaraderie illuminated by the flickering stove. The painting's depth of mood and intimacy marked a shift in Rockwell's work toward greater subtlety and emotional resonance, earning it lasting acclaim as one of his finest achievements.

- New creative energy arrived in Arlington in the form of Don Trachte, a cartoonist best known for his long-running work on the popular comic strip *Henry*. Moving with his family to Arlington, Trachte quickly became part of the artists' informal community, forming close friendships with Rockwell, Hughes, and others. With his background in comics and shared connection to *The Saturday Evening Post*, Trachte contributed to the ongoing creative exchange that defined Arlington in the mid-century years.

1951

- In 1951, Rockwell painted *Saying Grace*, a scene of quiet reverence and compassion that depicts a grandmother and young boy bowing their heads in prayer at a bustling lunch counter (see Plate 46). Drawn from an idea suggested by a reader of *The Saturday Evening Post*, the painting struck a powerful chord with audiences across the country. It was voted the *Post* readers' favorite cover of the year and is now widely regarded as one of Rockwell's greatest artistic triumphs.

- That same year, Rockwell's *Saturday Evening Post* cover *Soldier's Return* was included in an exhibition showcasing alumni of New York's Art Students League, highlighting the enduring influence of his early training and lifelong dedication to narrative realism.

- The year also marked a more difficult personal chapter for the artist as Mary began receiving treatment for depression at the Austen Riggs Center in Stockbridge, Massachusetts. The family maintained their home in Arlington, but Mary's regular commutes to Stockbridge foreshadowed the town's growing presence in their lives and the family's eventual relocation there.

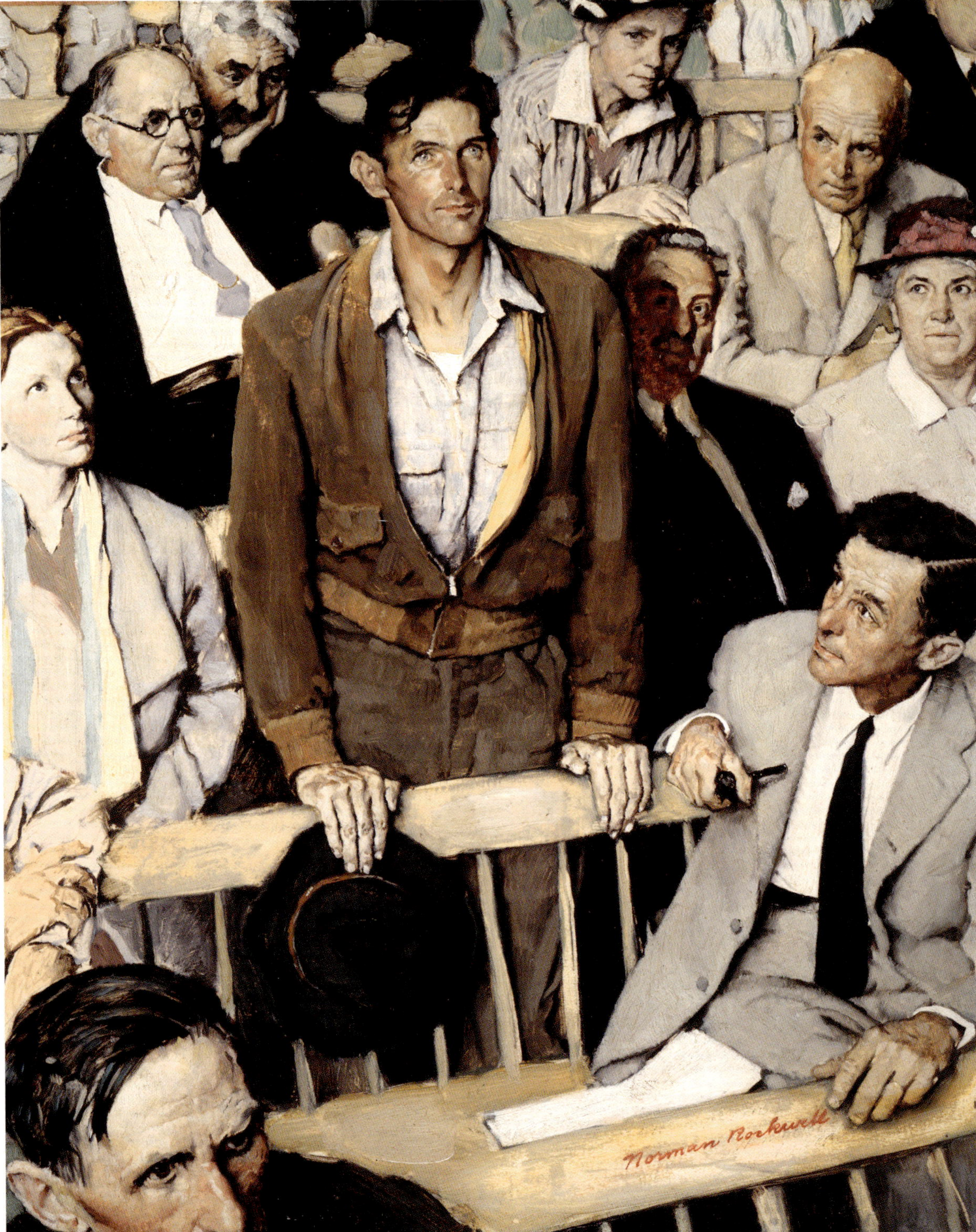

Fig. 39
Norman Rockwell, *Town Meeting*, 1943. Study for cover illustration for *The Saturday Evening Post*, February 20, 1943. Oil on composition board, 21¼ × 17¼ in. The Metropolitan Museum of Art, George A. Hearn Fund, 1952. 52.164. Licensed by Art Resource, NY. Artwork Approved by the Norman Rockwell Family Agency.

1952

- In 1952, Rockwell traveled to Washington, D.C., to paint a formal portrait of General Dwight D. Eisenhower, then a World War II hero and soon-to-be presidential candidate, for *The Saturday Evening Post*. The portrait reflected Rockwell's keen ability to humanize national figures.

- Rockwell appeared on national television, where he was celebrated as Vermont's "Good Will Ambassador Extraordinary." In this role, he praised his adopted home state for its beauty, its people, and its inspiration.

- The year also saw the Metropolitan Museum of Art's acquisition of Rockwell's *Town Meeting*, an oil study for his celebrated *Freedom of Speech* (Fig. 39). This acquisition represented a rare institutional recognition of an artist often dismissed by critics as "merely an illustrator." Meanwhile, the Arlington artist circle suffered a profound loss with the sudden death of Atherton, who passed away unexpectedly during a fishing trip in New Brunswick, Canada.

1953

- In 1953, Rockwell's *The Young Lady with the Shiner* appeared in *The Saturday Evening Post* (see Plate 3). This was one of the last paintings Rockwell created in Arlington prior to his move out of state, and also the last work featuring a model from this community. The triumphant young girl in the painting, despite her fresh black eye and impending discipline, is Mary Whalen, a favorite model of Rockwell.

- This year also marks the departure of the Rockwell family, who left Arlington for Stockbridge, Massachusetts, seeking proximity to Mary's ongoing treatment and a fresh start after more than fourteen transformative years in Vermont.

1954

- Now working from his new studio in Stockbridge, Rockwell continued to produce beloved *Saturday Evening Post* covers that revealed the enduring influence of his Arlington years. Works such as *Girl at Mirror* and *Breaking Home Ties* (both 1954) demonstrated a deepened emotional sensitivity and psychological insight while maintaining the narrative clarity that had defined his earlier Vermont compositions.

1955

- In 1955, Rockwell returned to Arlington to reunite with old friends and fellow artists during the town's Street Fair event, rekindling the spirit of camaraderie that had characterized his years there. His affection for Vermont remained strong, and he continued to accept commissions that tied him to the region's artistic and industrial landscape, including paintings for the Rock of Ages Corporation in Barre, Vermont: *Kneeling Girl* (see Plate 34), completed this year, followed by *The Craftsman* (see Plate 35) in 1963.

NOTES

Small Town, Big Picture

1. Dorothy Canfield Fisher, *Vermont: A Guide to the Green Mountain State* (Boston: Houghton Mifflin, 1937), 4. Fisher was highly involved in advocacy for the arts in Vermont and was instrumental in Rockwell's time in Arlington. She is perhaps most well-known as the founding editor of the Book-of-the-Month Club. Today, we recognize that she played a controversial role in the eugenics movement in Vermont; she worked with the Vermont Commission on Country Life on the Committee for the Preservation of Vermont Literature and Ideals, which had ties to the Eugenics Survey of Vermont. More on this can be found in Perri Klass, "The Author Who Brought the Montessori Method to Life in Her Fiction," *New Yorker*, February 27, 2023, https://www.newyorker.com/books/second-read/the-author-who-brought-the-montessori-method-to-life-in-her-fiction.
2. Fisher, *Vermont*, 4. The presidency of Calvin Coolidge, who served from 1923 to 1929, increased national attention on his home state of Vermont.
3. For a brief time, in 1777, Arlington was also Vermont's state capital. For further insight into Arlington's rich history, see Fisher, *Memories of Arlington, Vermont* (New York: Duell, Sloan, and Pearce, 1957); Christopher S. Wren, *Those Turbulent Sons of Freedom: Ethan Allen's Green Mountain Boys and the American Revolution* (New York: Simon & Schuster, 2014); and William P. Budde, *Arlington, Vermont: Its First 250 Years* (Arlington, VT: Arlington Townscape Association, 2014). The Russell Vermontiana Collection at the Martha Canfield Library in Arlington also contains a large selection of historical documents and town records.
4. Pelham, who had previously known Rockwell in New Rochelle, worked as Rockwell's studio assistant in Arlington. As his assistant, Pelham would primarily act as Rockwell's photographer, taking pictures from which Rockwell worked from to create his paintings, as well as source props and build sets. More on this can be found in Ron Schick, *Norman Rockwell: Behind the Camera* (New York: Little, Brown & Company, 2009), 27–28.
5. Rockwell quoted in Lois Henderson Bayliss, "Artist Likes Rural Folks for Models," *Manchester Journal*, October 26, 1939, 4.
6. While Rockwell and his family spent most of their time in Vermont, there were periods when the artist felt isolated in the rural state. In his letters to friends, he expressed loneliness during the long winters when the seasonal people left. More on this can be found in Deborah Solomon, "Norman Rockwell's New England," *New York Times*, November 1, 2013, https://www.nytimes.com/2013/11/03/travel/norman-rockwells-new-england.html. He would, therefore, periodically travel across the East Coast and to California for extended visits, as shared in "Among Other Things," *Saturday Evening Post*, November 29, 1941, 4.
7. The Rockwells stayed at this home until Rockwell's studio burnt down in a fire in 1943. They purchased a new property in West Arlington, where he built a new studio. The family remained there until their relocation to Stockbridge, Massachusetts, in 1953.
8. Rockwell discusses how he and Mary found themselves in Arlington and purchasing their new home in detail in his autobiography. Norman Rockwell, *My Adventures as an Illustrator* (New York: Doubleday, 1960), 357–59.
9. Melinda Pelham Murphy, daughter of Gene Pelham, discussed the Coca-Cola machine that was in Rockwell's studio and offered to his models. Melinda Pelham Murphy, interview by Carolyn Bauer, April 16, 2025.
10. Rockwell quoted in Bayliss, "Artist Likes Rural Folks for Models," 4.
11. Norman Rockwell, "Commonplace," *American Magazine*, May 1936, 11.
12. This was the last painting by Rockwell began in Vermont before his move to Stockbridge, Massachusetts.
13. In his advertisement, Rockwell claimed he could not find any black eyes in either Arlington or nearby Bennington. So he sent out an inquiry through the local newspaper asking for a "black eye, fresh enough for a good color picture." "Rockwell in Market for Shiners," *Burlington Daily News*, January 23, 1953, 1.
14. The toddler, Tommy Forsberg of Worcester, Massachusetts, had the best black eyes for reproducing on Whalen. Forsberg earned twenty-five dollars from Rockwell and had his picture in the local newspapers. "Perfect Shiners," *Montpelier Evening Argus*, February 20, 1953, 1.
15. Rockwell and his family's deep involvement in these events and more is described in newspaper articles from their Vermont years, including "Battenkill Grange Hears Three Artists," *Manchester Journal*, July 22, 1948, 4; "500 Enjoy PTA Square Dance," *Manchester Journal*, June 28, 1951, 1; "Norman Rockwell Is Rotary Speaker," *Manchester Journal*, October 26, 1939, 1; "Famous Vermonters to Appear at Fair," *Manchester Journal*,

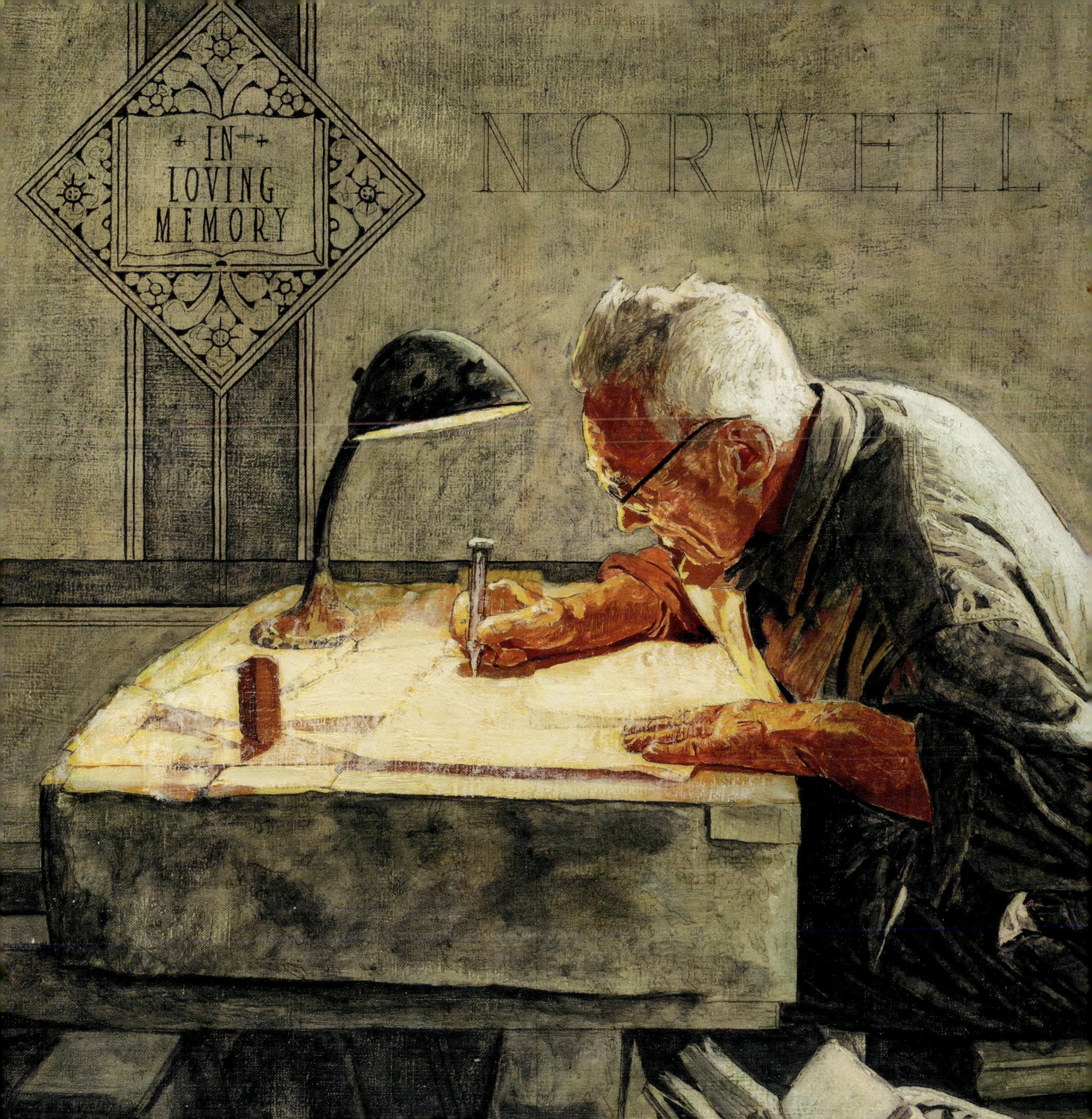
IN
LOVING
MEMORY
NORWELL

November 11, 1948, 1; "An All-Star Cast," *Manchester Journal*, July 17, 1952, 5; and "Artist Norman Rockwell Is Part Owner of a Cemetery," *Barre Daily Times*, June 23, 1951, 7.

16. As mentioned previously, several of these artists, such as Schaeffer and Pelham, knew Rockwell when they lived in New Rochelle. Atherton and Schaeffer were also drawn to this area because of the exceptional fishing opportunities near the Battenkill River.
17. In 1951, Rockwell and Atherton collaborated on the painting *The Kansas City Spirit*, which was commissioned by Hallmark founder J. C. Hall. Rockwell painted its central heroic figure, but he recruited his friend to render the rest of the painting, which includes Kansas City's skyline and representations of agriculture, commerce, and transportation.
18. Rockwell, *My Adventures as an Illustrator*, 365.
19. Atherton quoted in Dorothy C. Miller and Alfred H. Barr Jr., *American Realists and Magic Realists* (New York: Museum of Modern Art, 1943), 26.
20. "Rock of Ages Ads to Feature Rockwell Painting," *Times Argus* (Barre and Montpelier, VT), August 29, 1962, 12.
21. Greenhill has argued that paintings like this reflect both Rockwell's mastery of genre and his awareness of the broader art world: "something beyond the pale of the ordinary Rockwell picture is at work here." Jennifer A. Greenhill, "The View from Outside: Rockwell and Race in 1950," *American Art* 21, no. 2 (Summer 2007): 70–95.
22. "I Like to Please People," *Time*, June 21, 1943, 41.
23. In August 1951, Clement Greenberg and Helen Frankenthaler paid a visit to Rockwell's studio, where they became smitten with him and the work on his easel, his initial start for the painting *Saying Grace*. More on this visit can be found in Alexander Nemerov, *Fierce Poise: Helen Frankenthaler and 1950s New York* (New York: Penguin Books, 2020), 40–41.
24. Rockwell received a solo exhibition at Bennington College from June 23 to September 5, 1977, as noted in Christine Graham, "Memo to Non-term Committee Members," March 21, 1977, Bennington College Archives. More about exhibitions featuring contemporary abstract artists at Bennington College can be found in *Manchester Journal*, November 8, 1951, 7, and "Bennington College Art Exhibit Opens Tomorrow," *Rutland Daily Herald*, March 19, 1953, 5.
25. Dorothy Canfield Fisher, "Vermont," *Holiday Magazine*, November 1949, typescript, Special Collections, Bailey-Howe Library, University of Vermont.
26. Dona Brown, "Vermont as a Way of Life," *Vermont History* 85, no. 1 (Winter/Spring 2017): 54.
27. "Her pictures are never phony," Rockwell reflected on Moses's artwork: "they were good, honest pictures. She has an unerring sense of color and somehow the source of her paintings—her memories—remains fresh and vital, so that no matter how many times she does a winter scene it still retains its charm and sense of life." Rockwell, *My Adventures as an Illustrator*, 413.
28. Bernard DeVoto, "New England: There She Stands," *Harper's Magazine*, March 1932, 413.
29. Schaeffer used Atherton, Atherton's wife Maxine, and his own wife, Elizabeth, as the models in this illustration.
30. Rockwell, *My Adventures as an Illustrator*, 393.
31. "Four Top-Notch Artists of Arlington Make Exhibit," *Suburban List*, August 18, 1949, 16.
32. Fisher helped lure Alan Carter, founder of the Vermont Symphony Orchestra, to the area. She continued to be a vocal advocate for the organization, delivering a speech at a benefit in its honor. For more on this, see Dorothy Canfield Fisher, "Remarks for a VSO Benefit Concert at Rutland," carton 30, folder 21, Dorothy Canfield Collection, Special Collections, University of Vermont Libraries.
33. Rockwell quoted in Rufus Jarman, "Profiles: U.S. Artist," *New Yorker*, March 17, 1945, 36.

Looking North

1. For a magisterial exploration of the role of the "ad man" in American culture, see Jackson Lears, *Fables of Abundance: A Cultural History of Advertising in America* (New York: Basic Books, 1994). Rockwell's peer Maxfield Parrish was tagged with this nickname; see Sylvia Yount, *Maxfield Parrish, 1870–1966* (New York: Harry N. Abrams in association with the Pennsylvania Academy of the Fine Arts, 1999), 108.
2. William H. Truettner and Roger B. Stein, eds., *Picturing Old New England: Image and Memory* (Washington, DC: National Museum of American Art, Smithsonian Institution; New Haven: Yale University Press, 1999); Julia B. Rosenbaum, *Visions of Belonging: New England Art and the Making of American Identity* (Ithaca, NY, and London: Cornell University Press, 2006).
3. Lawrence Buell, *New England Literary Culture: From Revolution through Renaissance* (Cambridge: Cambridge University Press, 1986), especially chap. 13, "The Village as Icon"; Joseph S. Wood, *The New England Village* (Baltimore: Johns Hopkins University Press, 1997), especially chap. 7, "A World We Have Gained."
4. Stephen Nissenbaum, "New England as Region and Nation," in Edward L. Ayers, Patricia Nelson Limerick, Stephen Nissenbaum, and Peter S. Onuf, *All Over the Map: Rethinking American Regions* (Baltimore: Johns Hopkins University Press, 1996), 39. For a study of this

phenomenon in New England visual culture, see William H. Truettner, "Small Town America," and Bruce Robertson, "Small Town America," in Truettner and Stein, *Picturing Old New England*.

5. Truettner and Stein, *Picturing Old New England*, 111–12.
6. To plot this arc, see Marc Simpson, *Winslow Homer: Paintings of the Civil War* (San Francisco: Fine Arts Museums of San Francisco, 1988), and Bruce Robertson, *Reckoning with Winslow Homer: His Late Paintings and Their Influence* (Cleveland: Cleveland Museum of Art in cooperation with Indiana University Press, 1990).
7. Margaret C. Conrads, *Winslow Homer and the Critics: Forging A National Art in the 1870s* (Princeton: Princeton University Press, 2001), 1.
8. My thinking about Homer is developed in Thomas Denenberg, *Winslow Homer and the Poetics of Place* (Portland: Portland Museum of Art, 2010), and Thomas Denenberg, ed., *Weatherbeaten: Winslow Homer and Maine* (New Haven: Yale University Press, 2012), especially chap. 1, "Weatherbeaten."
9. *The Crayon* quoted in Charles O. Vogel, "Wanderings after the Wild and Beautiful: The Life and Career of Benjamin Champney," *Historical New Hampshire* 51, nos. 3 and 4 (Fall/Winter 1996): 80.
10. "Summer in the Country," *Appletons' Journal of Literature, Science, and Art* 1, no. 15 (July 10, 1869): 465.
11. John Wilmerding, *Signs of the Artist: Signatures and Self-Expression in American Paintings* (New Haven: Yale University Press, 2003), 151.
12. Jennifer A. Greenhill, *Playing It Straight: Art and Humor in the Gilded Age* (Berkeley: University of California Press, 2012), especially chap. 1, "Winslow Homer's Visual Deadpan."
13. "The Strange Hermitage of Winslow Homer on the Maine Coast," undated press clipping, Bowdoin College Museum of Art, Scrapbook: Clippings about Winslow Homer and His Work, 1867–1941 (1964.649.185), 65.
14. Rockwell Kent, *World Famous Paintings* (New York: Wise & Company, 1939), entry 93.
15. Lawrence Alloway, "The Return of Maxfield Parrish," *Show* 4 (May 1964): 62–67, quoted in Yount, *Maxfield Parrish, 1870–1966*, 16.
16. "The House of Mr. Maxfield Parrish," *The Architectural Record* 22, no. 4 (October 1907): 276.
17. It comes as no surprise, perhaps, to discover that such images were often clipped out and framed to decorate middle-class homes in the Jazz Age.
18. Sylvia Yount, *Maxfield Parrish, 1870–1966* (New York: Harry N. Abrams in association with the Pennsylvania Academy of the Fine Arts, 1999), 113.
19. "Three New York Exhibitions," *The American*, May 19, 1888, 74, quoted in Nicolai Cikovsky Jr. and Franklin Kelly, *Winslow Homer* (Washington, DC: National Gallery of Art; New Haven: Yale University Press, 1995), 288.
20. Joyce Hill Stoner, "Wyeth Vertigo: On Land and Sea, In the Air, and at the Dinner Table," in *Wyeth Vertigo*, ed. Thomas Denenberg (Shelburne, VT: Shelburne Museum; Hanover: University Press of New England, 2013), 26.
21. Laurie Norton Moffatt, "The People's Painter," in *Norman Rockwell: Pictures for the American People*, ed. Marueen Hart Hennessey and Anne Knutson (New York: Harry N. Abrams, 1999), 23–28.
22. Although many of Frost's most famous poems are about decisions or places in between, I have in mind "The Secret Sits" from 1936 and thank Joel Gardner for reminding me of this work. For a salient exploration of the Janus-faced nature of art and illustration see Richard J. Boyle, *Double Lives: American Painters as Illustrators, 1850–1950* (Lebanon: University Press of New England, 2008). In general, historians have become increasingly comfortable describing culture as fluid; see Lawrence W. Levine, *Highbrow/Lowbrow: The Emergence of Cultural Hierarchy in America* (Cambridge: Harvard University Press, 1988).

Rock and Stone

1. Herman Melville, *The Confidence-Man: His Masquerade*, ed. Hershel Parker (1857; New York: Norton, 1971), 20.
2. Søren Kierkegaard, *The Concept of Anxiety*, trans. Alistair Hannay (1844; New York: Liveright, 2014), 180.
3. See Richard Murray, "Abbott Thayer's 'Stevenson Memorial,'" *American Art* 13 (Summer 1999): 2–25.
4. H. P. Lovecraft, "The Tomb" (1922), in *The Gothic Tales of H. P. Lovecraft*, ed. Xaxier Aldana Reyes (London: British Library, 2018), 13–24.
5. Osip Mandelstam, "On the Addressee" (1913), in *Modern Russian Poets on Poetry*, ed. Carl R. Proffer, trans. Jane Gary Harris (New York: Ardis, 1976), 52–59.
6. Ruth Stone, "Being a Woman," in *The Essential Ruth Stone*, ed. Bianca Stone (Port Townsend, WA: Copper Canyon Press, 2020).
7. Eric Aho, conversation with the author, September 12, 2025.
8. Alexander Pope, "The Rape of the Lock: Canto One" (1712), Poetry Foundation, accessed October 21, 2025, https://www.poetryfoundation.org/poems/44906/the-rape-of-the-lock-canto-1.
9. See Søren Kierkegaard's *Fear and Trembling*, trans. Alastair Hannay (1843; London: Penguin, 1985), which, in a "shudder of thought," meditates on the story of Abraham and Isaac as beyond reason; there is no way, Kierkegaard says, to grasp faith.

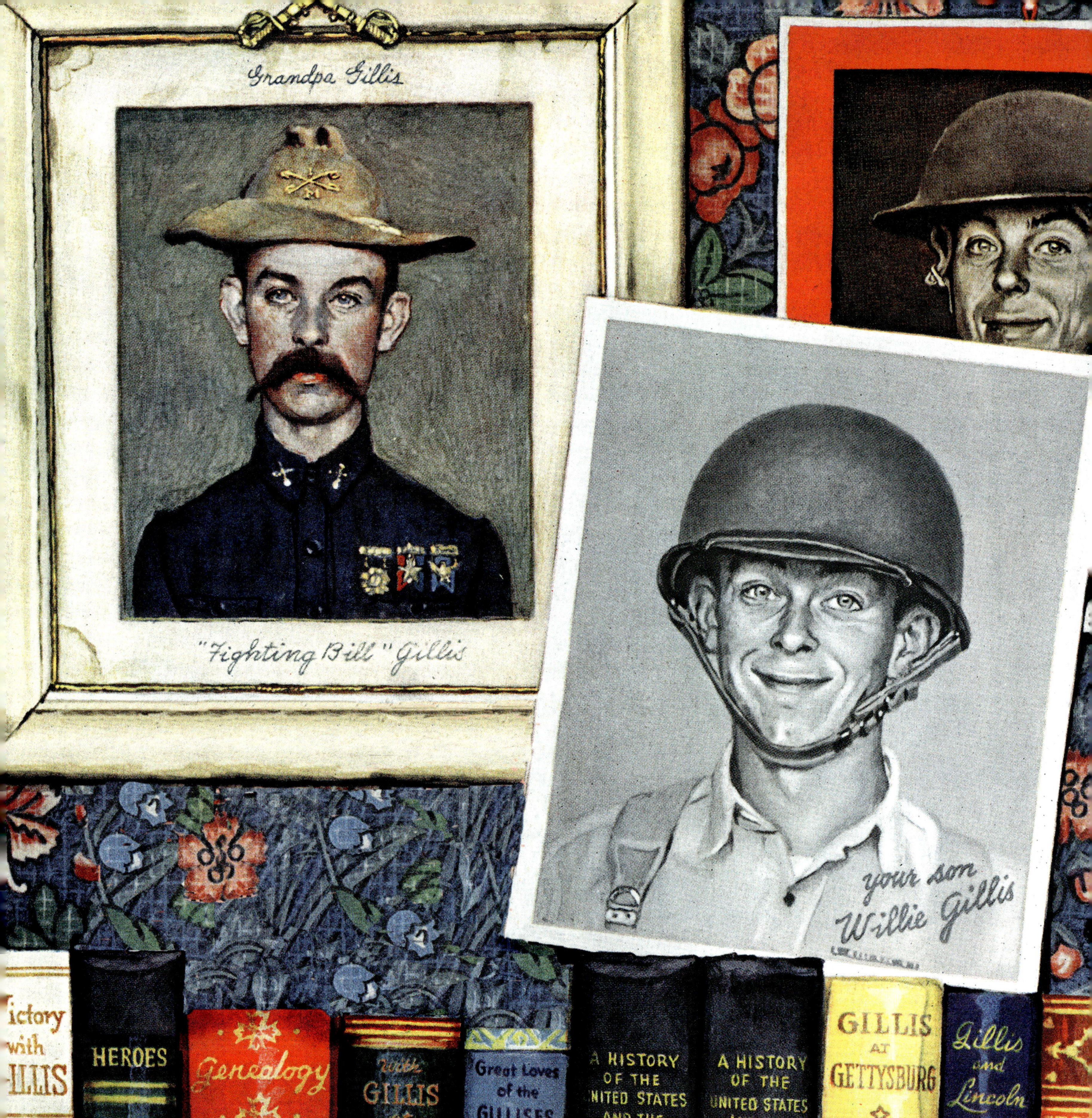

Grandpa Gillis
"Fighting Bill" Gillis
your son Willie Gillis
HEROES
Genealogy
GILLIS
Great Loves of the
A HISTORY OF THE
A HISTORY OF THE UNITED STATES
GILLIS AT GETTYSBURG
Gillis and Lincoln

SELECTED BIBLIOGRAPHY

Ayers, Edward L., Patricia Nelson Limerick, Stephen Nissenbaum, and Peter S. Onuf. *All Over the Map: Rethinking American Regions*. Baltimore: Johns Hopkins University Press, 1996.

Barter, Judith A., ed. *America after the Fall: Painting in the 1930s*. With essays by Judith A. Barter, Sarah L. Burns, Teresa A. Carbone, Annelise K. Madsen, and Sarah Kelly Oehler. Chicago: The Art Institute of Chicago, 2016.

Bauer, Fred. *Norman Rockwell's Faith in America*. New York: Abbeville Press, 1996.

Budde, William P. *Arlington, Vermont: Its First 250 Years*. Arlington, VT: Arlington Townscape Association, 2014.

Buechner, Thomas S. *Norman Rockwell: A Sixty Year Retrospective*. New York: Harry N. Abrams, 1972.

———. *Norman Rockwell: Artist and Illustrator*. New York: Harry N. Abrams, 1970.

Buell, Lawrence. *New England Literary Culture: From Revolution through Renaissance*. Cambridge: Cambridge University Press, 1986.

Canfield Fisher, Dorothy—see Fisher, Dorothy Canfield.

Claridge, Laura. *Norman Rockwell: A Life*. New York: Random House, 2001.

Conrads, Margaret C. *Winslow Homer and the Critics: Forging a National Art in the 1870s*. Princeton: Princeton University Press, 2001.

Cohn, Jan. *Creating America: George Horace Lorimer and "The Saturday Evening Post."* Pittsburgh: University of Pittsburgh Press, 1989.

Coyle, Heather Campbell. *Jazz Age Illustration*. Wilmington: Delaware Art Museum, 2024.

Cullen, Jim. *The American Dream: A Short History of an Idea That Shaped a Nation*. Oxford: Oxford University Press, 2003.

Denenberg, Thomas. *Winslow Homer and the Poetics of Place*. Portland: Portland Museum of Art, 2010.

———, ed. *Weatherbeaten: Winslow Homer and Maine*. New Haven: Yale University Press, 2012.

———, Jamie Franklin, Dina Korzenik and Alexander Nemerov. *Grandma Moses: American Modern*. Shelburne, VT: Shelburne Museum; Bennington, VT: Bennington Museum; New York: Skira Rizzoli Publications, 2016.

Edgerton, James A. "Buddy" and Nan O'Brien. *The Unknown Rockwell: A Portrait of Two American Families*. Essex Junction, VT: Battenkill River Press, 2009.

Ermoyan, Arpi. *Famous American Illustrators*. New York: Chartwell Books, 2002.

Fairbrother, Trevor. *Painting Summer in New England*. Salem, MA: Peabody Essex Museum; New Haven: Yale University Press, 2007.

Finch, Christopher. *Norman Rockwell: 332 Magazine Covers*. New York: Abbeville Press, 1979.

———. *Norman Rockwell's America*. New York: Harry N. Abrams, 1975.

Fisher, Dorothy Canfield. *Memories of Arlington, Vermont*. New York: Duell, Sloan, and Pearce, 1957.

———. *Vermont: A Guide to the Green Mountain State*. Boston: Houghton Mifflin, 1937.

Flythe, Christopher, Donald Stoltz, and Marshall Stoltz. *Norman Rockwell and the Saturday Evening Post: The Early Years, the Middle Years, the Later Years*. New York: Fine Communications, 1997.

Greenhill, Jennifer A. *Playing It Straight: Art and Humor in the Gilded Age*. Berkeley, CA: University of California Press, 2012.

Guptill, Arthur L. *Norman Rockwell Illustrator*. New York: Watson-Guptill Publications, 1946.

Haggerty, S. T. *Norman Rockwell's Models: In and Out of The Studio*. Lanham, MD: Rowman & Littlefield, 2023.

Hennessey, Maureen Hart, and Anne Knutson, eds. *Norman Rockwell: Pictures for the American People*. Atlanta: High Museum of Art; New York: Harry N. Abrams, 1999.

Kent, Rockwell. *World Famous Paintings*. New York: Wise & Company, 1939

Kierkegaard, Søren. *The Concept of Anxiety.* Translated by Alistair Hannay. 1844; New York: Liveright, 2014.

——. *Fear and Trembling.* Translated by Alastair Hannay. 1843; London: Penguin, 1985.

Kirchhoff, Katie Wood, ed. *Luigi Luccioni: Modern Light*. With essays by David Brody, Thomas Denenberg, Katie Wood Kirchhoff, Alexander Nemerov, Nancie Ravenel, and Richard Saunders. Shelburne, VT: Shelburne Museum; New York: Rizzoli Electra, 2022.

Lacy, Susan, and Elena Mannes. *Norman Rockwell: Painting America.* New York: Educational Broadcasting Corp., 1998.

Lears, Jackson. *Fables of Abundance: A Cultural History of Advertising in America.* New York: HarperCollins, 1994.

Levine, Lawrence W. *Highbrow/Lowbrow: The Emergence of Cultural Hierarchy in America.* Cambridge: Harvard University Press, 1988.

Lovecraft, H. P. "The Tomb" (1922). In *The Gothic Tales of H. P. Lovecraft,* edited by Xavier Aldana Reyes. London: British Library, 2018.

Marling, Karal Ann. *Norman Rockwell.* New York: Harry N. Abrams in association with the National Museum of American Art, Smithsonian Institute, 1997.

McGrath, Robert L. *Gods in Granite: The Art of the White Mountains of New Hampshire.* Syracuse, NY: Syracuse University Press, 2001.

Melville, Herman. *The Confidence-Man: His Masquerade.* Edited by Hershel Parker. 1857; New York: Norton, 1971.

Meyer, Susan E. *America's Great Illustrators.* New York: Harry N. Abrams, 1985.

——. *Norman Rockwell's People*. New York: Harrison House, 1987.

———. *Norman Rockwell's World War II: Impression from the Homefront*. San Antonio: USAA Foundation, 1991.

Michaelis, David. *N.C. Wyeth: A Biography.* New York: Alfred A. Knopf, 1998.

Miller, Dorothy C., and Alfred H. Barr Jr. *American Realists and Magic Realists.* New York: Museum of Modern Art, 1943.

Moffatt, Laurie Norton. *Norman Rockwell: A Definitive Catalogue.* 2 vols. Stockbridge, MA: Norman Rockwell Museum at Stockbridge, 1986.

——. "The People's Painter." In *Norman Rockwell: Pictures for the American People,* edited by Maureen Hart Hennessey and Anne Knutson. Atlanta: High Museum of Art; New York: Harry N. Abrams, 1999.

Moline, Mary. *Norman Rockwell Encyclopedia: A Chronological Catalog of the Artist's Work, 1910–1979.* Indianapolis: Curtis Publishing Co., 1979.

Murray, Stuart. *Norman Rockwell At Home in Vermont: The Arlington Years, 1939–53.* Bennington, VT: Images from the Past, 1997.

Nemerov, Alexander. *Fierce Poise: Helen Frankenthaler and 1950s New York.* New York: Penguin Books, 2020.

Patterson, Cynthia Lee. *Art for the Middle Classes: America's Illustrated Magazines of the 1840s.* Jackson: University Press of Mississippi, 2010.

Pero, Linda Szekely. *American Chronicles: The Art of Norman Rockwell.* Stockbridge, MA: Norman Rockwell Museum, 2007.

Plunkett, Stephanie Haboush, and James J. Kimble. *Enduring Ideals: Rockwell, Roosevelt, and the Four Freedoms.* New York: Abbeville Press, 2018.

Rafael, Anita, and Lyman Orton. *For The Love of Vermont: The Lyman Orton Collection.* Manchester, VT: Vermont Country Store, 2023.

Robertson, Bruce. *Reckoning with Winslow Homer: His Late Paintings and Their Influence.* Cleveland: Cleveland Museum of Art in cooperation with Indiana University Press, 1990.

Rockwell, Norman. "Commonplace." *American Magazine,* May 1936, 11.

——. *My Adventures as an Illustrator.* As told to Thomas Rockwell. New York: Abbeville Press Publishing, 2019. Originally published in 1960 by Doubleday.

——. *The Norman Rockwell Albumn.* New York: Doubleday, 1960.

——. *Rockwell on Rockwell: How I Make a Picture.* New York: Watson-Guptill Publications, 1979.

Rosenbaum, Julia B. *Visions of Belonging: New England Art and the Making of American Identity.* Ithaca, NY, and London: Cornell University Press, 2006.

Rosen, Dana. *Norman Rockwell: The Artist and His Work.* Norman Rockwell Museum at Stockbridge. Reprint ed. Fairfax, VA: Friedman/Fairfax Publishers, 1995.

Roy, Jennifer Rozines, and Gregory Roy. *Norman Rockwell: The Life of an Artist*. Berkeley Heights, NJ: Enslow Publishers, 2002.

Schick, Ron. *Norman Rockwell: Behind the Camera*. New York: Little, Brown & Company, 2009.

Schwartz, Lew Sayre, dir. *Norman Rockwell and "The Saturday Evening Post."* VHS. Video Arts, 1986.

Searls, Paul M. *Repeopling Vermont: The Paradox of Development in the Twentieth Century*. Barre: Vermont Historical Society, 2019.

Solomon, Deborah. *American Mirror: The Life and Art of Norman Rockwell*. New York: Farrar, Straus & Giroux, 2013.

Sommer, Robin Langley, ed. *Norman Rockwell: A Classic Treasury*. London: Bison Boooks, 1993.

Stone, Ruth. "Being a Woman." In *The Essential Ruth Stone,* edited by Bianca Stone. Port Townsend, WA: Copper Canyon Press, 2020.

Stoner, Joyce Hill. *Wyeth Vertigo,* edited by Thomas Denenberg. Shelburne, VT: Shelburne Museum; Hanover: University Press of New England, 2013.

Tomasi, Mari, and Roaldus Richard. *Men Against Granite,* edited by Alfred and Mark Wanner. Shelburne, VT: New England Press, 2004.

Truettner, William H., and Roger B. Stein, eds. *Picturing Old New England: Image and Memory*. Washington, DC: National Museum of American Art, Smithsonian Institution; New Haven: Yale University Press, 1999.

Vermont Development Commission. *Background for Living*. Promotional film. Bay State Film Productions, 1948. 24 min., 1 sec. https://vermonthistory.org/digitized-film-and-video-collections.

Walton, Donald. *A Rockwell Portrait: An Intimate Biography*. Kansas City: Sheed & Ward, 1978.

Wilmerding, John. *Signs of the Artist: Signatures and Self-Expression in American Paintings*. New Haven: Yale University Press, 2003.

Wood, Joseph S. *The New England Village*. Baltimore: Johns Hopkins Press, 1997.

Wren, Christopher S. *Those Turbulent Sons of Freedom: Ethan Allen's Green Mountain Boys and the American Revolution*. New York: Simon & Schuster, 2014.

WQED (Pittsburgh). *Norman Rockwell: An American Portrait*. Aired November 25, 1987. DVD, VIEW Video, 2002.

Yount, Sylvia. *Maxfield Parrish, 1870–1966*. New York: Harry N. Abrams in association with the Pennsylvania Academy of the Fine Arts, 1999.

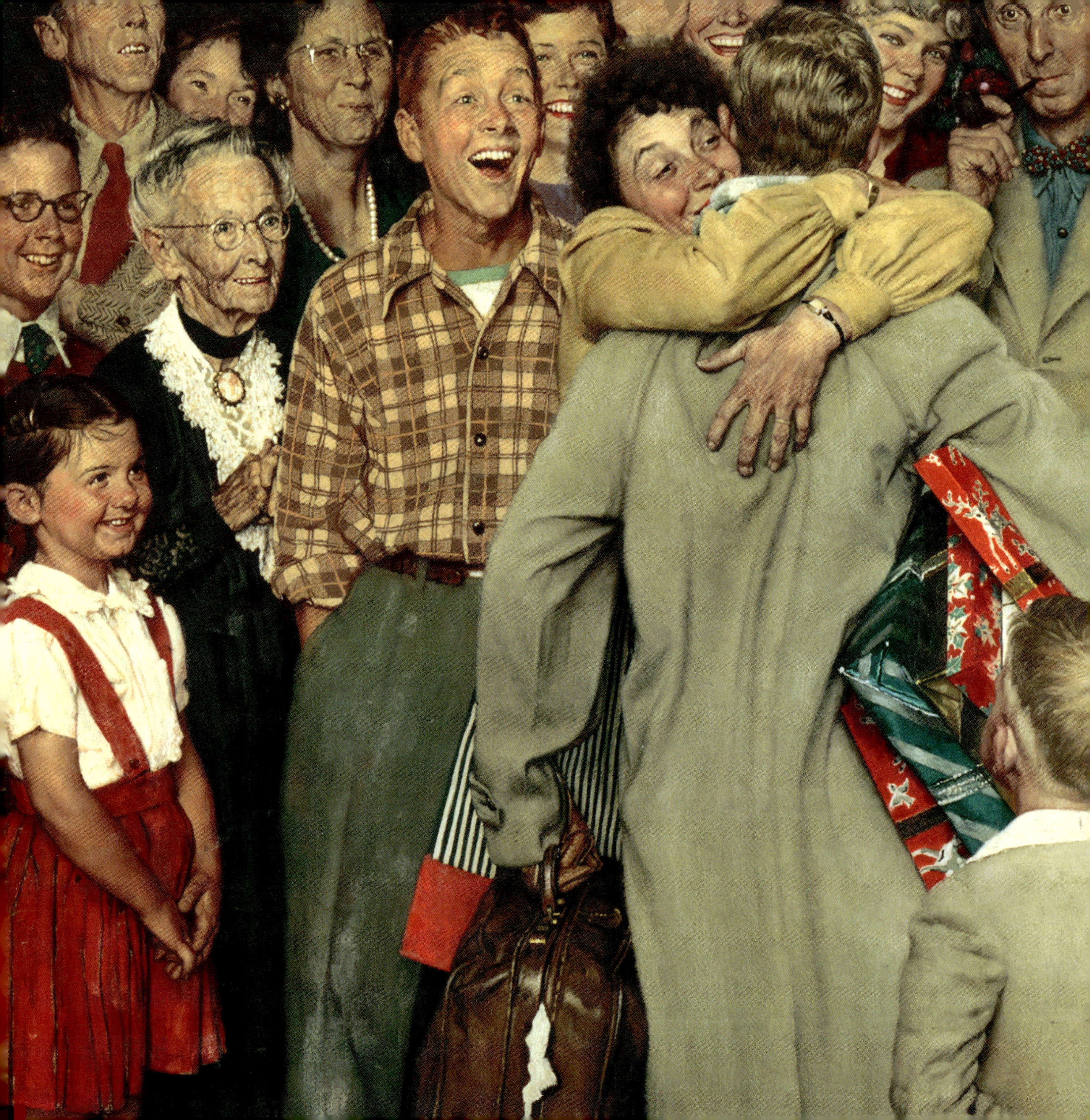

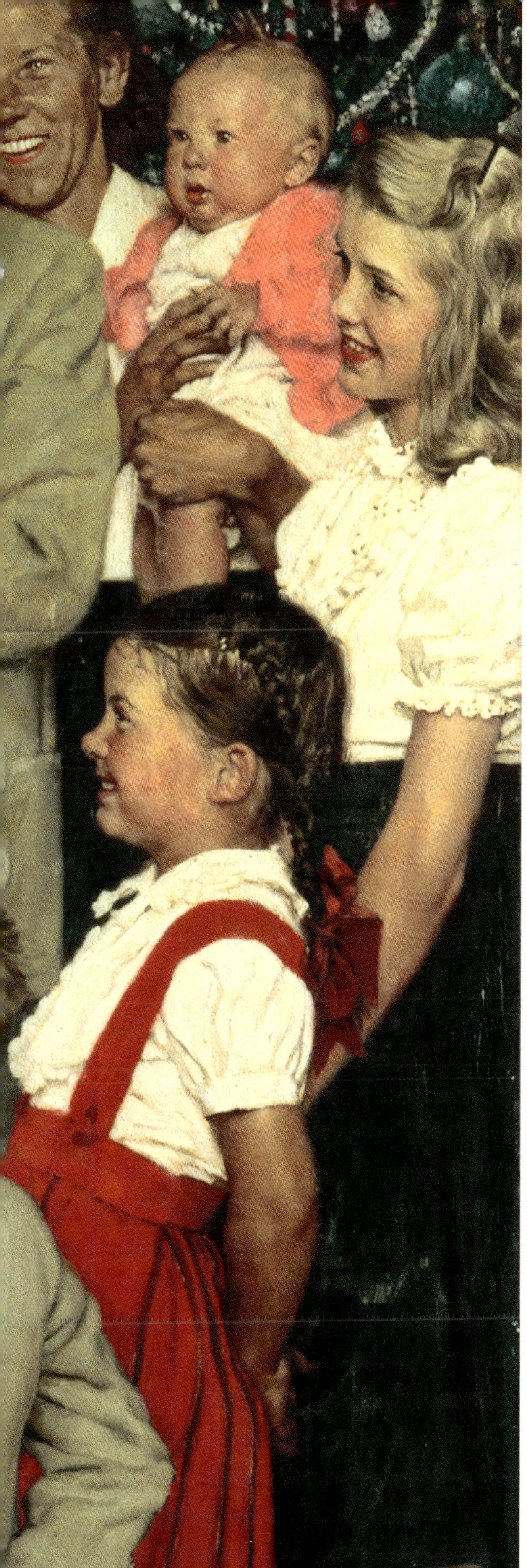

AUTHORS

Carolyn Bauer is the Marna and Chuck Davis Curator of American Art at Shelburne Museum.

Thomas Denenberg is the John Wilmerding Director & CEO at Shelburne Museum.

Alexander Nemerov is the Carl and Marilynn Thoma Provostial Professor in the Arts and Humanities at Stanford University.

PHOTO CREDITS

Figures

Marion Post Wolcott: Fig. 1: © Library of Congress Prints and Photographs Division

Artvue Post Card Company: Fig. 2: Image courtesy of Collection of Shelburne Museum

Gene Pelham: Fig. 3: Image Courtesy of the Norman Rockwell Museum Collection; Artwork Approved by the Norman Rockwell Family Agency; © Curtis Licensing

Unidentified photographer: Figs. 4, 31, 34, 38: Images Courtesy of the Norman Rockwell Museum Artwork Approved by the Norman Rockwell Family Agency
Fig. 6: Image courtesy of Bennington College Archives
Figs. 23, 24, 28: Images courtesy of Vermont Granite Museum

John Atherton: Fig. 5: Image courtesy of Collection of Shelburne Museum; Photography by Andy Duback

Unknown photographer: Fig. 6: Image courtesy of Bennington College Archives

Norman Rockwell: Fig. 7: Image courtesy of Bennington Museum; Artwork Approved by the Norman Rockwell Family Agency
Fig. 19: Illustration © SEPS licensed by Curtis Licensing; Artwork Approved by the Norman Rockwell Family Agency
Fig. 20: Image courtesy of Shelburne Museum; Photograph by Andy Duback; © Rock of Ages Corporation
Fig. 32: Image courtesy of the Norman Rockwell Museum Collection; © Curtis Licensing
Fig. 35: Image courtesy of the Norman Rockwell Museum; © Curtis Licensing; Artwork Approved by the Norman Rockwell Family Agency
Fig. 39: Licensed by Art Resource, NY; Artwork Approved by the Norman Rockwell Family Agency

Anna Mary Robertson "Grandma" Moses: Fig. 8: Image courtesy of Collection of Shelburne Museum; Photography by Bruce Schwarz; © Estate of Grandma Moses (Bridgeman Copyright)

Mead Schaeffer: Fig. 9: Illustration © SEPS licensed by Curtis Licensing

Adolf Dehn: Fig. 10: Image courtesy of Shelburne Museum; © Estate of Adolf Dehn, courtesy of D. Wigmore Fine Art, Inc.; Photography by Andy Duback

Winslow Homer: Fig. 11: Image courtesy Meyersphoto

John Karst: Fig. 12: Image courtesy of The Metropolitan Museum of Art

Abbott Fuller Graves: Fig. 13: Image courtesy of Shelburne Museum; Photography by Andy Duback

Maxfield Parrish: Fig. 14: Image courtesy of Shelburne Museum; Photography by Andy Duback
Fig. 15: Image courtesy of New Britain Museum of American Art; © 2025 Maxfield Parrish Family, LLC / Artists Rights Society (ARS), NY

N. C. Wyeth: Fig. 16: Image courtesy of Bank of America Collection
Fig. 17: Image courtesy of Shelburne Museum
Fig. 18: Image licensed by Bridgeman Images

Abbott Handerson Thayer: Fig. 21: Image courtesy of Smithsonian American Art Museum

Rembrandt: Fig. 22: Image courtesy of The Metropolitan Museum of Art

Eric Aho: Figs. 25, 27: Images Courtesy of the artist and DC Moore Gallery; Photography by Rachel Portesi
Fig. 30: Image Courtesy of the artist and DC Moore Gallery

Samuel Chamberlain: Fig. 29: Image courtesy of Shelburne Museum

Aldo Merusi: Fig. 33: Image courtesy of the Norman Rockwell Museum; Artwork Approved by the Norman Rockwell Family Agency

Arthur Johnson: Fig. 36: Image courtesy of the Norman Rockwell Museum; Artwork Approved by the Norman Rockwell Family Agency

Pagano Studios: Fig. 37: Image courtesy of the Norman Rockwell Museum; Artwork Approved by the Norman Rockwell Family Agency

Plates

Norman Rockwell: Plates 1, 2, 5, 8, 9, 10, 11, 12, 13, 14, 19, 20, 24, 25, 26, 28, 29, 30, 31, 32, 33, 36, 40, 42, 43, 44, 45, 46, 47, 48: Illustrations provided by SEPS through Curtis Licensing; Artwork Approved by the Norman Rockwell Family Agency

Plate 3: Image courtesy of Wadsworth Atheneum Museum of Art; Photography by Allen Phillips; Artwork Approved by the Norman Rockwell Family Agency

Plate 4: Image courtesy of Lucas Museum of Narrative Art; Artwork Approved by the Norman Rockwell Family Agency

Plate 6: Image courtesy of Norman Rockwell Museum; © 1941 Brown & Bigelow Licensing; Artwork Approved by the Norman Rockwell Family Agency

Plates 7, 15, 16, 17, 18, 37, 38, 41, 49: Images courtesy of Norman Rockwell Museum; © Curtis Licensing; Artwork Approved by the Norman Rockwell Family Agency

Plates 21, 27: Images courtesy of Norman Rockwell Museum; Artwork Approved by the Norman Rockwell Family Agency

Plate 22: Image courtesy of Crystal Bridges Museum of American Art, Bentonville, Arkansas; Photography by Dwight Primiano; Artwork Approved by the Norman Rockwell Family Agency

Plate 23: Image courtesy of Brooklyn Museum; Artwork Approved by the Norman Rockwell Family Agency

Plates 34, 35: Image courtesy of Shelburne Museum; Photography by Andy Duback; © Rock of Ages Corporation

Plate 39: Image courtesy of Fleming Museum of Art, University of Vermont; Artwork Approved by the Norman Rockwell Family Agency

Full-Page Details

Page 6: Norman Rockwell, *Freedom of Speech* (detail), 1943. Illustration for *The Saturday Evening Post*, February 20, 1943, p. 13. Oil on canvas, 45 ¾ × 35 ½ in. Norman Rockwell Museum Collection, Norman Rockwell Art Collection Trust. NRACT.1973.021. © 1943 SEPS: Licensed by Curtis Licensing, Indianapolis, IN. All rights reserved. Artwork Approved by the Norman Rockwell Family Agency.

Page 8: Norman Rockwell, *Willie Gillis in College* (detail), 1946. Cover illustration for *The Saturday Evening Post*, October 5, 1946. Oil on canvas, 36 × 35 in. Private Collection. Illustration provided by SEPS through Curtis Licensing. Artwork Approved by the Norman Rockwell Family Agency.

Page 10: Unidentified photographer, *Norman Rockwell and John Atherton* (detail), date unknown. Silver gelatin print, 7 ⅝ × 7 ⅝ in. Norman Rockwell Museum Collection, Famous Artists School Collection, gift of Magdalen & Robert Livesey. RC.2013.11.6.246. Artwork Approved by the Norman Rockwell Family Agency.

Page 48: N. C. Wyeth, *Young Maine Fisherman* (detail), 1933. Oil on canvas, 52 ⅜ × 48 ⅛ in. Bank of America Collection. 05106.

Page 84: Unidentified photographer, *Untitled* [Norman Rockwell painting *The Craftsman*], ca. 1963. Photograph, 10 × 8 ⅛ in. Vermont Granite Museum. 2021.74.512.

Page 120: Norman Rockwell, *Freedom from Want* (detail), 1943. Illustration for *The Saturday Evening Post*, March 6, 1943, p. 13. Oil on canvas, 45 ¾ × 35 ½ in. Norman Rockwell Museum Collection, Norman Rockwell Art Collection Trust. NRACT.1973.022. © 1943 SEPS: Licensed by Curtis Licensing, Indianapolis, IN. All rights reserved. Artwork Approved by the Norman Rockwell Family Agency.

Page 135: Norman Rockwell, *The Craftsman* (detail), 1963. Oil on canvas, 47 ¼ × 38 ¼ in. Collection of Shelburne Museum, gift of Polycor and Rock of Ages Corporation. 2024-12.1. Photography by Andy Duback. © Rock of Ages Corporation.

Page 138: Norman Rockwell, *Willie Gillis: Gillis Heritage* (detail), 1944. Cover illustration for *The Saturday Evening Post*, September 16, 1944. Oil on canvas, 13 ¼ × 10 ⅝ in. Private Collection. Illustration provided by SEPS through Curtis Licensing. Artwork Approved by the Norman Rockwell Family Agency.

Pages 142–43: Norman Rockwell, *Christmas Homecoming* (detail), 1948. Cover illustration for *The Saturday Evening Post*, December 25, 1948. Oil on canvas, 35 ½ × 33 ½ in. Norman Rockwell Museum Collection, Museum purchase, NRM.1978.10. © 1948 SEPS: Curtis Licensing, Indianapolis, IN. All rights reserved. Artwork Approved by the Norman Rockwell Family Agency.

Page 147: Norman Rockwell, *Rosie the Riveter* (detail), 1943. Cover illustration for *The Saturday Evening Post*, May 29, 1943. Oil on canvas, 52 × 40 in. Crystal Bridges Museum of American Art, Bentonville, Arkansas. 2007.178. Photography by Dwight Primiano. Artwork Approved by the Norman Rockwell Family Agency.

Page 150: Norman Rockwell, *War News* (detail), ca. 1945. Unpublished cover for *The Saturday Evening Post*. Oil on canvas, 41 ¼ × 40 ½ in. Norman Rockwell Museum Collection, Museum purchase. NRM.1976.02. Artwork Approved by the Norman Rockwell Family Agency.

End Pages

Designed by Norman Rockwell, *Marble Champion (Girl Playing Marbles)*, *The Saturday Evening Post*, September 2, 1939. Cover illustration tear sheet, 14 ¼ × 11 ¼ in. Norman Rockwell Museum Collection, Gift of John A. & Laura C. Savio. RC.2007.1.186. © 1939 SEPS: Curtis Licensing, Indianapolis, IN. All rights reserved.

Designed by Norman Rockwell, *Willie Gillis: Food Package*, *The Saturday Evening Post*, October 4, 1941. Cover illustration tear sheet, 14 ¼ × 11 ¼ in. Illustration provided by SEPS through Curtis Licensing.

Designed by Norman Rockwell, *Rosie the Riveter*, *The Saturday Evening Post*, May 29, 1943. Cover illustration tear sheet, 14 ¼ × 11 ¼ in. Illustration provided by SEPS through Curtis Licensing.

Designed by Norman Rockwell, *The Tattoo Artist*, *The Saturday Evening Post*, March 4, 1944. Cover illustration tear sheet, 14 ¼ × 11 ¼ in. Illustration provided by SEPS through Curtis Licensing.

Designed by Norman Rockwell, *The Homecoming*, *The Saturday Evening Post*, May 26, 1945. Cover illustration tear sheet, 14 ¼ × 11 ¼ in. Illustration provided by SEPS through Curtis Licensing.

Designed by Norman Rockwell, *Willie Gillis in College*, *The Saturday Evening Post*, October 5, 1946. Cover illustration tear sheet, 14 ¼ × 11 ¼ in. Illustration provided by SEPS through Curtis Licensing.

Designed by Norman Rockwell, *Going and Coming*, *The Saturday Evening Post*, August 30, 1947. Cover illustration tear sheet, 14 ¼ × 11 ¼ in. Illustration provided by SEPS through Curtis Licensing.

Designed by Norman Rockwell, *The Gossips*, *The Saturday Evening Post*, March 9, 1948. Cover illustration tear sheet, 14 ¼ × 11 ¼ in. Illustration provided by SEPS through Curtis Licensing.

Designed by Norman Rockwell, *Christmas Homecoming*, *The Saturday Evening Post*, December 25, 1948. Cover illustration tear sheet, 14 ¼ × 11 ¼ in. Illustration provided by SEPS through Curtis Licensing.

Designed by Norman Rockwell, *Game Called Because of Rain (Tough Call)*, *The Saturday Evening Post*, April 23, 1949. Cover illustration tear sheet, 14 ¼ × 11 ¼ in. Illustration provided by SEPS through Curtis Licensing.

Designed by Norman Rockwell, *New Television Set*, *The Saturday Evening Post*, November 5, 1949. Cover illustration tear sheet, 14 ¼ × 11 ¼ in. Illustration provided by SEPS through Curtis Licensing.

Designed by Norman Rockwell, *The Young Lady with the Shiner*, *The Saturday Evening Post*, May 23, 1953. Cover illustration tear sheet, 14 ¼ × 11 ¼ in. Illustration provided by SEPS through Curtis Licensing.

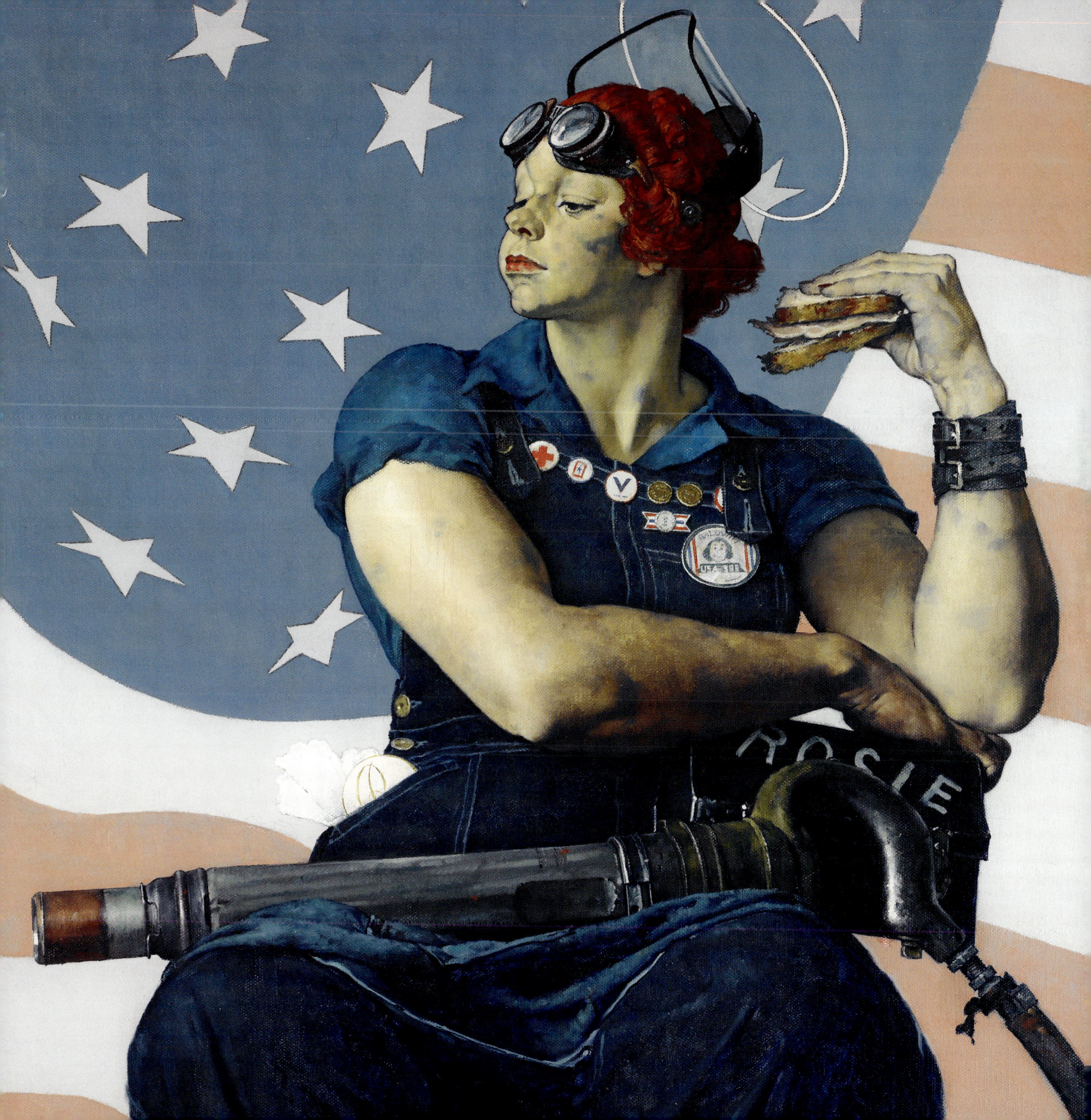
ROSIE

INDEX

Page numbers in *italics* refer to the illustrations

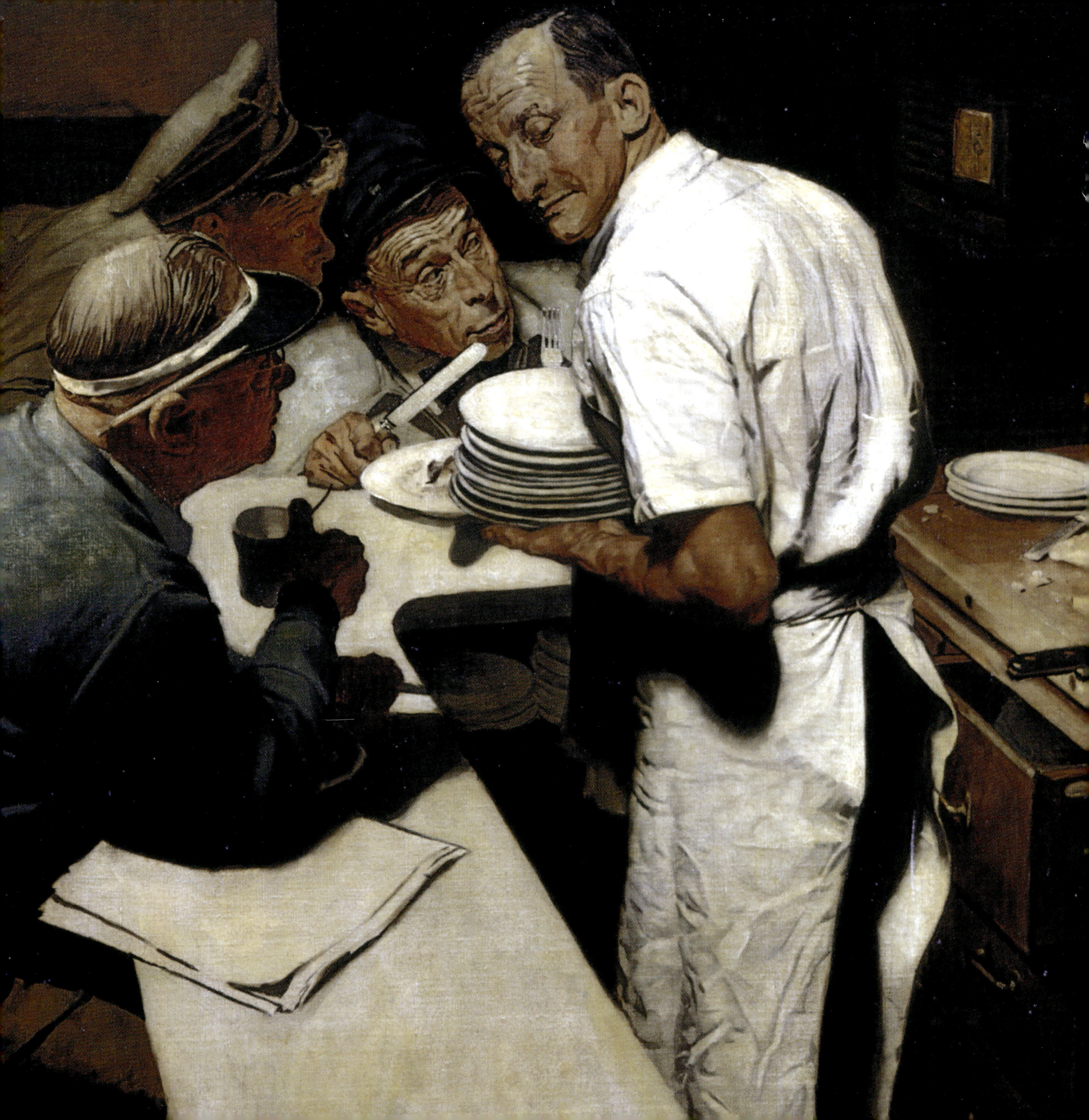

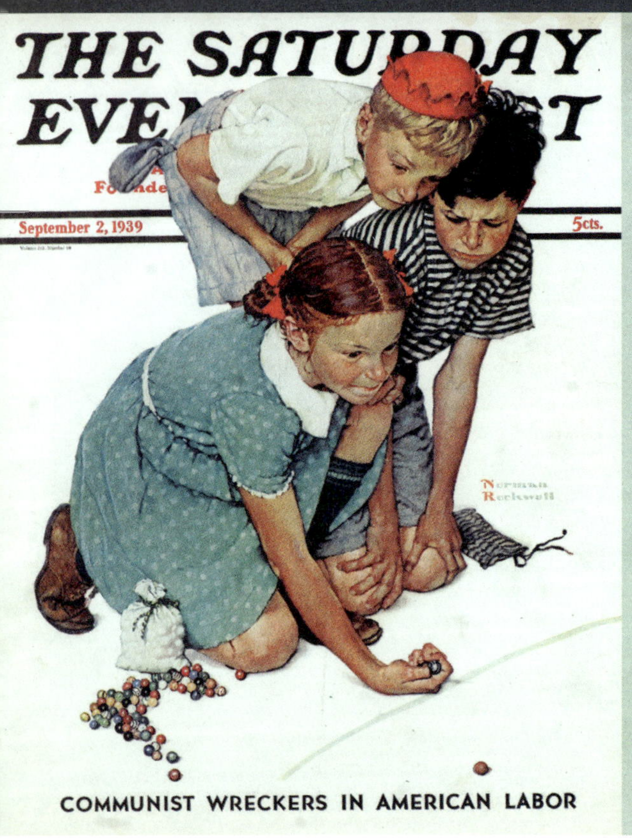

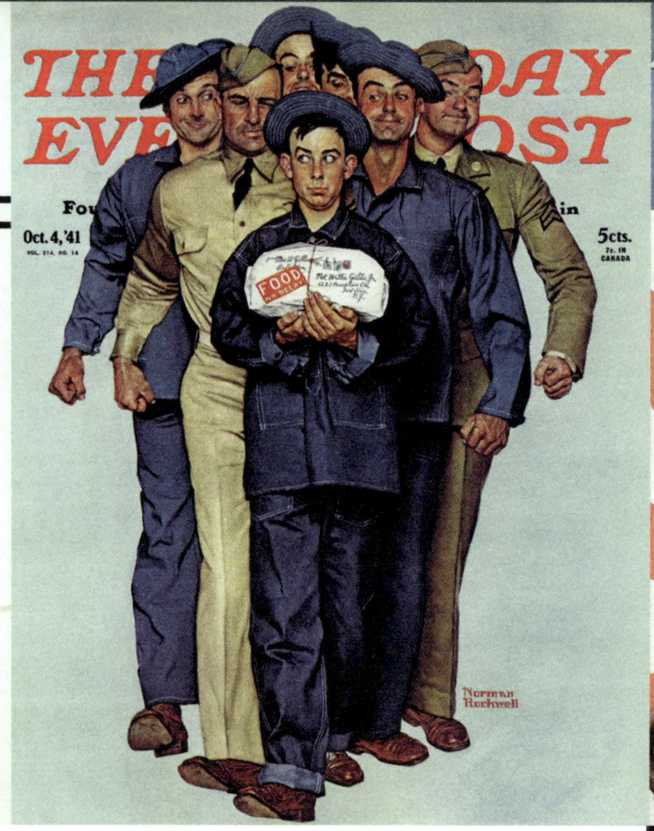

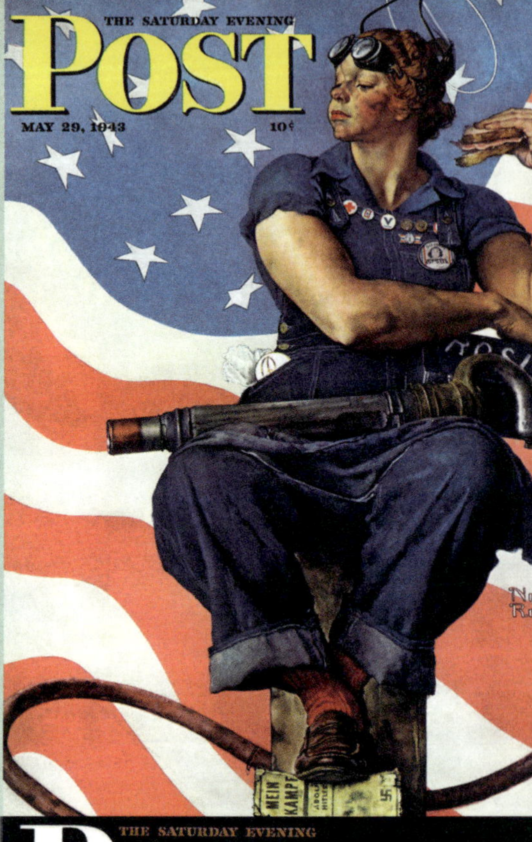

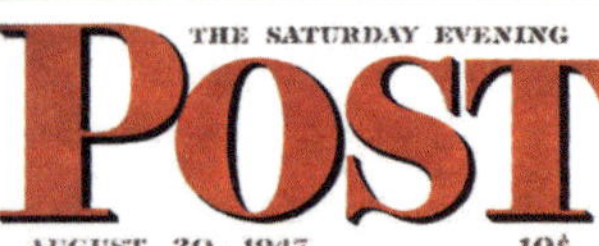

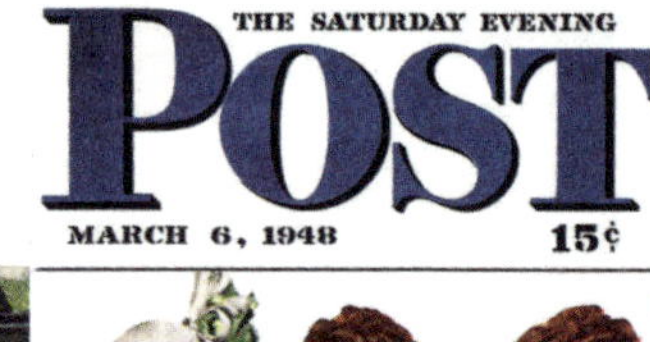

THE SATURDAY EVENING
POST
DECEMBER 25, 1946
15¢

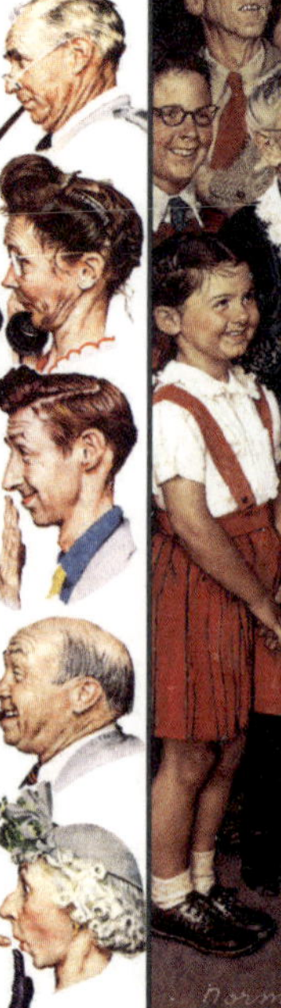

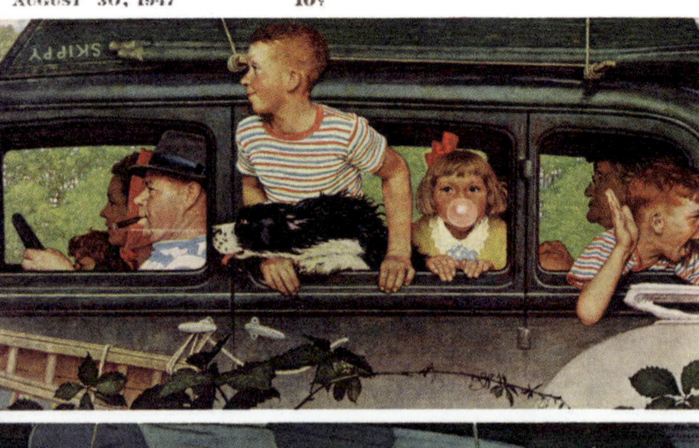

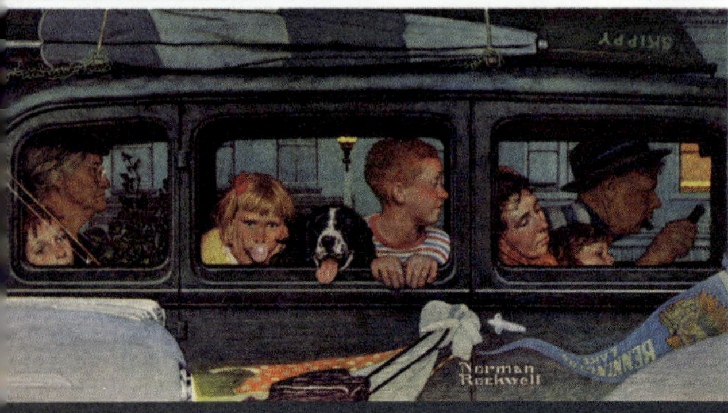

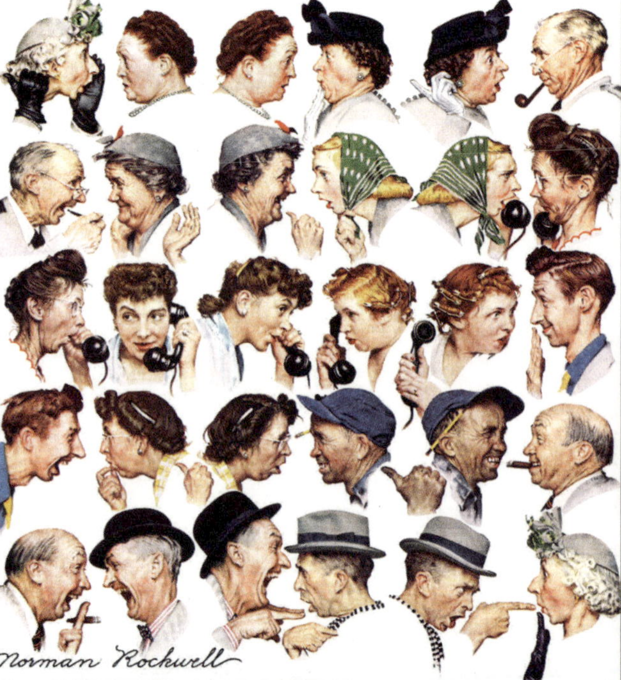

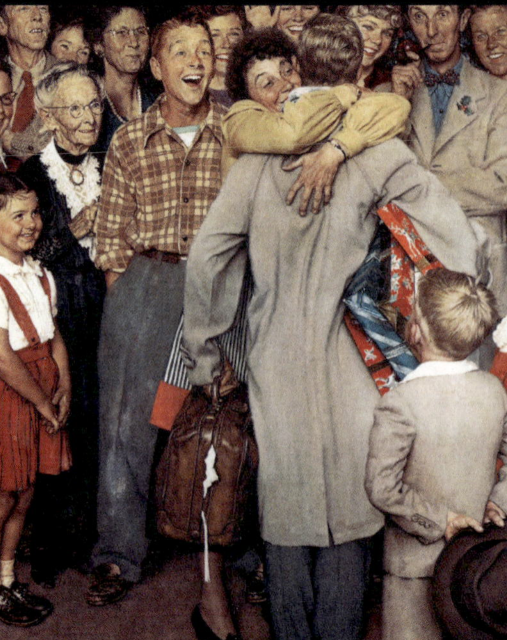